Left out of the Bargain

Stolen Asset Recovery (StAR) Series

The Stolen Asset Recovery Initiative (StAR) is a partnership between the World Bank Group and the United Nations Office on Drugs and Crime (UNODC) that supports international efforts to end safe havens for corrupt funds. StAR works with developing countries and financial centers to prevent the laundering of the proceeds of corruption and to facilitate more systematic and timely return of stolen assets.

The Stolen Asset Recovery (StAR) Series supports the efforts of StAR and UNODC by providing practitioners with knowledge and policy tools that consolidate international good practice and wide-ranging practical experience on cutting edge issues related to anticorruption and asset recovery efforts. For more information, visit star.worldbank .org.

Titles in the Stolen Asset Recovery (StAR) Series

Stolen Asset Recovery: A Good Practices Guide for Non-Conviction Based Asset Forfeiture (2009) by Theodore S. Greenberg, Linda M. Samuel, Wingate Grant, and Larissa Gray

Politically Exposed Persons: Preventive Measures for the Banking Sector (2010) by Theodore S. Greenberg, Larissa Gray, Delphine Schantz, Carolin Gardner, and Michael Latham

Asset Recovery Handbook: A Guide for Practitioners (2011) by Jean-Pierre Brun, Larissa Gray, Clive Scott, and Kevin Stephenson

Barriers to Asset Recovery: An Analysis of the Key Barriers and Recommendations for Action (2011) by Kevin Stephenson, Larissa Gray, and Ric Power

The Puppet Masters: How the Corrupt Use Legal Structures to Hide Stolen Assets and What to Do About It (2011) by Emile van der Does de Willebois, J. C. Sharman, Robert Harrison, Ji Won Park, and Emily Halter

Public Office, Private Interests: Accountability through Income and Asset Disclosure (2012)

On the Take: Criminalizing Illicit Enrichment to Fight Corruption (2012) by Lindy Muzila, Michelle Morales, Marianne Mathias, and Tammar Berger

Left out of the Bargain

Settlements in Foreign Bribery Cases and Implications for Asset Recovery

Jacinta Anyango Oduor
Francisca M. U. Fernando
Agustin Flah
Dorothee Gottwald
Jeanne M. Hauch
Marianne Mathias
Ji Won Park
Oliver Stolpe

STAR Stolen Asset Recovery Initiative

The World Bank • UNODC

ISBN (paper): 978-1-4648-0086-3
ISBN (electronic): 978-1-4648-0087-0
DOI: 10.1596/978-1-4648-0086-3

Cover photos: Shutterstock (front cover, "Approved" seal, ticker with reflected images); Thinkstock (front cover, money changing hands, stock ticker); iStockphoto (back cover). Used with permission; further permission required for reuse.
Cover design: Naylor Design.

Library of Congress Cataloging-in-Publication Data

Left out of the bargain : settlements in foreign bribery cases and implications for asset recovery / Jacinta Anyango Oduor, Francisca M.U. Fernando, Agustin Flah, Dorothee Gottwald, Jeanne M. Hauch, Marianne Mathias, Ji Won Park, Oliver Stolpe.
    pages cm.
  Includes bibliographical references.
ISBN 978-1-4648-0086-3 (alk. paper) – ISBN 978-1-4648-0087-0
  1. Forfeiture. 2. Compromise (Law) 3. Reparation (Criminal justice) 4. Corporations–Corrupt practices. 5. Bribery. 6. Damages. 7. Political corruption–Prevention. I. Oduor, Jacinta, editor of compilation.
  K5107.L47 2014
  345'.02323–dc23

                                                                                        2013034128

Contents

Contributors   *ix*
Acknowledgments   *xi*
Abbreviations   *xiii*

Executive Summary   **1**
1. Key Findings   2
2. Additional Observations   3
3. StAR's Proposals   4

Introduction   **7**
1. Background   7
2. United Nations Convention against Corruption: Setting the Stage   11
3. Methodology and Overview of the Study   13

1. Settlements in Foreign Bribery Cases   **17**
1. Defining the Term *Settlement*   17
2. Legal Frameworks for Settlements   20
3. Shortened Criminal Procedures and Other Forms in Certain
   Civil Law Countries   21
      3.1 Switzerland   21
      3.2 Norway   23
      3.3 Italy   23
      3.4 Germany   25
4. Guilty Pleas, Civil Liability, and Other Forms in Certain Common
   Law Countries   26
      4.1 United Kingdom   26
      4.2 Canada   30
      4.3 Nigeria   30
      4.4 United States   32

2. Common Threads and General Observations about Settlements   **39**
1. Criteria for Understanding Settlements   39
      1.1 Forms of Legal Liability: Criminal, Civil, and Administrative   39
      1.2 Judicial Oversight   40
      1.3 Transparency   41
2. Terms Typically Included in Settlements   41

3. The Role of International Organizations in Settlements   44
4. The Rationale behind Settlements   45
5. Trends and Developments   50
   5.1 General Trends   50
   5.2 Developments in Countries Whose Officials Have Been
       the Object of Alleged Bribes   53

**3. The Impact of Settlements on Pending and Future
Cases in Other Jurisdictions**   **57**
1. The Principles of *Ne Bis in Idem* and Double Jeopardy   58
2. International Cooperation and Mutual Legal Assistance   62

4. Implications of Settlements on Asset Recovery   **67**
1. Recovering Assets in the Context of Settlements: The Current
   State of Affairs   67
   1.1 Combination and Ratio of Monetary Sanctions: Sample
       Jurisdictional Comparisons   69
   1.2 Monetary Sanctions Imposed   71
   1.3 Involvement of Public Procurement Contracts and State-Owned
       Enterprises   82
2. Barriers to Asset Recovery in the Context of Settlements   83
3. Modes of Participation in Criminal Enforcement Actions for the
   Purpose of Asset Recovery   86
   3.1 Participation of Affected Countries through Formal Legal Avenues   86
   3.2 Participation in Criminal Enforcement Action in Civil Law
       Jurisdictions   87
   3.3 Restitution and Compensation in Common Law Jurisdictions 91
   3.4 Participation of Affected Countries in Settlements through Other
       Avenues   94
4. Conclusion   96

5. Conclusions   **97**

6. Case Summaries   **101**
  1. Alcatel-Lucent (Costa Rica and United States)   101
  2. Alstom (Switzerland, Tunisia, Latvia, Malaysia, and World Bank)   105
  3. BAE Systems (Tanzania, United Kingdom, and United States)   107
  4. Daimler (More than 22 Countries)   110
  5. Haiti Teleco (Haiti and United States)   112
  6. Innospec (United Kingdom and United States)   115
  7. Johnson & Johnson (Greece, United Kingdom, and United States)   117
  8. Mabey & Johnson (Ghana, Iraq, Jamaica, and United Kingdom)   121
  9. Macmillan Publishers (United Kingdom and World Bank)   123
 10. Mercator/Giffen et al. (Kazakhstan, Switzerland, and United States)   125
 11. Schneider Electric (Lesotho)   128
 12. Siemens AG (Germany, Greece, Italy, Nigeria, United States, and others)   131

13. Statoil (Norway and United States)   134
14. TSKJ Consortium (Nigeria, United Kingdom, and United States)   136

Appendix I Forms of Legal Remedies Relevant to Foreign Bribery Cases   **141**

1. Confiscation: Criminal, Civil, and Administrative   141
2. Compensation: Criminal and Civil   142
3. Disgorgement: Civil Remedy Variation on Confiscation   142
4. Restitution: Criminal and Civil   143
5. Fines: Criminal and Civil   143
6. Reparations: Gratuitous and/or Voluntary Payments   144

Appendix II U.K. Remedies   **145**

1. Criminal Remedies   145
2. Civil Remedies   145

Appendix III Settlements Cases Database: Methodology   **147**

StAR Database of Settlements of Foreign Bribery and Related Cases   147
1. Details of the Settlements Cases Database   148
    1.1 Time Period Covered   148
    1.2 "Case" Defined   148
    1.3 Sources Used   149
2. Explanation of Fields and a Sample Entry   150

Appendix IV Glossary   **159**

Boxes

I.1   *A Time for Action*, 2010 ICHA Meeting Report   10
1.1   Elements of a Deferred Prosecution Agreement: Alcatel-Lucent SA and
      the Department of Justice, in the United States District Court, Southern
      District of Florida   35
3.1   Practices to Promote International Cooperation in Cases of Prior or
      Pending Settlement   65
4.1   Components of Monetary Sanctions   68
4.2   NGOs as *Parties Civiles*   90

Figures

1.1   U.K. Settled Enforcement Actions by Legal Form of Settlement
      (as of July 3, 2012)   29
1.2   U.S. DOJ FCPA Enforcement Actions (June 1979–January 2012)   34
1.3   Principles of Federal Prosecution of Business Organizations and
      Prosecutors' Decisions to Decline Prosecution, Enter into a DPA or
      NPA, or Prosecute   37
2.1   Timeline of Settlements in Various Cases against Siemens   51
3.1   Settlements in Multiple Jurisdictions by a Multinational Corporation
      Involved in a Bribery Scheme Related to the Bonny Island Liquefied
      Natural Gas Project (Nigeria)   60

3.2	Settlements in Foreign Bribery Cases Settled across Multiple Jurisdictions	62
B4.1.1	Methods for Recovering the Proceeds of Corruption	68
4.1	Alstom: Swiss Settlement	70
4.2	BAE Systems: U.K. Settlement	70
4.3	Alcatel Lucent: U.S. Settlement	71
4.4	Monetary Sanctions in Settlements of Criminal Foreign Bribery and Related Cases	72
4.5	Monetary Sanctions in Civil and Administrative Settlements of Foreign Bribery and Related Cases	73
4.6	Total Monetary Sanctions and Assets Returned or Ordered Returned Where Jurisdiction of Settlement Differed from Jurisdiction of Foreign Public Officials	73
4.7	Sector Involvement in Foreign Bribery and Related Cases	83

Map

4.1	Assets Returned by 30 OECD Countries (2006–09)	81

Tables

1.1	Settlements of Foreign Bribery and Related Offenses Cases, 1999 through July 3, 2012	19
1.2	Settlements by Type of Legal System: Civil and Common Law Jurisdictions	19
2.1	Forms of Liability in Public Legal Actions: Criminal, Civil, and Administrative	40
2.2a	Settlements: Criminal Forms and Sanctions	43
2.2b	Settlements: Civil Forms and Sanctions	43
4.1	Assets Returned/Ordered Returned Where the Jurisdiction of Enforcement and the Jurisdiction of Allegedly Bribed Foreign Public Officials Were the Same	74
4.2	Assets Returned/Ordered Returned Where the Jurisdiction of Enforcement and Jurisdiction of Foreign Public Officials Were Different	76
4.3	Other Asset Returns	80
A3.1	Fields and Their Breakdowns in the Settlements Database	151
A3.2	Sample Entry in Settlements Database	155

Contributors

Jacinta Anyango Oduor
Jacinta Anyango Oduor holds a master's degree in law and has practical experience gained over a career of 23 years. Currently she works as a Senior Public Sector Specialist with the Stolen Asset Recovery Initiative (StAR)/World Bank. Ms. Oduor's experience includes working with the United Nations Office on Drugs and Crime (UNODC) as country Anti-Corruption Adviser for Southern Sudan and Senior Public Litigation Attorney/Prosecutor and Investigator, Anti-Corruption Agency-Kenya. She has worked in private practice and as a lecturer in graduate courses on gender. She is an accomplished trainer and has published numerous academic theses and papers. Ms. Oduor led the team in this study.

Francisca M. U. Fernando
Francisca M. U. Fernando is a Junior Professional Associate with the StAR Initiative and the Financial Market Integrity Unit of the World Bank. She holds a master of laws degree from the University of Toronto and a bachelor of laws from the London School of Economics and Political Science, where she was the Jones Markham Scholar. She is called to the Bar of England and Wales. Prior to joining the Bank, she interned with the Legal and Constitutional Affairs Division of the Commonwealth Secretariat and the Anti-Corruption Division of the Organisation for Economic Co-operation and Development.

Agustin Flah
Agustin Flah graduated as a lawyer from the University of Buenos Aires and holds an LL.M. from the London School of Economics (LSE). Prior to working at StAR he was the Argentine representative to the intergovernmental Financial Action Task Force. He formerly held the positions of Chief of Staff of the Secretary of Justice, Counsel to the Argentina Anti-Corruption Commission, and Legal Advisor to the Argentine Congress. He has won several awards during his career: the British Chevening Scholarship by the Foreign and Commonwealth Office, awarded to support graduate studies at the LSE; the Fulbright-Humphrey Fellowship granted for his commitment to public service; and appointment to the Georgetown Leadership Seminar.

Dorothee Gottwald
Dorothee Gottwald has been a crime prevention and criminal justice officer with UNODC since 2006. Her work focuses on the implementation of the United Nations

Convention against Corruption, in particular its chapter 5 on asset recovery. Before joining the United Nations, she served the German Federal Ministry of Interior. Dr. Gottwald holds a PhD in law from Goethe University Frankfurt am Main in Frankfurt, Germany, and a bar exam from Munich.

Jeanne M. Hauch

Jeanne M. Hauch is a consultant to StAR at the World Bank, where she has worked since 2009. She is concurrently on the faculty of the George Washington University Law School. Before joining the World Bank, she served as a federal prosecutor with the U.S. Department of Justice for many years, specializing in transnational crimes. Earlier, she practiced law in Washington, DC, and Brussels. She was a Fulbright scholar in France and served as a law clerk for Justice Anthony Kennedy of the United States Supreme Court. She was educated at Yale Law School and the Woodrow Wilson School of Public and International Affairs at Princeton University.

Marianne Mathias

Marianne Mathias was a consultant at the World Bank for six years, in the Financial Market Integrity Unit and with StAR. She is currently an anticorruption investigator at the Inter-American Development Bank in Washington, DC. Ms. Mathias holds a master's degree in laws from the University Pierre Mendes-France, Grenoble, France. Ms. Mathias has a law enforcement background in financial investigation. She successively served as a lawyer at the Customs Headquarters in Paris, France, as a financial investigator in the French Financial Intelligence Unit, and as a Special Advisor to the Prosecutor's Office in the Court of Justice of Paris in charge of money laundering and corruption crimes.

Ji Won Park

Ji Won Park is an attorney with two decades of experience in government, private sector, and civil society organizations in the United States and South Korea. Her projects at the World Bank and StAR include *The Puppet Masters: How the Corrupt Hide Stolen Assets Using Legal Structures*, Asset Recovery Watch cases database, and the G20 Anti-Corruption Working Group. Ms. Park also participated in the intergovernmental Financial Action Task Force study, *Money Laundering and Terrorist Financing Vulnerabilities of Legal Professionals*. She is a graduate of Columbia College and Georgetown University Law Center, where she was a Public Interest Law Scholar.

Oliver Stolpe

Oliver Stolpe is a Senior Advisor with the StAR initiative of the World Bank and UNODC. From 2008 until 2011, he managed UNODC's largest anticorruption project in Nigeria, where he also served as UNODC's representative. He has been working for UNODC since 1999, supporting the launch of UNODC's Global Programme against Corruption, assisting the negotiations of the UN Convention against Corruption, heading its Justice and Integrity Unit, and delivering technical assistance in Africa, Eastern Europe, and Asia. Dr. Stolpe holds a PhD in law with research focusing on strategies against organized crime, asset recovery, and anti-money-laundering in the fight against the Italian Mafia.

Acknowledgments

This study would not have been possible without the participation, guidance, and insights of many individuals within and outside the World Bank and United Nations Office on Drugs and Crime (UNODC), including civil and common law practitioners, agencies, international organizations, and civil society organizations around the world who gave generously of their expertise and time.

This publication was written by Jacinta Anyango Oduor (Task Team Leader, Senior Public Sector Specialist, Stolen Asset Recovery [StAR] Initiative); Francisca M. U. Fernando (Junior Professional Associate, StAR Initiative); Agustin Flah (Consultant, Legal Vice Presidency, World Bank); Dr. Dorothee Gottwald (Crime Prevention and Criminal Justice Officer, UNODC); Jeanne M. Hauch (Consultant, StAR Initiative); Marianne Mathias (Consultant, StAR Initiative); Ji Won Park (Consultant, StAR Initiative); and Dr. Oliver Stolpe (Senior Advisor, StAR Initiative). Robert A. Harrison (Consultant, StAR Initiative) assisted in different stages of the study.

The team is especially grateful to Jean D. Pesme (Coordinator, StAR Initiative) for his support and guidance.

The team benefited immensely from the insightful comments and discussions during the peer review process, which was chaired by Jean Pesme. The peer reviewers were Antenor Madruga (Partner at Barbosa Müussnich & Aragão Advogados, Brazil); Dr. Olaf Meyer (Senior Research Fellow, Centre of European law and Politics, University of Bremen, Germany); Maria Schnebli (Federal Prosecutor, Office of the Attorney General, Switzerland); Dr. Edward Hoseah (Director General, Prevention and Combating of Corruption Bureau, Tanzania); Charles Cain (Deputy Chief, Foreign Corrupt Practices Act [FCPA] Unit, Division of Enforcement, U.S. Securities and Exchange Commission [SEC]); Nathaniel Edmonds (Assistant Chief, Fraud Section, U.S. Department of Justice); Tracy Price (Assistant Director, FCPA Unit, Division of Enforcement, U.S. SEC); Teresa Turner-Jones (Senior Trial Attorney, Asset Forfeiture and Money Laundering Section, U.S. Department of Justice); Panagiotis Papadimitriou (Associate Crime Prevention and Criminal Justice Officer, UNODC); Vladimir Kozin (Crime Prevention and Criminal Justice Office, UNODC); Christina Biebesheimer (Chief Counsel, Legal Vice Presidency, World Bank); El Cid Butuyan (Senior Litigation Specialist, Integrity Vice Presidency, World Bank); and Jean Pierre Brun (Senior Financial Sector Specialist, Financial Market Integrity, World Bank).

Additionally, the team is grateful to Frank A. Fariello (Lead Counsel, Legal Vice Presidency, World Bank); Pascale Helene Dubois (Chief Suspension and Debarment Officer, Office of Suspension and Debarment, World Bank); and Mamta Kaushal (Advisor to the Director of Operations, Integrity Vice Presidency, World Bank) for their review and invaluable comments on the final draft of the study.

We would like to gratefully acknowledge the following individuals who shared with us their knowledge, insights, and experiences:

Steven Johnston (Crown Prosecutor, Specialized Prosecutions Branch, Alberta Justice Criminal Division, Canada); Judge Renaud Van Ruymbeke (Investigative Magistrate, Pole Financier, France); Loic Guerin (Public Prosecutor, France); Philippe Caillol (Senior Liaison Legal Advisor, Embassy of France, Washington, DC); William Bourdon (Lawyer, Sherpa, France); Richard Findl (Public Prosecutor, Germany); Dr. Nina Sophie Heintzeler (Public Prosecutor, Germany); Dr. Nicolas Kaczynski (Senior Public Prosecutor, Germany); Hildegard Baeumler-Hoesl (Presiding Judge, Germany); Maria Gavouneli (Professor, University of Athens, Greece); Olga Sewe (Coordinator, Legal Services, Ethics & Anti-corruption Commission, Kenya); Emmanuel Akomaye (Secretary, Economic and Financial Crimes Commission, Nigeria); Alexander Sierck (Lawyer, SERAP, Nigeria); Helen Garlick (in her capacity as member of the Norway-sponsored International Corruption Hunters); Stefan Lenz (Federal Prosecutor, Switzerland); Walter Maeder (Chief Federal Prosecutor, Switzerland); Nicolas Bottinelli (Deputy Federal Prosecutor, Switzerland); Richard Alderman (Director, U.K. Serious Fraud Office [SFO]); Rosemary Donnabella (Head of Policy, U.K. SFO); Clyde Marklew (International Assistance Manager, U.K. SFO); Anthony Wilson (Legal Adviser, International Assistance Unit, U.K. SFO); Dick Gould (Interim Head—Proceeds of Crime Unit and Intelligence, U.K. SFO); John Folan (Head, Overseas Anti-Corruption Unit of the City of London Police, U.K.); Charlie Monteith (Partner, White & Case, U.K.); Robert Amaee (Partner, Convington & Burling, U.K.); Kathleen Hammann (Trial Attorney, Fraud Section, U.S. Department of Justice [DOJ]); Jack de Kluiver (Assistant Chief, International Unit, Asset Forfeiture and Money Laundering Section, U.S. DOJ); Brigitte Strobel-Shaw (Chief, Conference Support Section, Corruption and Economic Crime Branch, UNODC); Yves Aeschlimann (Senior Financial Sector Specialist, Financial Market Integrity, World Bank); Francesco Clementucci (Consultant, Financial Market Integrity, World Bank); Lindy Muzila (Public Sector Specialist, StAR Initiative, World Bank); and the Anti-Corruption Division of the OECD Secretariat.

We would also like to thank Pranvera Recica (Consultant, StAR Initiative), and Alex Gold, Jialing Shen, and Ryan Voorhees, who worked under the supervision of the Professor Richard K. Gordon, Case Western Reserve University School of Law. The World Bank Law Library also provided valuable research assistance and support in the collection of legal documents.

A special thanks also to Michael S. Geller (Senior Program Assistant, Financial Market Integrity, World Bank) and Eli Bielasiak (Program Assistant, StAR Initiative, World Bank) for their support in the administration of the project.

Abbreviations

AECA	Arms Export Control Act (U.S.)
ARIS	Asset Recovery Incentivisation Scheme (U.K.)
CEO	chief executive officer
CPS	Crown Prosecution Service (U.K.)
CRO	Civil Recovery Order (U.K.)
CSO	civil society organization
DFID	Department for International Development (U.K.)
DOJ	Department of Justice (U.S.)
DPA	Deferred Prosecution Agreement
ECHR	European Court of Human Rights
ECJ	European Court of Justice
EFCC	Economic and Financial Crimes Commission (Nigeria)
FATF	Financial Action Task Force
FBI	Federal Bureau of Investigation (U.S.)
FCPA	Foreign Corrupt Practices Act (U.S.)
FGN	Federal Government of Nigeria
FHC	Federal High Court (Nigeria)
FIU	Financial Intelligence Unit
FSA	Financial Services Authority (U.K.)
ICE	Instituto Costarricense de Electricidad (Costa Rica)
ICHA	International Corruption Hunters Alliance
ICRC	International Committee of the Red Cross
INS	Instituto Nacional de Seguros (Costa Rica)
ITAR	International Traffic in Arms Regulations (U.S.)
KNAB	Corruption Prevention and Combating Bureau (Latvia)
LHDA	Lesotho Highlands Development Authority
LHWP	Lesotho Highlands Water Project
LNG	liquefied natural gas
MDB	multilateral development bank
MLA	mutual legal assistance
MOU	memorandum of understanding
NCB	non-conviction-based (forfeiture)
NGO	nongovernmental organization
NPA	Non-Prosecution Agreement
OACU	Overseas Anti-Corruption Unit (U.K., City of London Police)

OAG	Office of the Attorney General
OECD	Organisation for Economic Co-operation and Development
OFAC	Office of Foreign Assets Control (U.S.)
OFFP	Oil-for-Food Programme (UN)
Økokrim	National Authority for Investigation and Prosecution of Economic and Environmental Crime (Norway)
PEP	politically exposed person
POCA	Proceeds of Crime Act (U.K.)
RICO	Racketeer Influenced and Corrupt Organizations Act (U.S.)
SCC/SCCP	Swiss Criminal Code/Swiss Code of Criminal Procedure
SEC	Securities and Exchange Commission (U.S.)
SFO	Serious Fraud Office (U.K.)
SOE	state-owned enterprise
StAR	Stolen Asset Recovery Initiative
UNCAC	United Nations Convention against Corruption
UNODC	United Nations Office on Drugs and Crime

All dollars are U.S. dollars unless otherwise indicated.

Executive Summary

For let there be no doubt that corruption is not a victimless offense. Corruption is not a gentlemen's agreement where no one gets hurt. People do get hurt. And the people who are hurt the worst are often residents of the poorest countries on the face of the earth, especially where it occurs in the context of government infrastructure projects, contracts in which crucial development decisions are made, in which a country will live by those decisions for good or for bad for years down the road, and where those decisions are made using precious and scarce national resources.

United States Acting Assistant Attorney General announcing
the settlement in the Siemens case December 15, 2008

The fight against the bribery of foreign public officials is critical to the global fight against corruption overall. It entails pursuing with equal determination those who pay bribes and those who accept them. Over the past decade, there has been significant progress in battling foreign bribery, with the clear trend of many cases being resolved through settlements rather than full trials. A settlement may be defined as any procedure short of a full trial.

This trend raises a number of questions that should be considered by the international community: What happens to the money associated with the settlements, and is it being returned to those most directly harmed by the corrupt practices? What are the effects of uneven transparency and varying levels of judicial review of these settlements? What is the impact of settlements on legal actions against the givers and recipients of bribes, in particular, on actions by the countries whose officials have allegedly been bribed?

Using the lens of the United Nations Convention against Corruption (UNCAC), the Stolen Asset Recovery Initiative (StAR) undertook the study *Left Out of the Bargain* to answer these questions and provide policy makers, practitioners, and others with greater understanding of the nature of settlements and, in particular, their implications for asset recovery. The StAR Initiative hopes that this study will spur a more informed and sharper discussion on settlements and asset recovery. StAR also hopes to encourage a global and collective effort toward tackling the challenges to asset recovery posed by settlements.

Left Out of the Bargain addresses the core issue of how the imposition of monetary sanctions through settlements compares to the requirements of UNCAC on the recovery and return of the proceeds of corruption. The study also examines the effect of settlements in one jurisdiction upon investigations into corruption in another: as legal practitioners, policy makers, civil society organizations, and others have asked, how might settlements affect mutual legal assistance or other forms of international cooperation in criminal matters?

This study represents the outcome of extensive research covering developments through April 2013 on settlements in foreign bribery cases. It is based on publicly available resources—including reports by the Organisation for Economic Co-operation and Development Working Group on Bribery and supplemental data—as well as on information collected through discussions with practitioners and experts. *Left Out of the Bargain* maps the contours of settlements in foreign bribery cases in both common and civil law jurisdictions. The objective is to identify the main features of settlements and recommend best practices, informed by the UNCAC requirements for asset recovery.

1. Key Findings

The study found that across the globe there is an increased use of settlements to enforce foreign bribery laws. This growth in the use of settlements is taking place in jurisdictions irrespective of either common law or civil law tradition and in both developed and developing countries.

Progress has been made in recent years in the prosecution of foreign bribery cases. However, the report illustrates in detail for the first time how little of the monetary sanctions collected by the countries of enforcement has been returned to the countries whose officials have been—or are alleged to have been—bribed.

Left Out of the Bargain looked at 395 settlements cases that took place between 1999 and mid-2012. These cases resulted in a total of $6.9 billion in monetary sanctions. Nearly $6 billion of this amount resulted from monetary sanctions imposed by a country different from the one that employed the bribed or allegedly bribed official. Most of the monetary sanctions were imposed by the countries where the corrupt companies (and related individual defendants) are headquartered or otherwise operate. Of the nearly $6 billion imposed, *only about $197 million, or 3.3 percent, has been returned or ordered returned* to the countries whose officials were bribed or allegedly bribed.

The main conclusion of the report is that significant monetary sanctions have been imposed with hardly any of the respective assets being returned to the countries whose officials have allegedly been bribed. The report highlights how the overwhelming majority of the jurisdictions harmed by foreign bribery are in the developing world and that the vast majority of the settlements involve state-owned enterprises and public procurement contracts, including projects that range from tens to hundreds of millions of dollars in infrastructure and natural resources sectors.

The reality is that, in the majority of settlements, the countries whose officials were allegedly bribed have not been involved in the settlements and have not found any other means to obtain redress.

2. Additional Observations

- Countries whose officials were allegedly bribed should step up their own efforts to mount effective investigations and prosecutions against the providers and recipients of these bribes. This would greatly improve their prospects of recovering assets and bolster deterrence against active and passive corruption.
- All jurisdictions negotiating settlements should proactively inform other affected countries of the legal avenues, both criminal and civil, available to them to seek redress and to recover assets. The study identifies innovative ways in which countries whose officials have been (or allegedly been) bribed could pursue the return of proceeds of corruption or other monetary compensation in the context of an enforcement action in another jurisdiction.
- Countries should consider pursuing legal proceedings irrespective of whether a settlement has taken place or may be under way in another jurisdiction. Prohibitions on trying the same crime twice (the principles of double jeopardy and *ne bis in idem*) may not necessarily preclude cases from being brought elsewhere, especially given the likely variations in the facts and the parties. Settlements do not change any legal obligation on the country where the settlement is concluded to respond to a request for international assistance.
- In the vast majority of settled cases, the jurisdictions whose officials were allegedly bribed have played little role in the settlement process, providing them limited opportunity to recover any of the proceeds of such settlements, and they have not often undertaken their own prosecutions of such offences following settlements outside their jurisdictions. The report highlights a small number of cases to date in which such roles have been available and under what circumstances and illustrates future possibilities. The report provides examples of assets being returned in the form of reparations, restitution, and voluntary payments and even under a three-country memorandum of understanding. The funds have been returned directly to countries or to special funds administered by government or nongovernmental organizations for the benefit of the people of the affected countries. In chronicling these examples, the study calls for affected countries to be involved in settlement negotiations and to establish other ways in which they can seek redress for the corrupt acts.
- This study calls for greater transparency in settlements. The negotiation of settlements takes place between the authorities and implicated parties behind closed doors. One critical step would be to inform affected jurisdictions that a negotiation toward a settlement is taking place. The study shows that forms of settlements (such as Non-Prosecution Agreement, Deferred Prosecution Agreement, penalty notice, or a guilty plea) provide varying degrees of transparency. In some jurisdictions, the outcomes of settlements are publicly available, illustrating that greater transparency is possible. Most settlements are negotiated with little oversight by a judge and sometimes without any public hearing at the conclusion. The report emphasizes that once an agreement has been reached, it should not be shielded from public view. More transparency helps ensure fairness to all affected jurisdictions and parties.

3. StAR's Proposals

As settlements have become more common, parties affected by corruption must take advantage of their options for redress, being mindful of the potential consequences financially and legally.

Left Out of the Bargain aims to generate discussion about asset recovery and foster practical action among jurisdictions. The aim is to see affected countries made whole from financial harm stemming from corrupt acts. StAR believes that the settlement of foreign bribery cases should follow the growing global trend for the return of stolen assets and allow countries that are harmed by foreign corruption to seek recovery of assets in line with the UNCAC objectives.

This study suggests a range of potential options to address these settlement-specific challenges:

- Countries should develop a clear legal framework regulating the conditions and process of settlements.
- Countries pursuing settlements should, wherever possible, transmit information spontaneously to other affected countries concerning basic facts of the case, in line with Article 46, paragraph 4 and Article 56 of UNCAC.
- Where applicable, countries pursuing corruption cases should inform other potentially affected countries of the legal avenues available to participate in the investigation and/or claim damages suffered as a result of the corruption.
- Countries should consider permitting their courts or other competent authorities to recognize the claims of other affected countries when deciding on confiscations in the context of settlements, consistent with Article 53 (c) of UNCAC.
- Countries should further proactively share information on concluded settlements with other potentially affected countries. Such information could include the exact terms of the settlement, the underlying facts of the case, the content of any self-disclosure, and any evidence gathered by the investigation. This information could enable other affected countries to conduct several activities:
  - Initiate law enforcement actions within their own jurisdictions against the payers and recipients of bribes as well as any intermediaries
  - Seek mutual legal assistance and other forms of international cooperation
  - Pursue the recovery of assets through international cooperation in criminal matters
  - Pursue the recovery of assets through private civil litigation
  - Participate formally in the initiating jurisdiction's investigation and/or prosecution, with a view to pursuing compensation for damages suffered
  - Seek to modify, annul, or rescind any public contracts, permits, and the like that were concluded in the context of bribery cases as well as consider public debarment
  - Where settlements include such conditions, monitor the compliance of companies with any resolutions of the settlement, obligating them to establish

or reinforce their respective internal anticorruption measures when conducting business transactions within their jurisdiction

Through the implementation of these concrete measures, the progress in the fight against foreign bribery hopefully will continue and the nearly 170 States Parties to the UNCAC, along with other concerned members of the international community, will strengthen their commitment to fulfilling their promises of asset recovery, which lies at the heart of this international treaty.

Introduction

Corruption is an insidious plague that has a wide range of corrosive effects on societies. It under-mines democracy and the rule of law, leads to violations of human rights, distorts markets, erodes the quality of life and allows organized crime, terrorism and other threats to human security to flourish .... Corruption hurts the poor disproportionately by diverting funds intended for development, undermining a Government's ability to provide basic services, feeding inequal-ity and injustice and discouraging foreign aid and investment. Corruption is a key element in economic underperformance and a major obstacle to poverty alleviation and development.

Kofi Annan, *Secretary-General of the United Nations (1997–2006)*
From the Foreword to the UN Convention against Corruption, 2004

1. Background

It is a conservative estimate that every year, through corruption, between $20 billion and $40 billion are diverted from developing countries and find safe haven in foreign jurisdictions.[1] The tracing, seizure, and return of assets looted through corrupt practices have become major concerns of the international community. Multiple international forums, including the General Assembly of the United Nations, the G8 (Group of Eight), the G20 (Group of Twenty), and the Organisation for Economic Co-operation and Development (OECD) Development Assistance Committee, have declared that the identification, confiscation, and return of assets are a priority in the context of enhanced action for development.[2]

One hundred sixty-eight countries have now ratified the United Nations Convention against Corruption (UNCAC),[3] which establishes asset recovery as a "fundamental principle of the Convention."[4] In accordance with their obligations under UNCAC, countries have put into place new domestic laws, amended and simplified existing pro-cedures (particularly in relation to international cooperation in criminal matters), and enhanced the capacities of their relevant authorities in tracing, seizing, and confiscating

---

1. See United Nations Office on Drugs and Crime (UNODC) and World Bank, *Stolen Asset Recovery (StAR) Initiative: Challenges, Opportunities, and Action Plan* (Washington, DC: World Bank, 2007), 1. The StAR Initiative is a partnership between the World Bank Group and UNODC that supports international efforts to end safe havens for corrupt funds. StAR works with developing countries and financial centers to prevent the laundering of the proceeds of corruption and to facilitate more systematic and timely return of stolen assets.
2. UN General Assembly Resolutions 55/188, 56/186, 57/244, 59/242, and 60/207; The G20 Seoul Summit Leaders' Declaration, 11–12 November 2010, and its annex 3; the G20 Anti-Corruption Action Plan; and the OECD Convention on Combating Bribery of Foreign Public Officials in International Business Transactions (OECD Anti-Bribery Convention).
3. Status as of October 24, 2013.
4. See United Nations Convention against Corruption (UNCAC), Chapter 5, Article 51, General Provision.

the proceeds of corruption. Under UNCAC, countries are required to adopt a more proactive approach to asset recovery. Despite these measures, countries mounting international asset recovery efforts continue to face multiple, often insurmountable, barriers.[5] Although UNCAC came into force in 2005, efforts to trace, seize, confiscate, and return the stolen assets are frequently thwarted. In some cases, in the wake of these efforts, frictions and misunderstandings have arisen between the states or governments involved, perhaps due to frustration at uneven rates of progress in asset recovery.

While obstacles to recovery remain, over the past decade significant strides have been made in enforcing foreign bribery laws,[6] especially in countries signatory to the OECD Convention on Combating Bribery of Foreign Public Officials in International Business Transactions (commonly referred to as the OECD Anti-Bribery Convention). In the period examined for this study, 1999 to mid-2013, more countries have successfully pursued cases, and the monetary sanctions assessed against offenders, especially companies (legal persons), have become heavier.

In several countries that are party to the OECD Anti-Bribery Convention, a very high proportion of cases of foreign bribery and related offenses have been resolved short of a full trial. These methods of resolving cases have become known as *settlements*. This study adopts a broad definition of *settlements*, covering various procedures for concluding foreign bribery cases short of a full trial, whether in civil law or common law jurisdictions. The authorities in the enforcement countries generally consider such resolutions to be a highly effective way of concluding complex cases, ensuring comparatively quick punishment of the offenders, and, in the case of companies, imposing significant monetary sanctions and recovering the proceeds of corruption.[7]

Meanwhile, outside of the home countries of the bribe payers (where many of the cases are settled), those countries whose officials were bribed or allegedly bribed have struggled to bring prosecutions against either the public officials in question or the foreign bribe payers. In the vast majority of such cases, these countries have not been involved in the settlements concluded in the jurisdictions pursuing the bribe payers, nor have they found any other way of obtaining redress.

Anticorruption practitioners and policy makers in countries where officials were allegedly bribed have (along with other interested stakeholders) therefore raised concerns about whether settlements might impede their own criminal/enforcement investigations and

---

5. See Kevin M. Stephenson, Larissa Gray, Ric Power, Jean Pierre Brun, Gabriele Dunker, and Melissa Panjer, *Barriers to Asset Recovery: An Analysis of the Key Barriers and Recommendations for Action* (Washington, DC: World Bank and StAR, 2011).

6. See UNCAC, Article 16, Bribery of Foreign Public Officials and Officials of Public International Organizations.

7. In several OECD countries, up to half of their cases of foreign bribery have been resolved through settlements. With regard to cases against legal persons, in a number of countries (e.g., the United Kingdom and Italy), *all* the foreign bribery cases against legal persons have been settled and not a single case has proceeded to trial. The use of settlements in the context of foreign bribery cases is typically no different than the use of settlements in other types of enforcement actions.

affect the liability of multinational companies in third countries. In particular, questions have surfaced about whether settlements may affect mutual legal assistance (MLA) or other forms of international cooperation in criminal matters, and if so, how. Furthermore, several countries, as well as civil society organizations,[8] have expressed concern about the eligibility of fines, confiscations, and other sums paid in the context of settlements to be returned to the countries whose officials were allegedly bribed; from their standpoint, these countries have suffered damage as a result of the acts of foreign bribery.

This debate gained momentum in late 2010, when a group of anticorruption officials from around the world came together in an effort to craft a truly global alliance against corruption at the inaugural meeting of the International Corruption Hunters Alliance (ICHA) convened at the World Bank.[9] During the proceedings, members of ICHA expressed interest in the growing practice in settlements and particularly the impact of settlements on asset recovery. As noted in box I.1, at the conclusion of the 2010 meeting the ICHA requested that the Stolen Asset Recovery (StAR) Initiative undertake a study on the topic.[10] The interest has continued to mount through the mid-2012 second meeting of ICHA, where a conference version of this study was presented and feedback was received from the participants.

This study represents the outcomes of this research to date. One component of this research was the compilation of a database of 395 settled cases involving foreign bribery and related offences, which include criminal, civil, and administrative settlements.[11] The study found that in the 395 settled cases, a total of about $6.9 billion has been imposed in monetary sanctions. This amount falls into three categories: (i) about $5.9 billion where the country of enforcement was different from the country where the official was bribed or allegedly bribed, (ii) about $556 million imposed by enforcing countries whose officials were bribed, and (iii) other cases totaling about $385 million in sanctions. Of the first category of cases ($5.9 billion in sanctions), the study found that only about $197 million, or 3.3 percent, had been returned or ordered returned to the countries whose officials were bribed or allegedly bribed.

With such minimal returns, it will come as no surprise that countries whose officials were allegedly bribed crave knowledge as to how they may benefit from the settlement trend

---

8. The UNCAC Coalition (http://www.uncaccoalition.org/) is a global network of over 350 civil society organizations in more than 100 countries committed to promoting the ratification, implementation, and monitoring of UNCAC. Established in August 2006, it mobilizes civil society action for UNCAC at international, regional, and national levels.

9. Joined by representatives of international organizations, the private sector, and civil society organizations, more than 250 anticorruption officials from 134 countries met at the World Bank to strengthen enforcement through information-sharing and coordinated action.

10. See note 1 for more on StAR. See also ICHA, *A Time for Action,* 2010 ICHA meeting report (Washington, DC: World Bank, 2010), http://siteresources.worldbank.org/INTDOII/Resources/ICHA _Meeting_Report.pdf.

11. For the purpose of the study, the database Settlements of Foreign Bribery and Related Cases was compiled for the period between 1999 and July 2012 (see appendix 3). The database can be accessed at StAR Corruption Cases Search Center at http://star.worldbank.org/corruption-cases/?db=All. However further research on actions taken by countries whose officials have been bribed was only completed in April 2013.

and, operationally, what legal tools they can mobilize to play a full part in the increasing global enforcement drive against foreign bribery. These countries have a vital interest in pursuing the wrongdoers (domestically and abroad) and in recovering assets as well as in obtaining redress for harm suffered as a result of the foreign bribery. Expanding knowledge about the effects of settlements of prosecutions and other enforcement actions is likely to help countries in their anticorruption and asset recovery efforts. More generally, all countries could benefit from greater clarity regarding the settlement process and how it may impact their own anticorruption efforts, including their adherence with UNCAC.

This study seeks to fill this knowledge gap by (i) informing policy makers and practitioners about the frameworks for settlements in various legal systems, (ii) examining settlements in practice and their implications for international cooperation, and (iii) analyzing how settlements relate to asset recovery in foreign bribery cases. An additional goal is to inform the general public (including civil society organizations) about these frameworks.

Before proceeding further, it is helpful to consider the terminology regarding the consequences of foreign bribery. This study has opted to use the word *victim* sparingly, when it refers to domestic legislation that uses such terminology. *Affected country* is understood as any country that may claim harm as a result of transnational bribery, which includes in particular the countries whose officials were allegedly bribed. Countries whose facilities are used, whose nationals serve as intermediaries, or whose markets are touched by transactions may also take the position that they are affected. While the concept of *victim* may readily be understood in its general meaning, in a legal context the question of who may be considered a victim, and under what circumstances, is determined by domestic laws, with many variations and subtleties.[12] In the context of corruption, there is no commonly agreed upon definition of *victim* at the global level.

The question of who is or should be considered a victim in the context of corruption is not only important but also complex in relation to transnational bribery. In a particular case, whether harm was suffered, by whom, and where may be difficult to identify and quantify.[13] The concept of a *victim country* is even more complicated and deserving of a thorough debate. That debate, however, would go beyond the scope of this study. Nonetheless, certain elements in this study (addressing participation as a civil party to a criminal action and conditions for qualifying for restitution) may serve as points of departure for further discussions.[14]

2. United Nations Convention against Corruption: Setting the Stage

Asset recovery represents a relatively new field of international law and international cooperation. As of yet, there have been relatively few cases where countries have been able to recover the proceeds of corruption. In 2011, StAR estimated that the total of stolen assets recovered over the past 15 years probably does not exceed $5 billion.[15]

Chapter 5 of UNCAC establishes asset recovery as one of its fundamental principles. UNCAC provides the necessary legal framework to enable countries effectively to prevent the transfer of proceeds of corruption and to detect, trace, freeze, forfeit, and return funds obtained through corrupt activities and moved across jurisdictions. More specifically, UNCAC sets forth procedures and conditions for asset recovery, such as the facilitation of civil and administrative actions, recognition of and actions based on foreign confiscation orders, and return of property to requesting states and other

---

12. Domestic laws often confer victim status. International organizations have also sought to define victims and ways to provide redress. More information can be found on the website of the International Criminal Court Trust Fund for Victims, http://www.trustfundforvictims.org/.

13. On the issue of quantification, see OECD/World Bank, *Identification and Quantification of the Proceeds of Bribery: A Joint OECD-StAR Analysis* (OECD, 2011), http://dx.doi.org/10.1787/9789264174801-en, which presents information on methods used by different countries to calculate illicit gains made by companies that pay bribes to win contracts or gain unfair advantages.

14. See chapter 4, section 3 for more on modes of participation in criminal/enforcement actions in the context of settlements.

15. Stephenson et al., 1.

legitimate owners.[16] The convention requires States Parties to establish a regime and procedures for the receipt, processing, recognition and enforcement of a request received by another State Party for the purpose of confiscation, either through the freezing, seizure or confiscation of assets by its competent national authorities or by means of direct enforcement of foreign orders (Articles 55 and 54).

In Article 57, the convention establishes some mandatory requirements and general rules upon which States Parties shall base their procedures for the return and disposal of confiscated assets, once the proceeds of corruption have been traced, frozen, and confiscated. Article 57 begins with the principle that confiscated property "shall be disposed of, including by return to its prior legitimate owners." More specifically Article 57 recognizes the following:

- Where property has been obtained through the embezzlement of public funds, the property *must* be returned, provided that the requesting state has obtained a "final judgment" (a requirement that can be waived).[17]
- Assets *must* also be returned in cases where the requesting State Party can demonstrate "prior ownership" or "damage" suffered as a consequence of acts of corruption, provided that the requesting State has obtained a "final judgment" (a requirement that can be waived).[18]
- In "all other cases," the requested State Party shall still "give *priority consideration* to returning confiscated property to the requesting State Party, returning such property to its prior legitimate owners, or compensating the victims of the crime."[19]

In the obligation to return confiscated assets to the requesting State Party, the provision departs significantly from other earlier conventions. In all cases, a requesting State Party needs to act proactively.

Asset recovery efforts through criminal proceedings have often suffered setbacks because of obstacles such as the immunity of some high-ranking public officials, an inability to reach the required standard of proof in criminal cases, or the death or flight of defendants.[20] Therefore, to supplement the more traditional proceedings for recovering assets

---

16. Measures relevant to asset recovery are contained in other parts of the convention as well. Other relevant provisions include (i) measures to prevent and criminalize the laundering of the proceeds of corruption (Articles 14, 16, 23, and 24); (ii) measures to allow for the effective freezing, seizure, and confiscation of the proceeds of corruption domestically (Article 31); (iii) measures allowing the victims of corruption, whether entities or persons, to claim damages suffered as a result of corruption and to obtain compensation (Article 35); and (iv) procedures related to the request and provision of mutual legal assistance and law enforcement cooperation (Articles 1[b], 43, 46, and 48). In particular, with regard to the tracing, seizing, confiscation, and return of the proceeds of corruption, the convention provides a range of avenues for asset recovery, including direct civil litigation (Article 53) as well as by the more traditional means of international cooperation in criminal matters (Articles 54, 55, and 57).
17. Article 57(3)(a).
18. Article 55 and 57(3)(b).
19. Article 57(3)(c). Italics added.
20. See generally Stephenson et al.

through international cooperation in criminal matters, Article 53 of the convention provides for facilitating the recovery of assets through direct (private) civil litigation.[21]

Chapter 5 of UNCAC underlines the proactive spirit of the convention when it comes to going after the proceeds of corruption. Among other provisions, Article 56 encourages States Parties to forward any information about known or suspected proceeds of corruption to another State Party *without prior request* when the requesting state believes that the disclosure of such information might assist the receiving party in initiating or carrying out investigations, prosecutions, or judicial proceedings or when such information might trigger a request for international cooperation. Article 35 is also relevant within this context, as it requires States Parties to ensure that entities or individuals who have suffered damages as a result of corruption have the right to initiate legal proceedings to obtain damages or compensation from those responsible.

The convention further foresees, in its Article 37, paragraph 2, that each State Party shall consider providing for the possibility, in appropriate cases, of mitigating punishment of an accused person who provides substantial cooperation in the investigation or prosecution of an offence established in accordance with the convention. In sum, these UNCAC provisions make up the highly innovative architecture of legal, institutional, and operational measures aimed at materializing the return of assets. As the convention is in only the early stages of implementation, it will be years before all the technical implications of this framework are fully explored. Nonetheless, at this stage, in light of the possibilities for countries to take advantage of the various options opened by the convention to recover assets, concerns have been voiced as to whether—and how—settlements can have an impact on those possibilities. Against this backdrop, settlements appear to be an important tool that requires careful analysis in the context of UNCAC.

3. Methodology and Overview of the Study

This study describes and analyzes, both qualitatively and quantitatively, settlements in cases of foreign bribery and related offenses, and their implications for international cooperation and asset recovery.

The following categories of cases fall within the scope of this study:

- Cases involving public enforcement by criminal, civil, or administrative law against both legal and natural persons (with the emphasis on cases against legal persons, since any monetary sanctions and other forms of relief tend to be more substantial, making them of greater interest in the context of asset recovery)[22]

---

21. As for Article 53, since this study focuses on settlements resulting from enforcement actions by states, the avenue of civil private litigation under this provision of the convention is only indirectly relevant.
22. To define the category, the study used as its starting point the work done by the OECD, the only major public body to have compiled comprehensive reliable enforcement data by country on foreign bribery. In addition to the self-reported cases from the OECD data, this study has drawn on other sources. See appendix 3 on methodology.

The study does not cover the following categories:

- Cases brought only against assets in the context of civil forfeiture procedures as available in some common law jurisdictions (i.e., cases not against natural or legal persons),[23] unless such cases also involved a foreign bribery or related offense charged against a legal or natural person
- Private civil lawsuits, when a state acting in its private capacity files a civil claim in the courts of another state[24]

To define the category of cases examined, the study used as its starting point the work done by the Organisation for Economic Co-operation and Development (OECD) Working Group on Bribery. Member countries self-report cases fulfilling their obligations under the OECD Anti-Bribery Convention. These include foreign bribery cases and those "related" cases arising under other offenses covered by the OECD convention, which addresses the "supply side" of foreign bribery (i.e., offenses committed by the bribe payers or alleged bribe payers).[25]

The study does not itself define a case as "related" to foreign bribery but relies on the selection of cases put forward by States Parties to the OECD convention. In addition to using cases self-reported to the OECD, and because of the variance in reporting dates for countries, this study has drawn on other sources to include similar data announced by countries subsequent to their most recent OECD reports. Where readily available, the study has also included similar data regarding settlements in non-OECD member countries, such as Costa Rica and Nigeria.[26]

Although most of the cases used were mentioned in the countries' OECD Phase 3 Peer Review Reports, not all countries reported all of their enforcement actions in cases arising under the "UN Oil-for-Food" scandal as foreign bribery cases,[27] since the cases were sometimes prosecuted under statutes not specific to foreign bribery. To be consistent, the study included in its database all UN Oil-for-Food enforcement actions that

---

23. Similarly, another kind of procedure, known as *asset sharing*, is not part of this study. Asset sharing generally refers to laws or policies that provide a share of the monetary proceeds or forfeited assets from a case to a law enforcement agency of another jurisdiction that assisted the primary jurisdiction that prosecuted the case and generated the recovery. That is very different from asset recovery to countries whose officials were allegedly bribed, the focus of this study.

24. The World Bank plans a future study on this important aspect of asset recovery. These are lawsuits contemplated by Article 53 of UNCAC.

25. The OECD convention criminalizes not only the offering of bribes but also related accounting, auditing, books, and record-keeping offenses. The convention also places sanctions on the laundering of bribes and proceeds of foreign bribery. It does not address the receipt of bribes, the so-called demand side.

26. See appendix 3 for greater explanation.

27. The Oil-for-Food Programme was designed to soften the impact on the Iraqi people of sanctions against the government of Iraq by allowing some sales of oil. However, many companies were found to have made kickback payments to the regime of Saddam Hussein.

were resolved by settlements. Finally, the study considered settlements in cases against the recipients of bribes where such data was available.[28]

Following extensive research through publicly available sources, this study created the database of 395 settlements in foreign bribery and related cases mentioned earlier,[29] building on the research that had been conducted for the StAR Asset Recovery Watch Database as well as the StAR Asset Recovery Handbook.[30] These sources were supplemented with open-source materials. Cases for which there were no official sources were not included in the database.[31] As noted, the database includes cases of foreign bribery and related offenses, against both legal and natural persons, whether prosecuted by criminal, civil, or administrative methods. In addition, the study selected 14 cases of primary relevance to settlements and asset recovery for in-depth review. These case summaries illustrate the principles, trends, and developments highlighted in the analysis throughout and have been included as a final section to this study.

Moreover, the study team consulted with practitioners and policy makers working in global financial centers and in the developing world, with a view to drawing from their practical experience in concluding settlements in foreign bribery cases. The study team also sought further guidance and analysis regarding the interpretation of some of the source material and collected additional materials where available. The aim was to gain a more precise understanding of the settlement process, especially where there is little or no publicly available documentation. These practitioners provided key insights into how settlements come about and the destinations of the monetary penalties collected as a result of settlements. In addition, the study team reached out to 28 countries to seek further information on efforts taken by the countries whose public officials had allegedly been bribed, whether such action had been taken in parallel to a case prosecuted or as follow-up actions to a settlement concluded in another jurisdiction.

The study team conducted an experts workshop to review a draft in progress, with the participation of civil and common law practitioners from the developed and

---

28. For example, if the case of the bribe taker is part of the same cluster of cases reported to the OECD, it is considered. To illustrate, if a country reported a case of company X paying bribes to person A, the database also includes the case of person A. See, for example, chapter 6, case 5, the Haiti Teleco case, where the United States reported its enforcement actions against both bribe payers and foreign public officials who were the bribe takers.

29. Like the OECD data, the study includes cases that are concluded on the basis of offenses other than bribery, since many cases begin with the bribery offense and, because of self-reporting and cooperation in the investigation, lack of sufficient evidence, scarce law enforcement resources, or other factors, are settled on the basis of other, lesser charges.

30. Available at http://star.worldbank.org/corruption-cases/arw. The StAR Asset Recovery Watch Database is a publicly available database that collects and systematizes information about completed and ongoing asset recovery cases with international dimensions.

31. StAR used similar methods for both the database created for Emile van der Does de Willebois et al., *The Puppet Masters: How the Corrupt Use Legal Structures to Hide Stolen Assets and What to Do about It* (Washington, DC: International Bank for Reconstruction and Development/World Bank, 2011) and the StAR Asset Recovery Watch Database. See StAR Corruption Cases Search Center at http://star.worldbank.org/corruption-cases/?db=All.

developing world. In addition, the study was peer reviewed by a panel of internal World Bank and external experts. A conference edition of the study was presented during the ICHA 2012 meetings, which included a panel discussion with civil and common law experts with experience in settlements cases in their respective jurisdictions. In addition, the team consulted with civil society organizations and reviewed relevant materials produced by such groups.

This report is structured as follows:

- Chapter 1 adopts a broad definition of settlements as various procedures short of trials and analyzes the legal frameworks in a number of civil and common law countries.
- Chapter 2 traces the general trends and developments in settlements and considers the rationale for settlements.
- Chapter 3 analyzes the impact of settlements in one jurisdiction on pending and future investigations in other countries, concentrating on any effects of *ne bis in idem/double jeopardy* principles and on international cooperation and mutual legal assistance.
- Chapter 4 explores the link between asset recovery and settlements through the lens of UNCAC.
- Chapter 5 offers conclusions.
- Chapter 6 presents detailed summaries of 14 significant cases.

1. Settlements in Foreign Bribery Cases

Settlements are part of the legal toolkit for depriving offenders of the proceeds of crime. Settlements are used in many countries of different legal traditions, both civil and common law. As noted in the Introduction, this study adopts a broad definition of *settlements* to include various procedures for concluding foreign bribery cases short of a full trial, whether in civil law or common law jurisdictions. Settlements may take a variety of forms, be reached through different means and be used for different reasons. In this chapter, we explore these topics in more detail.

1. Defining the Term *Settlement*

Over the past decade, in many countries around the world there has been a significant increase in the enforcement of foreign bribery laws. According to data from the Organisation for Economic Co-operation and Development (OECD), between the 1999 advent of the OECD Anti-Bribery Convention and December 2012, there were 90 legal persons (entities) and 216 natural persons (individuals) sanctioned under criminal proceedings alone for foreign bribery, by 13 out of the 40 States Parties to the convention.[1] National legal frameworks for addressing foreign bribery vary considerably. An examination of those civil law and common law jurisdictions that are most vigorous in their enforcement reveals that most of them are not using full trials but rather some form of abbreviated criminal proceedings. In fact, very few cases of foreign bribery (whether against natural or legal persons) have ever gone to trial anywhere. In other words, shortened procedures are becoming the norm rather than the exception, and this is especially true when cases involve legal persons.

Different jurisdictions conduct abbreviated procedures in different ways. Common law jurisdictions tend to prefer a negotiated process, in which the two sides—prosecution and defendant—reach a mutually acceptable agreement. This agreement is then usually presented to a judge for confirmation. The most widely used mechanism in such cases is the guilty plea. Settlements of this type, involving foreign bribery of legal persons, can be found in the United States, Canada, and the United Kingdom. However, other forms have also developed. These include civil settlements in the United Kingdom, deferred- and non-prosecution agreements in the United States, and out-of-court restitution arrangements in Nigeria.

In civil law countries, although negotiations may take place, the process tends to take the form of a proposal made by the prosecutor to the defendant to admit liability, agree

---

1. OECD Working Group on Bribery, *Annual Report 2013*, 9, http://www.oecd.org/daf/anti-bribery/AntiBriberyAnnRep2012.pdf.

to pay a specific sum of money or meet certain conditions, and thus avoid a long, drawn-out procedure. A few examples of this type of settlement are the summary punishment order against Alstom Network in Switzerland,[2] the *patteggiamento* used in the Pirelli case in Italy, the administrative and criminal procedures in Germany in the Siemens cases,[3] and the penalty notice used to end the Statoil case in Norway.[4]

While civil law practitioners would be unlikely to describe the procedures in use in their jurisdictions as "settlements," these procedures seem to have enough in common with what happens in common law jurisdictions to justify considering them as members of the same category, for purposes of this study. This provides an opportunity to consider similar developments with similar significant impact. In this study, therefore, we adopt a broad definition of the term "settlement," as any procedure short of a full trial.

As set out in the methodology, for the purposes of this study we compiled a database of relevant cases (the StAR Database of Settlements of Foreign Bribery and Related Cases). It contains 395 settlements that took place in 15 different jurisdictions and relate to both natural and legal persons from 1999 through mid-2012. Of these 395 cases, 391 are from national jurisdictions and four are cases from the administrative sanctions system of the World Bank Group.[5] The details are summarized in table 1.1.

Although we make no claim that our methodology is comprehensive or the database exhaustive,[6] the figures are enough to enable us to make some broad observations. First, the country with the most settlements was the United States, followed by Germany, the United Kingdom, and Switzerland, in that order.

When we further break down the data by legal system, we find that more than three-quarters of all settlements have occurred in common law jurisdictions. However, the vast majority of the common law settlements have occurred in the United States, so the percentages are not very probative. In common law jurisdictions, settlements have taken place in Canada, Lesotho, Nigeria, the United Kingdom, and the United States. In civil law jurisdictions, settlements have occurred in Costa Rica, Denmark, Germany, Greece, Italy, Japan, Kazakhstan, the Netherlands, Norway, and Switzerland. See table 1.2.

It must be noted that these jurisdictions are using not only criminal but also civil and administrative laws to prosecute foreign bribery and related offenses. The use of these provisions frequently overlaps, as is clear from the concurrent use of criminal enforcement by the U.S. Department of Justice (DOJ) and civil enforcement by the Securities and Exchange Commission (SEC) and the predominant use in Germany of criminal provisions against natural persons and administrative provisions against legal persons.

---

2. For a summary of the case, see chapter 6, case study 2.
3. For a summary of the case, see chapter 6, case study 12.
4. For a summary of the case, see chapter 6, case study 13.
5. Please see StAR Corruption Cases Search Center at http://star.worldbank.org/corruption-cases/?db=All to access the database.
6. See appendix 3 for methodology.

TABLE 1.1	Settlements of Foreign Bribery and Related Offenses Cases, 1999 through July 3, 2012			
			Cases pertaining to	
Country/ jurisdiction of settlement	Total cases (no.)	Total cases (%)	Individuals/ natural persons (no.)	Companies/ legal persons (no.)
Canada	2	0.51	0	2
Costa Rica	1	0.25	0	1
Denmark	2	0.51	0	2
Germany	42	10.63	35	7
Greece	1	0.25	0	1
Italy	11	2.78	7	4
Japan	2	0.51	2	0
Kazakhstan	1	0.25	0	0
Lesotho	2	0.51	1	1
Netherlands	8	2.03	0	8
Nigeria	7	1.77	0	7
Norway	3	0.76	1	2
Switzerland	15	3.80	1	13
United Kingdom	19	4.81	6	13
United States	275	69.62	87	187
World Bank	4	1.01	0	4
Total	395	100	140	252*

Source: StAR Database of Settlements of Foreign Bribery and Related Cases, http://star.worldbank.org/corruption-cases/?db=All.
* The cases pertaining to individuals/natural persons and companies/legal persons total 392 as opposed to the total of 395 in column 2. The Kazakhstan and Swiss settlements in the Kazakh Oil Mining case pertain to confiscated funds, and hence were not included in this tally.

TABLE 1.2	Settlements by Type of Legal System: Civil and Common Law Jurisdictions		
Jurisdiction by system		Cases (no.)	Cases (%)
Civil Law: Costa Rica, Denmark, Germany, Greece, Italy, Japan, Kazakhstan, Netherlands, Norway, and Switzerland		86	21.8
Common Law: Canada, Lesotho, Nigeria, United Kingdom, and United States		305	77.2
Other: World Bank		4	1.0
Total		395	100%

Source: Based on StAR Database of Settlements of Foreign Bribery and Related Cases, http://star.worldbank.org/corruption-cases/?db=All.

Usually, a foreign bribery case begins with the gathering of evidence by investigators, investigating magistrates, and/or prosecutors. This may consist of the following:

- Information disclosed by the wrongdoer him/her/itself
- Evidence obtained as a result of the efforts of law enforcement
- Information provided by another state or some other third party (e.g., an international organization that has conducted an inquiry)[7]

Settlements typically come into the picture (if at all) before or when criminal charges are filed. For example, in the United States most settlements of cases against legal persons occur prior to criminal charges being filed, or the agreed upon charges are filed contemporaneously with the settlement agreement. However, settlements can also occur during the course of a trial.

For the purpose of obtaining evidence located outside its border, a country may engage in international cooperation (cooperation prior to mutual legal assistance and formal mutual legal assistance requests) to obtain evidence. This phase of an investigation (whether prior to the filing of charges or not) may include securing the proceeds of crime and any instrumentalities that may be subject to confiscation (e.g., obtaining restraint or freezing orders on any assets).

2. Legal Frameworks for Settlements

As already noted, quite a number of jurisdictions have used settlement procedures to conclude foreign bribery cases. We have selected the legal frameworks of eight jurisdictions (four civil law and four common law jurisdictions) as likely to be most informative: Canada, Germany, Italy, Nigeria, Norway, Switzerland, the United Kingdom, and the United States. Within this scope, we focus on instances where settlements have been used to conclude cases against legal persons, as it is in such cases that financial sanctions are most significant. We also take account of:

- innovative features (especially with regard to asset recovery),
- depth of experience, and
- cases involving multiple jurisdictions.

Other jurisdictions (e.g., Costa Rica, Greece, and Lesotho) have also concluded settlements within the definition of this study and certainly offer beneficial lessons.[8] The achievements of some of these countries (and the jurisdictions discussed in detail below) in addressing foreign bribery are illustrated in the 14 in-depth case summaries given in chapter 6.

---

7. For example, the UN Oil-for-Food cases and the Macmillan case were sparked by disclosures to national authorities by international organizations (the United Nations and the World Bank, respectively).
8. See chapter 2, section 5.2.

The next section examines typical cases, focusing on the procedural framework and how these shortened procedures work in practice in both civil and common law jurisdictions.

The discussion begins with civil law jurisdictions (in order, Switzerland, Norway, Italy, and Germany), which have only recently begun to use shortened procedures.[9] It then turns to the common law systems (United Kingdom, Canada, Nigeria, and the United States). Finally, there is a brief look at the role of administrative sanctions by a nonstate actor (e.g., an international organization), as in some cases these have been linked to cases in the national systems.

In discussing each national legal framework, particular attention has been paid to three aspects of each system, consistent with the goals of this study in assessing the impact of settlements:

- Form of the liability: whether the offender can be held liable under criminal, civil, or administrative law or some combination of the above.
- Judicial oversight: whether the court is involved and to what extent the court will review and approve the settlement.
- Transparency of the settlement: whether and to what extent the content and terms of the settlements are public.

3. Shortened Criminal Procedures and Other Forms in Certain Civil Law Countries

3.1 Switzerland

According to Section 352 of the Swiss Code of Criminal Procedure (SCCP), under certain conditions the prosecutor may conclude a case without bringing it to court if the prosecutor considers that the charges do not merit a penalty of greater than six months' imprisonment and a fine of Sw F 5 million, with any confiscation component to be unlimited. Another provision, SCCP 358, provides for a negotiated resolution or so-called simplified procedure, in which the accused can negotiate the sentence in exchange for recognizing the facts of the offense in documentation approved by the court. The imprisonment penalties can be up to five years, and monetary penalties have no limit.

In the first case of liability of a legal person under its foreign bribery laws, the Swiss authorities investigated a French energy and transport company. They found that the company, using its Swiss subsidiary, had engaged in a wide-ranging scheme to pay

---

9. The trend of civil law countries using shortened procedures to settle criminal foreign bribery cases could potentially expand to other countries, such as France, which has recently enacted legal reforms to permit the prosecutor and defendant to agree on a pecuniary sentence in foreign bribery cases. See newly redacted Article 495–7 of the French Criminal Procedure Code, extending the Comparution sur Reconnaissance Préalable de Culpabilité to classes of offenses including corruption and foreign bribery.

bribes to obtain contracts in Latvia, Tunisia, and Malaysia.[10] The Swiss prosecutors informed the subsidiary, Alstom Network Schweiz AG, that it was ready formally to file charges and proposed to the subsidiary company a *summary punishment order* to conclude the case.[11] The company accepted. Under that order, the company agreed to admit to and be convicted of failing to prevent bribery[12] and to pay a specified fine of Sw F 2.5 million and confiscation of Sw F 36.4 million plus procedural costs. The confiscation was for the amount of profits earned as a result of the offenses.

The Swiss prosecutors wrote up a statement of the facts (setting out the foreign bribery scheme in about eight pages) and the terms of the agreement. The prosecutor and the company signed the statement. The prosecutor acted as judge and placed a copy of the document in the nonpublic files of the court. The summary punishment document was then posted publicly on the Internet for a period of 14 days to alert any affected parties.[13] If the subsidiary had refused the summary punishment order, the prosecution would have filed charges in court and the case likely would have proceeded to full trial.

For the French parent company of the Swiss subsidiary, Swiss prosecutors negotiated a separate voluntary reparation payment of Sw F 1 million to a humanitarian foundation for the benefit of people in the three countries whose officials had been bribed. In light of the resolution of the case against its subsidiary and the reparation payment, Swiss prosecutors determined that it was appropriate to waive the prosecution under a section of Swiss criminal procedure permitting the waiver if full reparations have been made.[14] Both the summary punishment and reparations provisions have existed in Swiss law for quite some time. What is new is their application to a legal person for the offense of foreign bribery.

Under the summary punishment procedure and the reparations procedure, the punishment is determined through a proposal by the prosecutor and agreement by the defendant without the involvement of the court. The only aspect visible to the public is the posting of the settlement documents for 14 days, unless the defendant chooses to release the document or other information.[15]

---

10. See Case EAII.04.0325-LEN, Alstom Network Schweiz AG, summary punishment order under Article 352 of the Swiss Code of Criminal Procedure (SCCP) (22 November 2011). For a summary of the case, see chapter 6, case 1.
11. Section 352 of SCCP.
12. See SCCP Article 102, Section 2, and Article 322.
13. After that time, the summary punishment document would be available only by special request to the prosecutor's office, based on demonstration of a legal need for it. While the 14 days is not specified by law, Swiss authorities indicated it is a practice likely to be followed in future cases against legal persons.
14. Under the reparations provision, SCCP 53, if the public interest and the interest of the victim in prosecuting the defendant are insignificant and if the "defendant has compensated for the damage or made all efforts that could reasonably be expected to correct the wrong that was caused, the competent authority can waive prosecution." SCC Articles 53 and 42. See the summary at chapter 6, case 1.
15. In the case of Alstom Network, the company chose to provide an unofficial translation of the settlement document (in English) on its own website for a longer period of time.

3.2 Norway

Norway as well has resolved foreign bribery-related cases through a shortened criminal procedure similar to that of Switzerland. In Norway, the prosecution may issue a *penalty notice*[16] to a natural or legal person if the prosecutor determines that the case should be decided by the imposition of a fine or confiscation or both and not by a sentence of imprisonment (in the case of natural persons). The Norwegian penalty notice cites the provision of law alleged to be violated, describes the violation, and sets forth the proposed monetary penalty.[17] The defendant may accept the penalty (pay that amount) or elect to proceed to trial.[18]

For example, the Norwegian petroleum company, Statoil, entered into a consultancy arrangement to make payments for the benefit of an Iranian official, including paying a "success fee" upon obtaining certain rights to develop new oil reserves and contributing to "charities" chosen by the official. The Norwegian anticorruption authority, Økokrim, filed corruption charges against the company and carried out search warrants to obtain more evidence. About nine months later, Økokrim concluded its investigation of the company by issuing penalty notices. Under the penalty notices, the company agreed to pay a fine of NKr 20 million ($3 million) and the implicated employee agreed to pay a fine of NKr 200,000 (about $30,000).[19] In addition to the Statoil case mentioned above, one other company has admitted criminal liability under the penalty notice procedure.[20]

When a defendant accepts the penalty notice in Norway, it has the same legal consequences as a conviction.[21] The penalty notices are made public on Økokrim's website, along with a press release.

3.3 Italy

In Italy, all the foreign bribery cases in which sanctions have been imposed have been prosecuted under a procedure called the *patteggiamento*.[22] Akin to a plea-bargaining

---

16. Also referred to as *optional penalty writs*.
17. For natural persons, the penalty notice should also specify the sentence of imprisonment to be served if the fine and/or confiscation is not paid.
18. OECD, *Phase 3 Report on Implementing the OECD Anti-Bribery Convention in Norway* (Paris: OECD, 2011), 7–8, 20–21, http://www.oecd.org/daf/anti-bribery/anti-briberyconvention/Norwayphase3reportEN .pdf. For a summary of the case, see chapter 6, case 13. In a parallel proceeding, Statoil settled with the U.S. DOJ and SEC. The U.S. authorities took into account the financial penalties already paid in Norway.
19. See chapter 6, case 13.
20. SINTEF Petroleum Research was issued a penalty notice of NKr 2 million, in connection with a consulting contract signed with an Iranian company in 2002. See SINTEF's press release at http://www .sintef.no/home/Press-Room/Press-Releases/SINTEF-Petroleum-Research-accepts-fine/.
21. OECD, *Phase 3 Report: Norway*, 21.
22. See OECD, *Phase 3 Report on Implementing the OECD Anti-Bribery Convention in Italy* (2011), 4 and 7, http://www.oecd.org/daf/anti-bribery/anti-briberyconvention/Italyphase3reportEN.pdf. Italy has imposed final sanctions against three legal persons and nine individuals using this procedure. The cases against legal persons were two against Pirelli/Telecom and one against COGIM. For natural persons,

process, after the prosecution has decided upon a charge, the prosecution and defense can jointly ask the judge to impose a substitute penalty or a fine on which they both agree. The judge can accept that penalty or reject it but cannot modify the monetary sanctions on which the parties agreed. If the offender compensates the "victim" and takes steps to eliminate the consequences of the offense, the offender may be able to reduce its fine.[23]

The court hearing where the *patteggiamento* is pronounced is open to the public. However, it appears that only those persons who can justify an "interest" in receiving communication of the written disposition would have access to the decision, and the criteria for determining when a person has such an interest remain unclear. An additional advantage of the *patteggiamento* for the defendant is that the disposition will not appear in the criminal record of the defendant. This particular feature could be an impediment for successful international cooperation in money-laundering cases.[24]

For example, Italian authorities investigated the Italian company Pirelli and determined that it had made payments of about €200,000 in connection with the bribery of a French public official to obtain business authorizations.[25] Italian prosecutors contacted the defense counsel. Both sides agreed jointly to ask the court to impose a substitute penalty through a *patteggiamento*. In arriving at the monetary penalty, the prosecution determined the proposed fine based on what it would have considered adequate if imposed in a trial and then reduced that amount by a third as a benefit for using the *patteggiamento* rather than proceeding to trial.[26] Prosecutors lodged at the court a charge that company officials had failed adequately to supervise a lower-level employee to prevent the risk of bribery and proposed the agreed-upon penalty to the court.[27] After a hearing, the court approved the agreement, and the company was fined €400,000.[28]

---

the *pattegiamento* is limited to offenses for which the maximum penalty does not exceed five years of imprisonment (Articles 444 to 448 CCP).

23. OECD, *Phase 3 Report: Italy,* 19, 20. The operative provision is Article 12.2 of LD 231/2001. The recent evaluation by the OECD remarked that it was not clear to whom these reparations would be paid in a foreign bribery case. The enforcement through *patteggiamento* has been credited by the OECD working group on bribery with providing Italian companies a strong incentive to implement internal compliance programs.

24. Preliminary investigations in transnational money-laundering cases usually start by gathering information from foreign financial intelligence units and usually consist of checking the criminal records in the requested country in order to find out if the transactions detected in the requesting country can be linked to a predicate offense. If there is no criminal record in Italy due to a previous *patteggiamento*, the requesting country will not be informed that the suspect was previously caught for bribery.

25. OECD, *Phase 3 Report: Italy,* 18.

26. OECD, *Phase 3 Report: Italy,* 20.

27. OECD, *Phase 3 Report: Italy,* 15.

28. OECD, *Phase 3 Report: Italy,* 20. See also C. Milan, Div. of Investigating Judge and Judge of Precourt Hearings, 28 May 2010, n. 25194/08 RGNR and n. 6330/09 RGGIP.

3.4 Germany

Germany has also resolved foreign bribery cases through procedures other than full criminal trials. For example, the German authorities investigated a bribery scheme involving the large German multinational company Siemens AG, following up on an internal investigation by the company itself. Several hundred million dollars had been dispensed across multiple jurisdictions over an extended time period. Since German law does not provide for the criminal liability of legal persons, German prosecutors needed to seek other mechanisms to address the foreign bribery by the company. The sheer magnitude of the schemes, generating hundreds of potential cases, posed a challenge to German law enforcement resources under a system in which prosecution is mandatory.

For the prosecution of legal persons, German prosecutors found a solution in the provisions of the country's administrative law. A legal person can be liable when there is evidence that one of its representatives committed a criminal or administrative infraction that violates the obligations of the legal person or enriches it.[29] The fine is limited to €500,000 in case of negligence or €1 million in case of intentional misconduct. However, if the gain from the offense exceeds these amounts, a higher fine can be imposed, in addition to the confiscation of the illegal gains.[30] The criminal court can order the participation of the company in the criminal proceedings against the natural person. In the Siemens case, the proceedings against the natural persons were for both criminal (bribery) and administrative offenses (insufficient supervision of personnel).[31]

Moreover, a provision recently introduced in the German Criminal Procedure Code provides for negotiated sentencing agreements.[32] The provision refers to natural persons in the regular criminal trial and to legal persons if their participation in the criminal procedure is ordered as described above. The subject matter of the agreement may comprise only the legal consequences, procedural measures, and the conduct of the participants during the trial, not the verdict of guilt (although a confession forms an integral part of the negotiated sentencing agreement). The prosecutor in principle has to present the same level of evidence as in a full trial. The court announces the possible content of the negotiated agreement, which enters into effect if the defendant and the prosecution agree. This procedure was used in one of the Siemens cases to sanction both the company and individual offenders.[33]

There are two varieties of shortened procedures, namely, the *penal order* (Strafbefehl) and the *conditional exemption* from prosecution, that apply to natural persons only. Under the penal order, which applies only to misdemeanors,[34] the court, at the request

---

29. The relevant provision of administrative law is Article 30 of the Ordnungswidrigkeitsgesetz (OWiG), in English, the Administrative Offenses Act.
30. Article 17, para. 4, OWiG.
31. Article 130, OWiG.
32. Article 257 (c) of the Criminal Procedure Code.
33. See chapter 6, case 12.
34. Article 407 of the Criminal Procedure Code.

of the prosecutor, can issue a written penal order without a main hearing. There is no room for negotiation with the defendant, but the defendant has two weeks within which to object. If he does not, the penal order enters into force. If he does object, the prosecutor will open proceedings in court.

Under the conditional exemption from prosecution, the prosecutor may, with the consent of the accused and of the court, provisionally refrain from filing public charges and impose conditions, if these are considered to be sufficient to satisfy the public interest and the degree of guilt of the defendant does not present an obstacle. In practice, there can be some negotiation between the defendant and the court before they consent. The conditional exemption does not form a record of conviction and does not become public.[35] If the defendant rejects conditional exemption, the matter goes to full trial.[36]

Armed with these options, Germany has disposed of a large number of foreign bribery cases. With regard to foreign bribery cases, approximately half the cases were concluded through conditional exemption from prosecution between defendants and prosecutors. Between 2005 and 2010, Germany sanctioned 69 individuals (including 30 criminal convictions, 35 conditional exemptions from prosecution under the Criminal Procedure Code, and 4 administrative sanctions) and 7 legal persons (all sanctioned by use of administrative law, the Ordnungswidrigkeitsgesetz).[37]

Court hearings, whether for administrative or criminal proceedings, are open to the public. Court decisions are published, although decisions do not disclose the names of the parties.[38] The same cannot be said of conditional exemption from prosecution under the criminal provisions just outlined. Since these cases do not proceed to trial, there is no public hearing. Moreover, the content of a conditional exemption from prosecution is not made public.[39] In cases of a negotiated sentencing agreement, there is a public hearing.

4. Guilty Pleas, Civil Liability, and Other Forms in Certain Common Law Countries

4.1 United Kingdom

The United Kingdom has a long tradition of settlements through guilty pleas. The authorities have imposed liability in foreign bribery cases through criminal means, civil means, and administrative enforcement.[40] In fact all of its cases against legal persons

---

35. OECD, *Phase 3 Report on Implementing the OECD Anti-Bribery Convention in Germany* (2011), 33, http://www.oecd.org/germany/Germanyphase3reportEN.pdf.
36. OECD, *Phase 3 Report: Germany*, 33.
37. OECD, *Phase 3 Report: Germany*, 8.
38. OECD, *Phase 3 Report: Germany*, 7.
39. OECD, *Phase 3 Report: Germany*, 16.
40. Certain related matters involving failure to adopt adequate compliance measures to prevent corruption have also been dealt with through the Financial Services Authority (FSA) of the United Kingdom. See the Aon

involving foreign bribery have been resolved by way of settlements with none proceeding to trial.

As an example of a criminal case, the U.K. construction firm Mabey & Johnson (Mabey) had been caught inflating contract prices to fund kickbacks to Iraqi officials involved in a major contract to build bridges in Iraq, as well as paying bribes to officials in Ghana and Jamaica. In 2009, Mabey entered into a plea agreement with the prosecuting Serious Fraud Office (SFO), where Mabey pleaded guilty to two counts of conspiracy to corrupt and agreed to accept the monetary sanctions determined by the court.

After signing the plea agreement, the next step is for the defendant, defense counsel, and prosecution to appear before a judge who will hold a hearing, at which he or she will ask the defendant (or its representative if it is a legal person) a series of questions to determine if the defendant understands what he/she/it is doing by admitting guilt and is familiar with the terms of the plea agreement.[41]

In the United Kingdom, a key term of the plea agreement is that the defendant admits responsibility for the alleged criminal conduct. In return, the prosecution commits itself to certain terms, which may include dismissing some of the charges, recommending a certain range of sentence (including a particular amount of confiscation or fine), or addressing various other terms desired by the defendant. Many defendants plead guilty with the expectation of receiving a lesser sentence than they would have received if they had proceeded to trial. Some of the terms of the agreement will be the same for all defendants, such as giving up the right to have a trial, while other terms will vary based on the case. There are few legal limits on what terms could be included.

To return to the example, as part of the plea agreement, Mabey agreed to pay reparations to the Development Fund for Iraq, to Ghana, and to Jamaica in amounts to be determined ultimately by the judge. The plea involved several hearings in open court. At the sentencing, the judge determined the amount and structure of the monetary penalties. The court ordered Mabey to pay reparations in the amount of £1,415,000 (including £658,000 to Ghana, £139,000 to Jamaica, and £618,000 to Iraq). In the United Kingdom, two other legal persons, Innospec and BAE, have been convicted by guilty plea of foreign bribery or closely related offenses.[42]

---

and Willis matters summarized at OECD, *Phase 3 Report on Implementing the OECD Anti-Bribery Convention in the United Kingdom* (2012), 72, http://www.oecd.org/daf/anti-bribery/UnitedKingdomphase3reportEN .pdf.
41. Common law systems require a public hearing before a judicial officer when a guilty plea is entered, and the process tends to be similar among systems. Moreover, the process differs little whether a natural or legal person is pleading guilty to criminal charges. See, e.g., on the U.S. system, *Bench Book for U.S. District Court Judges,* 5th ed. (Washington, DC: Federal Judicial Center, 2007), 71–85, http://www.fjc.gov/public /pdf.nsf/lookup/Benchbk5.pdf/$file/Benchbk5.pdf. It describes in detail what questions the judge must ask of a natural or legal person in federal courts of the United States before a judge is permitted to accept a guilty plea.
42. See summaries in chapter 6, cases 3 (BAE) and 6 (Innospec).

Other recent cases in the United Kingdom have been resolved by way of civil enforcement actions, through prosecution by the SFO. For example, in the context of contracts to supply educational materials, a United Kingdom publishing house, Macmillan Publishers Limited, was found to have been operating in a manner that "potentially presented a bribery and corruption risk"[43] in three countries in Africa and "may have received revenue from unlawful conduct."[44] Under the United Kingdom Proceeds of Crime Act, Macmillan entered into an agreement with the SFO obligating it to acknowledge responsibility and to pay £11 million pursuant to a *Civil Recovery Order* or CRO (a form of consent order). The CRO procedure involves the prosecutor drafting an order reflecting the agreed-upon monetary sanctions and then submitting that order to a High Court judge who enters it into the court registry. No hearings are required. Several other recent cases have been resolved by CRO.[45] For a summary of the U.K. legal forms of settlements as of July 2012, see figure 1.1.

As demonstrated by the brief descriptions just presented, under U.K. procedures the amount of judicial involvement in settlements varies considerably between criminal and civil resolutions. Criminal settlements are negotiated between the prosecutors and the defendant. The plea agreement must be in writing and contain an admission of facts constituting the offenses. Then the plea must be entered in a hearing in open court before a judge. While the parties can confer in advance about what is an appropriate sentence and monetary punishment, they cannot agree on an exact sentence.[46] At sentencing, the judge will listen to the arguments of the parties and then decide on a sentence.

By contrast, in civil settlements the prosecutor and the defendant can agree on a specific penalty, and the prosecutor needs only to request a judicial order in that amount. The other component is a written agreement signed by the prosecutor and the defendant.

With regard to transparency, the U.K. system requires public hearings in the criminal settlements but does not file publicly the settlement documents. In a few cases, the court's sentencing remarks have been made publicly available.[47] The plea agreements

---

43. See U.K. Serious Fraud Office, "Action on Macmillan Publishers Limited," press release, 22 July 2011, http://cymraeg.sfo.gov.uk/press-room/press-release-archive/press-releases-2011/action-on-macmillan-publishers-limited.aspx.
44. U.K. Serious Fraud Office, "Action on Macmillan Publishers Limited."
45. These include the Johnson & Johnson/DePuy case (see summary at chapter 6, case 7), a Kellogg/TSKJ Consortium case (see summary at Part 6, 14) and the Balfour Beatty case.
46. See OECD, *Phase 3 Report: United Kingdom,* 19, citing *R. v. Underwood,* (2004); EWCA Crim, 1 Cr. App. R. 13, para. 6; Consolidated Criminal Practice Direction, para. IV.45.24; AG Guidelines on Acceptance of Plea, paras. C10, D9-D11, and E5; *R. v. Newton* (1983), 77 Cr. App. R. 13; *R. v. Innospec*; *R. v. Dougall.*
47. OECD, *Phase 3 Report: United Kingdom,* 20 (which includes the Innospec and BAE cases). Of course, the sentencing hearings are open to the public.

FIGURE 1.1

U.K. Settled Enforcement Actions by Legal Form of Settlement (as of July 3, 2012)

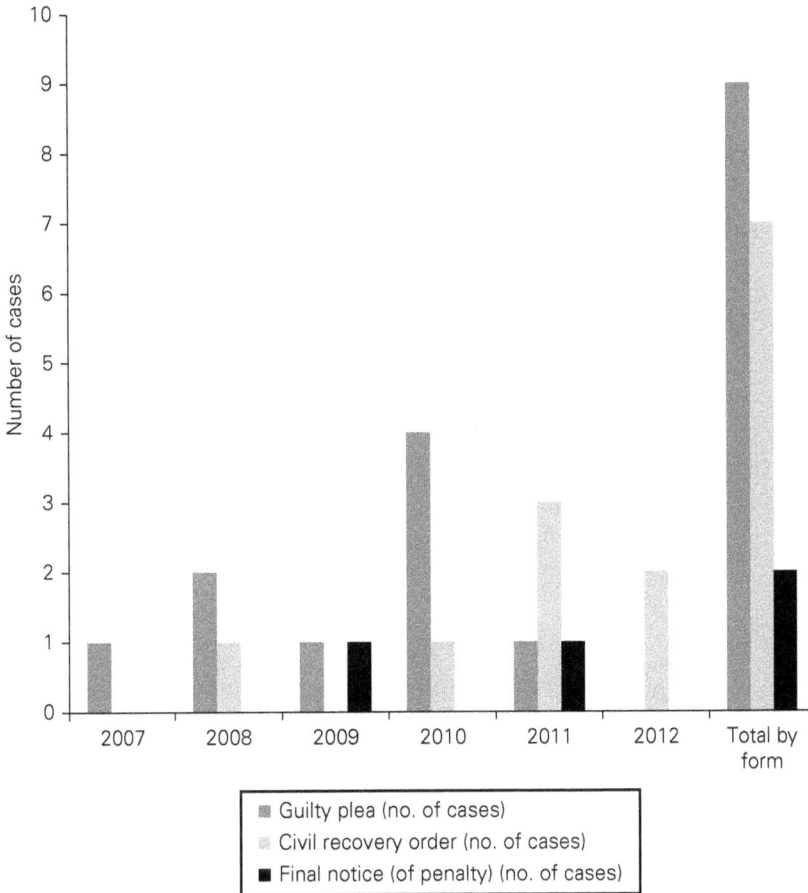

Number of cases (y-axis, 0 to 10)

x-axis categories: 2007, 2008, 2009, 2010, 2011, 2012, Total by form

Legend:
- Guilty plea (no. of cases)
- Civil recovery order (no. of cases)
- Final notice (of penalty) (no. of cases)

Source: Based on StAR Database of Settlements of Foreign Bribery and Related Cases, http://star.worldbank.org/corruption-cases/?db=All.

are not made public, with rare exceptions.[48] While certain pleadings in the cases are released sporadically to the public, most are not.

In the cases settled by CRO, the only document released is a press statement by the prosecution giving a brief synopsis of the matter and the penalty imposed. The exact nature of the conduct may not be specified, as was the case in the Macmillan matter. Finally, in some cases the prosecution has included in the settlement documents a confidentiality clause that obligates the prosecution not to disclose more details into the public domain.

48. OECD, *Phase 3 Report: United Kingdom,* 20. One exception is the BAE case, where the plea agreement was released. It can be found at http://www.caat.org.uk/issues/bae/bae-settlement-basis-of-plea.pdf. See also chapter 6, case 3.

4.2 Canada

Canada has a system of plea agreements similar to that of the United Kingdom and has begun to apply it to settle foreign bribery cases. Specifically, using criminal enforcement powers, Canada recently prosecuted a Canadian company for providing improper benefits to a government official in South Asia, obtaining a guilty plea by the company for violation of Canada's Corruption of Foreign Public Officials Act.[49]

In Canada's criminal process, as in that of the United Kingdom, a public hearing is held before a judge when a guilty plea is entered. The judge may accept or reject the guilty plea and has ultimate authority for imposing sentence. As in the United Kingdom, the plea agreements are not made public. However, unlike in the United Kingdom, the accompanying statement of facts in which a defendant admits the offenses is made public.[50]

A relevant feature of Canadian law is that fines in foreign bribery cases are subject to a unique levy of 15 percent in addition to any penalty handed down for a criminal code violation.[51] This *victim surcharge* is intended to finance Canada in-province victim services and does not go toward payment of restitution to persons who have directly suffered harm or loss because of the particular prosecuted offense.[52]

4.3 Nigeria

Nigeria has recently put into practice settlements in foreign bribery cases. With regard to guilty pleas in court, the judge must review the evidence to ensure it proves facts sufficient to support a finding of guilt as to the offense(s) to which the defendant is pleading guilty.

In Nigeria, there is no comprehensive legislation on plea bargaining, and the procedures in use come under the Federal High Court Act (FHC Act). The FHC Act contemplates that once charges have been filed, the parties may agree to the disposition of the case. The prosecution derives its authority from Section 174 of the Constitution of Nigeria, which grants the attorney general and his office the authority to commence, pursue, and end criminal actions at his discretion according to the interests of justice.

---

49. Royal Canadian Mounted Police, "Corruption Charge Laid Against NIKO Resources," press release, Ottawa, ON, Canada, June 24, 2011, http://www.rcmp-grc.gc.ca/ab/news-nouvelles/2011/110624-niko-eng.htm; *R. v. Niko Resources Ltd.*, Agreed Statement of Facts (Queen's Bench Alberta, 23 June 2011).
50. Additionally, see OECD, *Phase 3 Report on Implementing the OECD Anti-Bribery Convention in the Canada* (2011), 20, 22, http://www.oecd.org/daf/anti-bribery/anti-briberyconvention/Canadaphase3reportEN.pdf.
51. The case of Niko Resources Ltd., Agreed Statement of Facts (Queen's Bench Alberta, 23 June 2011), para. 57, illustrates this provision. Information on the Canadian surcharge may be located at Department of Justice (Canada), "Provisions of Interest to Victims of Crime," http://www.justice.gc.ca/eng/pi/pcvi-cpcv/code.html. While other nations have victim surcharges, most notably the United Kingdom, these are most often a small fixed fee added to court costs.
52. See Department of Justice (Canada), "Provisions of Interest to Victims of Crime," http://www.justice.gc.ca/eng/cj-jp/victims-victimes/code.html.

The anticorruption agency, the Economic and Financial Crimes Commission (EFCC), has prosecution powers and derives its authority from the same provision and from Section 14 of the EFCC Act. In addition, the Criminal Procedure Act, which regulates proceedings in the federal High Court, allows plea bargains. This may be done if the prosecutor and the defense agree to the amendment of the charges to enable the defense to plead guilty to a lesser offense that carries lesser punishment. The judge must consent to this agreement. A few states in the federation, however, have enacted laws to regulate plea bargains.

In addition, a plea of guilty will always be considered a mitigating factor, leading to a lower sentence than if that defendant had proceeded to trial. There is no distinction between natural persons and legal persons, so any criminal procedure applicable to an individual could in theory apply equally to a company.

In general, experts report that the criminal procedures of Nigeria are in need of reform, as the technical requirements of the current system provide opportunities for defendants to slow the process and impede efficient resolution of corruption cases.[53] Under such a system, out-of-court settlements are an attractive option for enforcement authorities.[54]

With regard to legal persons, Nigeria has concluded several out-of-court settlements against foreign companies that bribed Nigerian officials. For example, at the same time as a number of other jurisdictions were investigating the large multinational company Siemens in connection with allegations of foreign bribery, the Nigerian EFCC was carrying out its own investigation of suspected payments to Nigerian officials. In December 2008, coordinated simultaneous settlements against Siemens occurred in the United States and Germany. In October 2010, Nigeria filed charges against Siemens, alleging a foreign bribery scheme. In November, 2010, Nigeria entered into an out-of-court settlement with Siemens, agreeing to end all investigations and dismiss charges in exchange for millions of dollars in disgorgement and fines.[55]

Although the terms of the Siemens-Nigeria settlement and those of other similar cases in Nigeria have remained confidential, the Attorney General of Nigeria placed on the public record that the cases have been resolved and yielded a total of $170.8 million in monetary sanctions.[56] The attorney general further reported that the companies approached Nigerian prosecutors with various settlement options and, in light

---

53. Mohammed Bello Adoke (Attorney General of Nigeria), "Ministerial Media Briefing on the Activities of the Federal Ministry of Justice, Delivered at the Federal Ministry of Justice Annual Press Briefing, December 22, 2010," 10, 11. Adoke cited weaknesses in Nigerian criminal provisions concerning corporate liability reported that fewer than 10 percent of pending criminal cases had been resolved during the year 2010, noting "it is obvious that a substantial number of criminal cases are still pending in various courts."
54. See chapter 2, section 5.2.
55. This example and another similar case (the TSKJ Consortium) are discussed in detail in chapter 6, case 14.
56. Mohammed Bello Adoke, "Ministerial Media Briefing," 11.

of the "weaknesses of [Nigerian] penal provisions dealing with corporate criminal liability, as well as the need to ensure their early resolution in the greater national interest,"[57] Nigeria followed the example of what it called "best international practices, such as those of the United States of America" in deciding to resolve the matters.[58] The companies were made to "disgorge the proceeds of crime and to pay appropriate fines."[59]

4.4 United States

The United States has resolved more foreign bribery cases by way of settlement than any other nation and presents some unique procedural features.[60] It uses both criminal and civil enforcement in many foreign bribery cases. In its federal courts, the United States brings criminal prosecutions through the Department of Justice, resulting in monetary penalties for both legal and natural persons and possible imprisonment for natural persons. The United States often brings concurrent civil proceedings through the enforcement powers of the SEC to exact disgorgement of ill-gotten gains from natural persons and legal persons, as well as other civil monetary penalties. For the most part, the United States enforces its Foreign Corrupt Practices Act (FCPA), a law passed in 1977. Since there is abundant literature on the U.S. system,[61] this study will dispense with further description and move to the points most salient to settlements.[62]

As in other common law systems, in the United States the basic guilty plea is an agreement between the prosecution and the party under investigation to resolve the matter in a way satisfactory to both parties.[63] A judge must review and consent to the plea agreement.[64] The role of the judge is to determine if legal requirements are met,

---

57. Mohammed Bello Adoke, "Ministerial Media Briefing," 11, para. 40. The Nigerian Attorney General has directed a review of the laws regarding criminal liability of legal persons, with a view to appropriate amendments.

58. Mohammed Bello Adoke, "Ministerial Media Briefing," 11.

59. Mohammed Bello Adoke, "Ministerial Media Briefing," 11.

60. Indeed, the United States has led the world in enforcement of foreign bribery laws, based on number of cases and amounts confiscated and fines imposed. OECD Annual Report 2011, 14 (chart of enforcement). See also StAR Database of Settlements in Foreign Bribery and Related Cases, http://star.worldbank.org/corruption-cases/?db=All.

61. For readers looking for a primer on the U.S. enforcement system, a good starting point is OECD, *Phase 3 Report on Implementing the OECD Anti-Bribery Convention in the United States,* (Paris: OECD, 2010), http://www.oecd.org/daf/anti-bribery/anti-briberyconvention/UnitedStatesphase3reportEN.pdf.

62. Case summaries given in chapter 5 of this study cover a number of multijurisdictional U.S. cases, including Alcatel-Lucent, S.A.; BAE Systems, plc; Daimler AG; Haiti Teleco; Johnson & Johnson; Mercator/Giffen et al.; Siemens AG; Statoil; and TSKJ Consortium.

63. Note that it is also possible for the defendant to enter a guilty plea in the absence of any agreement, perhaps hoping for lenient treatment from the judge at sentencing.

64. Note that the variations of non-prosecution agreements (NPAs) and deferred prosecution agreements (DPAs) are generally not subject to judicial approval or supervision. The NPAs and DPAs exist only in the United States. The United Kingdom is reportedly giving some consideration to adopting DPAs. See Squire Sanders and Louise Roberts, "Ministry of Justice Confirms That Deferred Prosecution Agreements ('DPAs') Will Be Introduced in England and Wales," *Lexicology,* January 17, 2013, http://www.lexology.com/library/detail.aspx?g=e762e19a-52fb-4439-b943-502ec57a5592.

notably, that the facts constitute an offense. As in other common law jurisdictions, when a natural person admits responsibility, it is commonly called a *guilty plea,* whereas when a legal person (or corporation, as they are more often called in the United States) admits responsibility, it can be referred to as a criminal *settlement* or *resolution.*[65]

Unlike in the United Kingdom,[66] in some cases in the United States the plea agreement may recommend a specific sentence (in terms of a period of incarceration and/or a monetary penalty and/or other punishments) if the defendant enters a guilty plea under the agreement. In the United States, as a term of his plea agreement, the defendant may also agree to cooperate with the prosecution to generate evidence against other offenders or disclose the whereabouts of unidentified proceeds of crime. The prosecution may require the defendant to cooperate with foreign authorities as well,[67] a useful provision if requests for international cooperation from other jurisdictions are expected.[68]

The plea agreement is reduced to writing and signed by the prosecution, the defendant, and his/her counsel and lodged with the court pending approval. Attached to the plea agreement is a statement of facts describing at a minimum the conduct that constitutes the offense to which the defendant is pleading guilty but often describing more fully the foreign bribery scheme.[69]

At the plea hearing, the prosecution will be required to describe to the judge the evidence it would have used had the case gone to trial in order to prove that the defendant committed the offense to which it is pleading guilty. The judge will then ask the defendant if he/she agrees with the prosecutor's statements. The defendant must admit the facts described in the charging document and the statement of facts. Then the court may accept, reject, or modify the plea agreement.[70] If satisfied with the answers of

---

65. The term *settlement* is also commonly used to describe the termination of civil litigation between parties by mutual agreement. That kind of settlement is not the subject of this study (see discussion chapter 1, section 1).

66. In the United Kingdom, the prosecutor cannot recommend a specific sentence.

67. For purposes of sentencing, the term *cooperate* has a specific meaning in the United States, meaning to provide information on one's own wrongdoing. *Acceptance of responsibility* is the term used in that jurisdiction to acknowledge one's own wrongdoing. More generally, in the United States (and to some extent in the United Kingdom) a company may elect to "cooperate" and go to the authorities to disclose all its wrongdoing in the hope of obtaining more lenient treatment than it would receive if it waited for the authorities to use their coercive powers to go after it. The Macmillan case in the United Kingdom is an example. For a summary of the case, see chapter 6, case 9.

68. See, e.g., Johnson & Johnson case, discussed in chapter 6, case 7, which includes a non-prosecution agreement by which company agreed to help foreign authorities under direction of U.S. authorities with whom they settled. Note that this term is in line with Article 37(2) of United Nations Convention against Corruption (UNCAC), which encourages a mitigated punishment for cooperating defendants. UNCAC Article 37(2) states that each State Party "shall consider providing for the possibility of mitigating punishment of an accused person who provides substantial cooperation in the investigation or prosecution of an offense."

69. A written statement of facts is not required by U.S. law but is often used in foreign bribery cases.

70. See OECD, *Phase 3 Report: United States,* 31.

FIGURE 1.2 | U.S. DOJ FCPA Enforcement Actions (June 1979–January 2012)

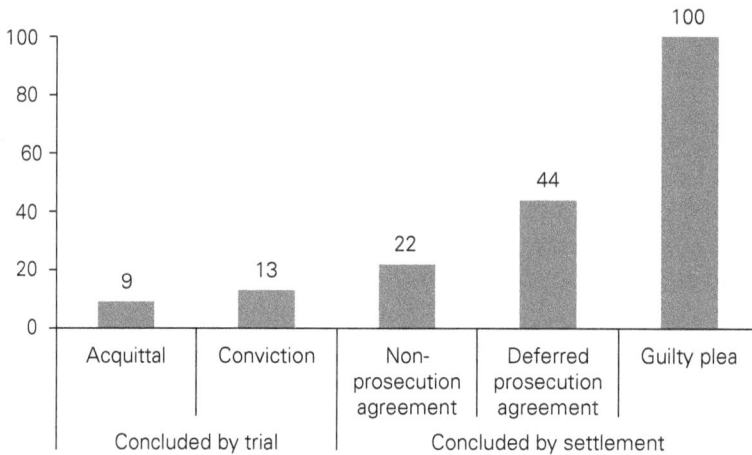

Source: Shearman & Sterling's FCPA Case Database, accessed 30 April 2012, http://fcpa.shearman.com/?_so_list_aat-04ff1aad45ab4a779ced52eb51756690=250. The site acknowledges 243 DOJ FCPA actions against individual and legal persons dating from July 10, 1979 to January 17, 2012. Of those 243, this figure excludes 55: 20 resulted in dismissal of charges, 2 ended in "civil settlement only," 25 have an "unresolved" status, and 8 are outstanding due to fugitive status.
Note: DOJ = Department of Justice; FCPA = Foreign Corrupt Practices Act.

the parties, the judge will accept the plea of guilty and enter a conviction for the offenses. If not, the judge may reject the plea. In that case, the parties may try to reach a new agreement or proceed to trial. When the judge approves and the defendant formally enters the guilty plea, the plea agreement is filed with the court and becomes a matter of public record, making the terms and underlying facts quite transparent. A guilty plea equals a conviction.

Unique even among the common law jurisdictions, the United States has two variations on the guilty plea that have been used to resolve many foreign bribery cases, the deferred prosecution agreement (DPA) and the non-prosecution agreement (NPA). The prosecution can propose to a defendant, a written agreement to admit responsibility and undertake certain obligations, in exchange for which the prosecutor will either not file charges (NPA) or will file charges but not immediately taking further action on those charges—in legal parlance, *deferring*—and then dismissing them at a later time once the defendant has satisfactorily fulfilled his or her side of the agreement (DPA).

In the United States, more than 88 percent of criminal foreign bribery and related cases have been resolved by settlement (guilty plea, DPA, or NPA), whereas only about 12 percent have proceeded to trial, as illustrated in figure 1.2.

DPAs generally require the defendant to admit relevant facts, commit to certain compliance and remediation measures, and pay a fine and/or other monetary penalties.

Elements of a Deferred Prosecution Agreement: Alcatel-Lucent SA and the Department of Justice, in the United States District Court, Southern District of Florida

- Criminal information and acceptance of responsibility
- Term of agreement
- Relevant considerations
- Payment of monetary penalty, using sentencing guidelines
- Conditional release from criminal liability
- Corporate compliance program
- Corporate compliance monitor
- Deferred prosecution
- Breach of agreement
- Sale or merger of Alcatel-Lucent
- Public statements by Alcatel-Lucent
- Limitation on binding effect of agreement
- Notice
- Complete agreement
- Signatories: Alcatel-Lucent and U.S. DOJ, Fraud Section

Attachment A: Statement of Facts
Attachment B: Certificate of Corporate Resolutions
Attachment C: Corporate Compliance Program
Attachment D: Independent Corporate Monitor

Source: U.S. v. Alcatel-Lucent, S.A., Case No. 10-cr-20907 (S.D. Fla.), Deferred Prosecution Agreement filed February 22, 2011, http://www.justice.gov/criminal/fraud/fcpa/cases/alcatel-etal/02-22-11alcatel-dpa.pdf.

If the defendant complies with the terms of the agreement, the prosecution dismisses the charge. While DPAs are technically subject to judicial review and approval, most judges accord considerable deference to the parties.[71] Box 1.1 outlines the different sections of a DPA in the United States, taking the Alcatel-Lucent case (see chapter 6, case 1) as an example.

Unlike a DPA, an NPA does not involve the court, but still the defendant is generally required to admit relevant facts. Under in the NPA, the government maintains a right to file charges but agrees not to do so. In return, the defendant is subject to terms similar to those often found in DPAs, such as (i) monetary sanctions; (ii) requirements that the company improve its compliance program; (iii) requirements that the company hire, at its own expense, an independent monitor to oversee compliance, review the effectiveness of a company's internal control measures, and determine whether the company has otherwise met the terms of the agreement; and (iv) extraordinary

---

71. OECD, *Phase 3 Report: United States*, 32.

restitution provisions, which are payments or services to organizations or individuals not directly affected by the crime.

While DPAs or NPAs could apply to natural persons, they are most commonly features in the resolutions of cases involving legal persons. DPAs and NPAs do not result in convictions. Authorities, including the OECD's Working Group on Bribery, have questioned whether it is possible to assess the impact of NPAs and DPAs in deterring foreign bribery by U.S. companies.[72] Like plea agreements, the DPAs and NPAs (which consist of letter agreements) and the accompanying statements of facts are publicly released by the U.S. DOJ. All of these documents are posted on the DOJ website, accessible to the public.

In the United States, of cases that settled (based on the data in figure 1.2), approximately 60 percent were guilty pleas, 27 percent were DPAs, and the remaining 13 percent were NPAs. In other words, the vast majority of cases involved judicial supervision. However the extent of such judicial supervision has varied.

Why are some companies prosecuted and others are not? In the United States, prosecutors use guidelines that examine various considerations, such as the severity of the offense, whether it is a first offense, remedial actions to date, and other factors normally common to a determination of penalty. Figure 1.3 presents how the Principles of Federal Prosecution of Business Organizations[73] in the United States guide and influence prosecutors' decisions to decline prosecution,[74] enter into an NPA or DPA, or prosecute the offense.

Prosecutors weigh these criteria, such as the seriousness of the violation in terms of how many bribes were paid and in what amounts, over what time period (short or extended), and whether the company had made efforts to prevent foreign bribery. After assessing all the considerations they deem relevant in a particular case, prosecutors decide whether the case should be declined or prosecuted and, if prosecuted, by full prosecution, DPA, or NPA.

As described in this chapter, in the past decade more jurisdictions have come to employ various forms of settlements, as provided for in their domestic legal framework, to resolve foreign bribery and related cases. The jurisdictions have included both common law and civil law systems. For some, the use of settlements is a recent

---

72. OECD, *Phase 3 Report: United States*, 19. Other parts of the U.S. government, civil society, and the OECD have raised the issue.

73. Text of the Principles of Federal Prosecution of Business Organizations can be found at http://www .justice.gov/opa/documents/corp-charging-guidelines.pdf. For brief background discussion, see Beth A. Wilkinson and Alex Young K. Oh, "Federal Prosecution of Business Organizations: A Ten-Year Anniversary Perspective," *NYSBA Inside* 27, no. 2 (Fall 2009): 8–11, http://www.paulweiss.com/media/1497187/pw _nysba_oct09.pdf.

74. *Declination* means a decision not to file any charges. Under U.S. law, and that of many common law systems, a prosecutor is not obligated to take action merely because there is evidence of an offense. By contrast, under the *legality principle*, civil law prosecutors must file charges.

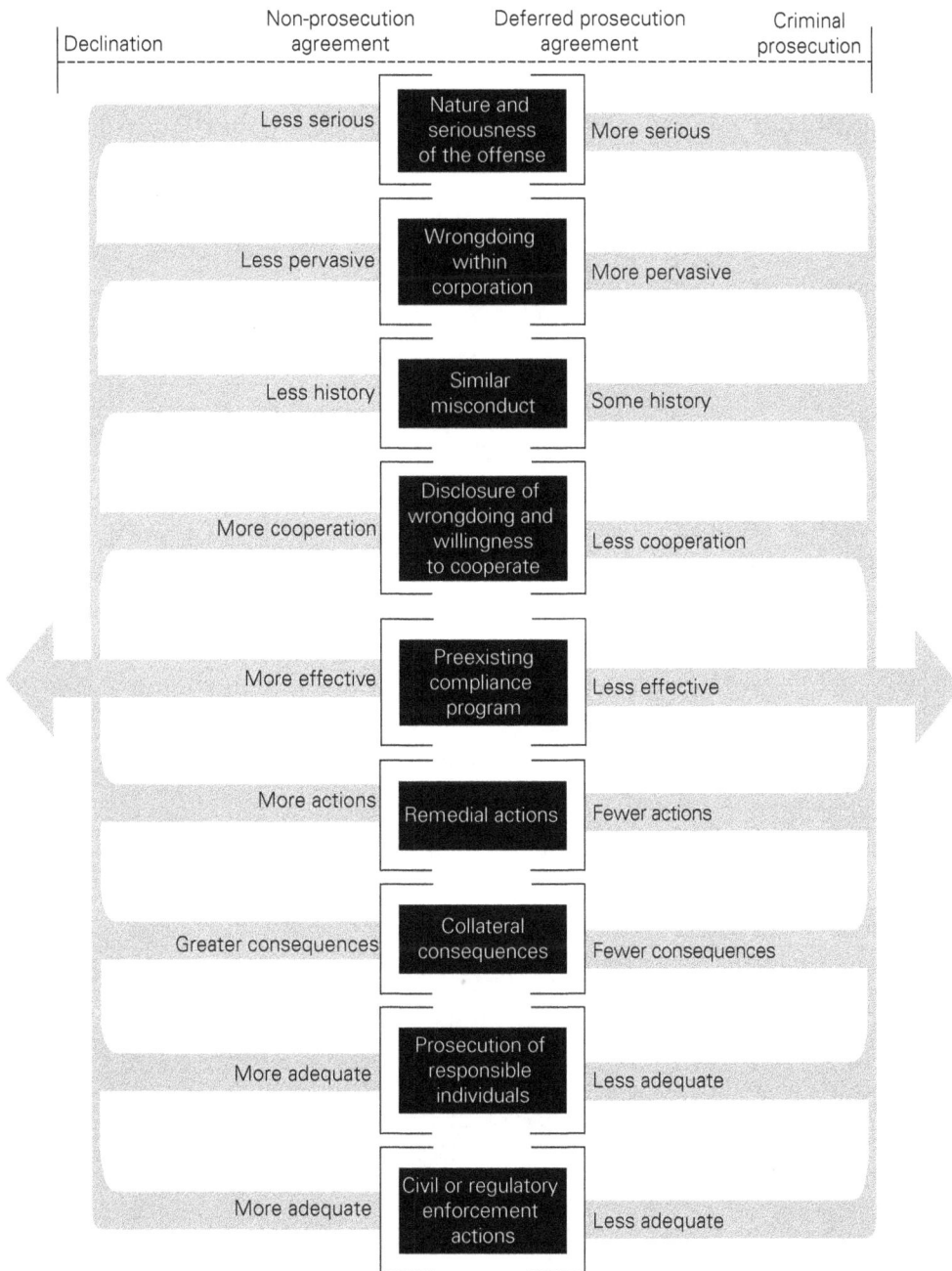

FIGURE 1.3 Principles of Federal Prosecution of Business Organizations and Prosecutors' Decisions to Decline Prosecution, Enter into a DPA or NPA, or Prosecute

| Declination | Non-prosecution agreement | Deferred prosecution agreement | Criminal prosecution |

| Less serious | Nature and seriousness of the offense | More serious |

| Less pervasive | Wrongdoing within corporation | More pervasive |

| Less history | Similar misconduct | Some history |

| More cooperation | Disclosure of wrongdoing and willingness to cooperate | Less cooperation |

| More effective | Preexisting compliance program | Less effective |

| More actions | Remedial actions | Fewer actions |

| Greater consequences | Collateral consequences | Fewer consequences |

| More adequate | Prosecution of responsible individuals | Less adequate |

| More adequate | Civil or regulatory enforcement actions | Less adequate |

Source: U.S. General Accounting Office, *Corporate Crime: DOJ Has Taken Steps to Better Track Its Use of Deferred and Non-Prosecution Agreements, but Should Evaluate Effectiveness* (Washington, DC: GAO, 2009), GAO-10-110, 10, http://www.gao.gov/new.items/d10110.pdf

undertaking, whereas other jurisdictions have a longer tradition of using various forms of settlements to resolve cases. The cases include criminal, civil, and administrative enforcement actions. The levels of transparency and judicial review vary considerably among the different jurisdictions and, depending on the form of settlement, within a given jurisdiction. The trend toward the use of settlements to resolve foreign bribery and related cases is likely to continue, as we shall see from the analysis in the next chapter.

2. Common Threads and General Observations about Settlements

We now look at common trends and developments in this field, as well as the more recent methods that are being used to take action against bribe payers by some countries whose officials have been bribed.

1. Criteria for Understanding Settlements

Three criteria were cited in chapter 1, section 2 as important to understanding settlements in various systems: form of liability, judicial oversight, and transparency of the settlement. Several general observations can be made about each.

1.1 Forms of Legal Liability: Criminal, Civil, and Administrative

The state can exercise its authority to punish and/or regulate through three forms of legal liability: criminal, civil, administrative, or some combination of these elements. The most essential difference among them is that only the criminal system can impose imprisonment (for natural persons). Table 2.1 illustrates basic criteria of each of the forms.

Multilateral treaties require States Parties to take measures in accordance with their own legal principles to establish the liability of legal persons for the bribery of a foreign public official. The United Nations Convention against Corruption (UNCAC) and the Organisation for Economic Co-operation and Development (OECD) Anti-Bribery Convention specify that such liability may be civil, criminal, or administrative;[1] countries are not limited to addressing the liability of legal persons for acts of foreign bribery through criminal law. For example, one civil law country, Germany, has relied exclusively on its administrative law to hold legal persons liable for foreign bribery, while several common law countries have supplemented criminal enforcement with enforcement through civil settlements.[2]

---

1. The United Nations Convention against Corruption (UNCAC), Article 26; OECD Convention on Combating Bribery of Foreign Public Officials in International Business Transactions (OECD Anti-Bribery Convention), Article 2 and Commentary 3 (explaining functional equivalence).
2. See OECD, *Phase 3 Report on Implementing the OECD Anti-Bribery Convention in Germany* (Paris: OECD, 2011), 18, http://www.oecd.org/germany/Germanyphase3reportEN.pdf for an example of functional equivalence.

TABLE 2.1	Forms of Liability in Public Legal Actions: Criminal, Civil, and Administrative		
	Criminal	**Civil**	**Administrative**

Possible punishments	Imprisonment
	
	Fines and other
	  monetary penalties
	Asset confiscation and
	  restitution
		Fines and other
		  monetary penalties
		Asset confiscation and
		  restitution
			Fines and other
			  monetary penalties
			Asset confiscation and
			  restitution
			Warnings
			Revocations/
			  suspensions of
			  licenses or permits

Source of authority	Written laws	Written laws or case law	Written laws or regulations
Burden of proof	Beyond a reasonable doubt or intimate conviction	Probability, more likely than not to have committed the infraction	Highly variable, usually lower than criminal standard
Objectives	Punish, deter, rehabilitate, restore victim's position	Punish, deter, confiscate profits derived from illegal activity, compensate for harm caused	Punish, deter, regulate activities
Enforcers	Prosecutors	Prosecutors, regulators	Regulators[a]

Examples of
  enforcement agencies
	U.S. Department
	  of Justice
		U.S. Securities and
		  Exchange Commission
			U.S. Securities and
			  Exchange Commission

	U.K. Serious Fraud
	  Office
		U.K. Serious Fraud
		  Office
			U.K. Financial Services
			  Authority[b]

[a] In some countries (including Germany), prosecutors have the power to enforce administrative laws.
[b] In April 2013, the Financial Services Authority became two separate regulatory authorities. The Financial Conduct Authority FCA (www.fca.org.uk) regulates the financial services industry in the United Kingdom. See http://www.fsa.gov.uk/.

1.2 Judicial Oversight

The second criterion for understanding settlements is the degree to which a judge plays a role in the proceedings.[3] The extent of judicial involvement in settlements varies widely, from none (as in Swiss summary punishment orders, Norwegian penalty notices, and Non-Prosecution Agreements in the United States) to supervision of a series of hearings (the case for guilty pleas in common law systems and the sanctioning

---

3. The definition may be complicated in systems where the prosecutor sometimes has the authority to act as a judge, as in Switzerland. In any event, judges or magistrates who run the courtrooms are generally a distinct category.

agreements in Germany). In general, if a judge oversees the process, the public will have more confidence in the outcome. Without the stamp of judicial approval, settlements may have less legitimacy.

1.3 Transparency

The third criterion is the degree to which a shortened procedure allows for transparency, as compared to a trial or full criminal proceeding. Most trials are public and hence highly transparent. Alternatives to trials vary considerably from jurisdiction to jurisdiction in terms of transparency. The relevant criteria for settlements may include whether there is a public hearing, whether the settlement agreement is made public, whether affected parties are informed, whether a statement of the facts to which the defendant is admitting is made public and whether the penalty and the method of penalty calculation are made public. There are wide differences in the degree of transparency of settlements among jurisdictions. For example, hearings on guilty pleas are public. In contrast, the publication of the settlement agreement itself may be the only public aspect of the case.

As far as settlement documents, some jurisdictions, like Norway and the United States, release most of the settlement documents on their websites, while the United Kingdom releases information selectively. [4] Many other jurisdictions, however, provide quite limited information, and their abbreviated procedures rarely involve public hearings. If there were public hearings, typically the public would have direct access to the proceedings or access to records of the proceedings.

2. Terms Typically Included in Settlements

Although settlement documents vary considerably, depending on the legal regime and the facts of the case, there are certain terms and conditions that most of them will contain. For example:

Admission of guilt: The defendant is usually required to admit to conduct that meets the definition of the offense that forms the legal basis of the settlement.[5] If the defendant

---

4. In the United States, court documents (with narrow exceptions, such as protection of privacy of personal identifier information or security-related concerns) filed in all federal and some state court cases can be accessed electronically, either for free or a nominal fee. In federal cases, the court filings may be accessed by PACER (Public Access to Court Electronic Records, at www.pacer.gov). However, in cases where restitution is ordered, the names of the recipients are not included in the publicly available judgment so as to provide privacy to the victims/restitution recipients. (For example, see the Haiti Teleco case summary in chapter 6.)

5. As noted in a January 2012 policy change statement issued by the U.S. Securities and Exchange Commission (SEC), under the commission's "traditional 'neither admit nor deny' approach, a defendant could be found guilty of criminal conduct and, at the same time, settle parallel SEC charges while neither admitting nor denying civil liability." The SEC announced that the "change applies to cases involving parallel (i) criminal convictions or (ii) NPAs [Non-Prosecution Agreements] or DPAs [Deferred Prosecution Agreements] that include admissions or acknowledgments of criminal conduct. Under the

specifically pleads guilty to the offense, the defendant must at least state that he/she/it has committed the crime in question. For example, in its simplest form, if the company is pleading guilty to foreign bribery, a statement to the effect that "Company X offered to pay bribes to foreign official Mr. Y in order to obtain public contracts" would be required.

Admission of offenses other than foreign bribery: In many cases, the defendant may settle on an offense other than foreign bribery. For example, it might admit to participating in a corrupt scheme or failing to keep proper books and records (thus enabling bribe money to be disguised in its accounts). Such offenses are usually associated in some way with foreign bribery,[6] and the penalties are typically less severe.[7] Admitting to these non–foreign bribery offenses may enable the company to avoid debarment.[8] In some jurisdictions (e.g., the United States), the defendant may be admitting to facts that constitute a more serious offense (e.g., foreign bribery) while actually settling on a lesser offense (e.g., failing to keep proper books and records). In other jurisdictions, however, the admissions may be very limited and amount to no more than a minimum of wrongdoing.

Payment of a monetary sanction: In cases of legal persons, the agreement will typically include payment of a monetary sanction made up of various components.[9] Natural persons are also subject to monetary sanctions, including asset forfeiture and payment of restitution, although sometimes they are not sentenced to pay monetary sanctions due to their inability to pay.

Implementation of a compliance program: Legal persons often must agree to implement or improve compliance programs, internal control systems designed to prevent future offenses of a similar nature. The company may need to engage a compliance monitor, an independent person to oversee implementation of a satisfactory program.

Appending of signatures: Both the defendant and the prosecuting authority are required to sign the settlement documents.

More specific terms: Settlements may also include other, more specific terms. These could include the following:

- The defendant shall fully disclose the extent of its wrongdoing and cooperate with any further investigations conducted by the prosecuting authority.

---

new approach, for those settlements we will: •Delete the 'neither admit nor deny' language from the settlement documents. •Recite the fact and nature of the criminal conviction or criminal NPA/DPA in the settlement documents...." Robert Khuzami, Director of the SEC's Division of Enforcement, *Public Statement by SEC Staff: Recent Policy Change,* Washington, D.C., January 7, 2012, http://www.sec.gov/news /speech/2012/spch010712rsk.html.

6. See appendix 3 (methodology).

7. For example, in the United States, while some of these are lesser offenses, some are also greater offenses. For example, the accounting violations under the Foreign Corrupt Practices Act (FCPA) carry higher statutory maximum penalties than those under the antibribery violations.

8. Debarment is the exclusion from eligibility to tender for public contracts.

9. See chapter 4, box 4.1, "Components of Monetary Sanctions."

- The defendant shall cooperate with other prosecuting authorities, under the direction of the prosecuting jurisdiction entering the settlement. This term is frequently applied in U.S. settlements.[10]
- The prosecuting authority reserves the right to require defendants to respond to requests for international cooperation. In some U.K. settlements, for example, it is included to emphasize the fact that prosecutors should and can cooperate with foreign authorities in investigations without breaching any promise they may have made to cease further investigation of the defendant for specific matters.
- The obligations in the agreement shall bind the signatory prosecuting authority but not any other agencies, domestic or foreign.[11] This prevents any confusion that may arise as to whether the settling jurisdiction intends to hinder other jurisdictions from going forward.

Table 2.2a and table 2.2b summarize typical forms and sanctions applied in settlements based on criminal offenses and settlements based on civil enforcement powers.

TABLE 2.2a Settlements: Criminal Forms and Sanctions	
Examples of forms of settlement	Examples of monetary sanctions
• Non-Prosecution Agreement	• Criminal fine
• Deferred Prosecution Agreement	• Forfeiture of criminal proceeds
• Guilty Plea	• Restitution
• Penalty Notice	• Contribution to investigations and/or prosecution costs
• Summary Punishment Order	• Contribution to charity (existing or newly created as part of the settlement)
	• Reparations

TABLE 2.2b Settlements: Civil Forms and Sanctions	
Examples of forms of settlement	Examples of monetary sanctions
• Civil recovery order	• Disgorgement of profits
• Consent to cease-and-desist order	• Prejudgment interest
• Consent	• Civil fine or penalty
• Consent to final judgment	• Asset forfeiture
• Consent to permanent injunction	• Debarment from future projects
• Penalty notice	• Payment of taxes owed
• Tax settlement	

---

10. U.S. Department of Justice (U.S. DOJ), Johnson & Johnson DPA, http://www.justice.gov/criminal/fraud/fcpa/cases/depuy-inc/04-08-11depuy-dpa.pdf.

11. U.S. DOJ, Johnson & Johnson. See also summary at chapter 6, case 7.

3. The Role of International Organizations in Settlements

Nation-states are not the only parties who have an interest in combating the bribery of their officials. International organizations, especially the larger ones (e.g., the United Nations and the World Bank), have an interest in rooting out foreign bribery and corruption on projects that they finance. Their interest includes bribery on the part of contractors, as such practices divert development resources. As a result, we have seen in recent years the emergence of another kind of investigation and enforcement, which sometimes overlaps and interacts with national enforcement.

- A number of foreign bribery cases have been initiated on the basis of information gathered by the United Nations and the World Bank and passed on to national authorities. Cases of this nature that have ended in settlements, such as the Macmillan and Mabey cases in the United Kingdom as well as several *patteggiamenti* in Italy.[12]
- A number of international institutions, such as the World Bank, have their own internal administrative procedures for addressing corruption-related offenses that involve the use of the institution's financing. These procedures allow for settlement agreements with offending companies.[13] For instance, when an administrative investigation reveals evidence indicating that firms or individuals have been engaging in fraudulent, corrupt, collusive, coercive, or obstructive practices in a project financed or administered by the World Bank, the Bank's investigative unit may launch proceedings, which may lead to the imposition of a sanction of debarment.[14] Since 2010, the Bank has had not only a full set of sanctions proceedings but also a mechanism to permit settlements, which include the agreement to sanctions.[15]
- Settlements by international organizations may concern the same or a similar set of facts as settlements made by national authorities. For example, in the foreign bribery case of the publisher Macmillan,[16] the World Bank reached a settlement with Macmillan that included debarment. In this case, the World Bank cooperated with

---

12. See a summary of the Macmillan case at chapter 6, case 9, and of the Mabey case at chapter 6, case 8.

13. In this context, such administrative systems are internal procedures at an institution designed to determine whether it will continue to engage in business dealings with certain persons, legal or natural, based on whether those persons have observed rules set up by the institution. Each of the regional multilateral development banks (MDBs) has its own sanctions regime. Under the "cross-debarment" agreement among the MDBs, however, a sanction by one MDB will be applied by all of the MDBs, subject to certain conditions and limitations. For example, if a company settles and agrees to be debarred by the World Bank for a period exceeding one year, the Asian Development Bank will normally apply that same period of debarment.

14. See World Bank, Integrity Vice Presidency, http://worldbank.org/integrity, for a description of the Bank's sanctions regime.

15. The World Bank's negotiated resolution agreements effectively end or, for settlements reached prior to their commencement, replace sanctions proceedings with an agreed sanction, which includes compliance by the respondent with certain conditions. The default sanction is debarment with conditional release, the introduction or improvement of an integrity compliance program and/or remedial measures such as disciplinary action against the wrongdoers, and, in exceptional cases, restitution. Cooperation with ongoing or future Bank investigations may also be a part of the terms of such a resolution.

16. For a summary of the case, see chapter 6, case 9.

U.K. authorities, who later settled their own prosecution of Macmillan through a civil recovery order. This demonstrates how international organizations and national authorities can work together to bring about settlements of parallel cases.

- Settlements by international organizations may also provide for restitution. For example, in February, 2012, the World Bank announced the sanctioning of Alstom.[17] The sanction, which included the debarment of two Alstom entities—Alstom Hydro France and Alstom Network Schweiz and their controlled affiliates—and the conditional nondebarment of all other Alstom entities, was agreed to under a settlement between the World Bank and Alstom, which also included a restitution payment totaling approximately $9.5 million. In an earlier matter, Siemens had agreed to a comprehensive settlement with the World Bank of corruption allegations regarding World Bank projects, including establishment of a $100 million fund to support global efforts to fight fraud and corruption.[18]

Settlement documents are reviewed by the World Bank's Legal Department to ensure legal adequacy and are then reviewed by the Bank's Suspension and Debarment Officer to confirm that the respondent entered into the settlement freely and that the agreed upon sanction fell within the four corners of the World Bank's publicly available sanctioning guidelines. The settlement agreements between the World Bank and respondent parties are confidential, but a summary of the agreements and facts are announced in press releases posted on the Bank's website.[19]

Not all World Bank cases are resolved through settlements. There is a two-tier adjudicative structure providing for a first instance of review by the World Bank's Office of Suspension and Debarment and, for cases that are appealed, a second instance of review by the World Bank Group Sanctions Board.

4. The Rationale behind Settlements

While in some jurisdictions, settlement of foreign bribery cases—generally by plea bargain—is a well-established part of criminal procedure, in others such practices have been introduced only recently. Available OECD statistics, the study's own database of

---

17. See World Bank, *Enforcing Accountability: World Bank Debars Alstom Hydro France, Alstom Network Schweiz AG, and their Affiliates,* press release, Washington, DC, February 22, 2012, http://web.worldbank .org/WBSITE/EXTERNAL/NEWS/0,,contentMDK:23123315~menuPK:34463~pagePK:34370~piPK:34424 ~theSitePK:4607,00.html.

18. See, for example, World Bank, *Siemens Settlement Agreement: Fact Sheet,* http://siteresources.worldbank. org/INTDOII/Resources/Siemens_Fact_Sheet_Nov_11.pdf. Siemens will provide funds to organizations and projects aimed at combating corruption through collective action, training, and education. The World Bank will have audit rights over the use of these funds and veto rights over the selection by Siemens of anticorruption groups or programs receiving funds.

19. See, for example, concerning the Macmillan case, World Bank, *The World Bank Group Debars Macmillan Limited for Corruption in World Bank-supported Education Project in Southern Sudan,* press release, April 30, 2010,
http://web.worldbank.org/WBSITE/EXTERNAL/NEWS/0,,contentMDK:22563910~menuPK:51062078 ~pagePK:34370~piPK:34424~theSitePK:4607,00.html.

foreign bribery and related cases, and evidence provided by experts consulted for the purposes of this study show that settlements have become a key tool in the arsenal of law enforcement agencies. Abbreviated procedures have also helped in no small measure to boost the enforcement of foreign bribery laws and regulations globally.

As noted earlier, in several countries party to the OECD Anti-Bribery Convention a very high proportion of cases of foreign bribery and related offenses do not go to trial but end with the imposition of substantial monetary sanctions.

- In Germany, approximately half the companies prosecuted for foreign-bribery-type offenses have been sanctioned through various forms of administrative settlements.
- In the United States, more than 90 percent of the foreign-bribery and related cases have been resolved through settlements.[20]
- In Italy, all the finalized foreign bribery cases that resulted in sanctions against individuals or corporations were obtained through the summary procedure known as a *patteggiamento*.[21]
- In Switzerland, most foreign bribery convictions have been concluded by summary punishment order.[22]
- In the United Kingdom, similarly, not a single successful foreign bribery case has proceeded to trial.[23]

In fact, the use of settlements seems to be related to factors such as growing caseloads and inadequate resources available to law enforcement authorities for fighting corruption. An increasing number of law enforcement agencies opt for settlements due to reasons such as the following:

- *Efficient use of law enforcement resources:* Where settlements have been introduced or are being used more frequently, law enforcement is using fewer resources to process comparatively more cases.
- *Convenient resolution of complex cases:* Settlements are seen as a way of dealing with highly complex financial crime, especially where legal persons are involved.[24] Such complexity certainly applies to cases involving the bribery of foreign officials; the schemes used for such purposes involve multiple offenders, various

---

20. See OECD, *Phase 3 Report on Implementing the OECD Anti-Bribery Convention in the United States* (2010), http://www.oecd.org/daf/anti-bribery/anti-briberyconvention/UnitedStatesphase3reportEN.pdf.

21. See OECD, *Phase 3 Report on Implementing the OECD Anti-Bribery Convention in Italy* (2011), 7, http://www.oecd.org/daf/anti-bribery/anti-briberyconvention/Italyphase3reportEN.pdf.

22. OECD, *Phase 3 Report on Implementing the OECD Anti-Bribery Convention in Switzerland* (2011), 9, http://www.oecd.org/daf/anti-bribery/anti-briberyconvention/Switzerlandphase3reportEN.pdf.

23. OECD, *Phase 3 Report on Implementing the OECD Anti-Bribery Convention in the United Kingdom* (2012), 7, http://www.oecd.org/daf/anti-bribery/UnitedKingdomphase3reportEN.pdf.

24. Complex financial crime cases present additional challenges to investigators, prosecutors, and courts. See OECD/World Bank, *Identification and Quantification of the Proceeds of Bribery: A Joint OECD-StAR Analysis* (Paris: OECD, 2011), http://star.worldbank.org/star/publication/identification-and-quantification -proceeds-bribery, which presents information on methods to calculate gains made by companies that pay bribes to win contracts or gain unfair advantages.

jurisdictions, and extended periods of time. Evidence is often hard to come by, and major offenders are often legal persons that can call on vast resources with which to defend themselves.

Similarly defendants, especially legal persons, benefit for a number of reasons:

- *Smaller or no penalties:* Given that most justice systems are structured to reward those who admit responsibility early by imposing lesser penalties,[25] companies can expect to receive lower monetary penalties by agreeing to settle rather than put the prosecution to the expense and uncertainty of a trial.
- *Financial ability to pay:* The defendant's financial ability to pay the full amount of the monetary sanctions is a factor taken into consideration in determining the amount payable.[26]
- *Less bad publicity:* By offering a quicker resolution, a settlement may help a company to limit its exposure to bad publicity and mitigate drops in share price. Certainly, publicity resulting from a settlement (the exact details of which may remain confidential) is likely to be far less intense than the media attention generated by pretrial proceedings and a public trial. Generally, a trial would entail testimony by live witnesses and consequently constitute a bigger story for the media.
- *Avoidance of debarment:* In the United States, a conviction for foreign bribery automatically debars a company from doing business with the government. In the European Union, a 2004 directive urged member countries to debar from public contracts any economic operator found guilty of corruption. The threat of debarment can be a powerful tool in the hands of enforcement agencies, and any settlement that avoids that outcome is highly desirable to companies.[27]

---

25. Commonly, natural person defendants who plead guilty receive significantly shorter prison sentences. For example, in one of the Haiti Teleco cases, recently an executive of a telecom company proceeded to trial in the United States on charges of fraud, money laundering, and paying bribes to officials in Haiti and was convicted. That executive was sentenced to 15 years in prison, while four other individuals who pleaded guilty to other roles in that scheme received sentences between six months and four years, nine months. See for further information, U.S. DOJ, "Executive Sentenced to 15 Years in Prison for Scheme to Bribe Officials at State-Owned Telecommunications Company in Haiti," press release, October 25, 2011, http://www.justice.gov/opa/pr/2011/October/11-crm-1407.html. See case summary in chapter 6, case 5.

26. For example, consider Regina v. Innospec Limited, Sentencing Remarks of Lord Justice Thomas, 26 March, 2010. For a summary of the case, see chapter 6, case 6. The corruption affected primarily two other countries (Indonesia and Iraq). U.S. and U.K. authorities and Innospec discussed a "global settlement" subject to court approval. The U.S. DOJ asked the U.S. courts to approve a fine of $14.1 million, a disgorgement order of $11.2 million to the U.S. SEC, and a $2.2 million penalty to the U.S. Department of Treasury's Office of Foreign Assets Control. The United Kingdom Serious Fraud Office asked the U.K. courts to approve a $6.7 million confiscation penalty and a $6 million civil recovery judgment. The U.K. courts very reluctantly agreed, while expressing concern that the total sums were inadequate to reflect the magnitude of the harm and cautioning that English courts would be unlikely to restrict their discretionary powers in future cases to accept such agreements among parties.

27. See Article 45 of the EU Procurement Contracts Directive http://eur-lex.europa.eu/LexUriServ/LexUriServ.do?uri=CELEX:32004L0018:en:NOT; Regulation 23 of the Public Contracts Regulations (2006) and Regulation 26 of the Utilities Contracts Regulations (2006) (U.K. implementation of the directive). See for example, the BAE case (chapter 6, case 3), in which the company pleaded guilty to one count of record-keeping violations, a bribery-related offense that does not cause mandatory debarment.

- *Reduced risk/more certain outcome:* Companies prefer to have as much certainty as possible as to what penalties they may face, so that they can plan and move ahead with their business strategies.[28] By negotiating a settlement, a company may be able to obtain that certainty. However, the extent to which a settlement can ensure certainty may vary, depending on the legal framework under which the settlement is concluded. Under most settlements in the United States, a company knows when it signs the settlement documents exactly what penalty it will get. This can also be true in the United Kingdom in the case of a civil recovery order, when the parties can agree a specific sum. However, in the case of a guilty plea, the parties can agree only on a range, and it is the judge who takes the final decision.

Despite their potential appeal to both defendants and prosecutors, however, such practices give rise to certain questions. For example, how do they affect the obligations of countries under various international anticorruption instruments, especially UNCAC? Given the fact that none of the existing conventions directly addresses the issue of settlements, no simple answer is available. We will consider such issues in more detail in chapter 4.

More generally, a lively debate is taking place about whether settlements are a satisfactory way of resolving foreign bribery cases. The following criticisms are frequently heard:

- *Inadequate or no judicial supervision:* If a settlement is made with little or no oversight by a judge, it leaves the power of the prosecutor largely unchecked.[29]

In the United States, debarment is discretionary. See, e.g., Federal Acquisition Regulation, 48 CFR Part 9, Subpart 9.4. See OECD, *Phase 3 Report: United States*, 40. With regard to debarment, it is worth noting that commentators have different views, with some commentators arguing that it can have an effect of distorting competition in markets.

28. One response to increased risk is that insurance companies have developed insurance products against FCPA enforcement by public authorities: "FCPA Corporate Response is the only insurance mechanism that provides cost of investigation coverage for both individuals and the organization. Designed for companies of all sizes that conduct business globally, FCPA Corporate Response reimburses companies for investigation costs including legal, accounting, auditing, and consulting fees due to a Foreign Corrupt Practices Act (FCPA) claim, provides coverage for both the organization and individuals for FCPA investigations, and acts as primary insurance to a directors and officers liability policy to immediately protect individual directors and officers." See Marsh USA, *Insurance Coverage for FCPA Investigation Costs*, July 11, 2011, http://usa.marsh.com/ProductsServices/MarshSolutions/ID/5042/Insurance-Coverage-for -FCPA-Investigation-Costs.aspx

29. The OECD recently voiced such concerns in its report on the United Kingdom, noting that "the Working Group [on Bribery] is concerned that, to settle foreign bribery-related cases, U.K. authorities are increasingly relying on civil recovery orders which require less judicial oversight and are less transparent than criminal plea agreements. The low level of information on settlements made publicly available by U.K. authorities often does not permit a proper assessment of whether the sanctions imposed are effective, proportionate and dissuasive. This also misses an opportunity for the United Kingdom to provide guidance and raise public awareness on foreign bribery-related issues. It is equally concerning that the SFO has in some cases entered into confidentiality agreements with defendants that prevent the disclosure of key information after cases are settled." OECD, *Phase 3 Report: United Kingdom*, 5.

- *Sanctions, both monetary and nonmonetary, are too low:* Settlements may not lead to the imposition of effective, proportionate, and dissuasive sanctions.[30] The implication may perhaps be that companies are being let off the hook, with the payment of fines becoming just another business cost. Under certain kinds of settlements, the size of fines is limited and may be too low to deter potential bribe payers.[31] Moreover, some settlements with companies have provided for immunity from prosecution for implicated individuals.

- *Not enough of a deterrent for individuals:* When settlements are concluded against legal persons, and no action is taken to address the criminal conduct of natural persons (either through jail or monetary sanctions), the deterrent effect may be inadequate.[32] Foreign bribery, like all crimes, is ultimately committed by people, not companies. An individual discovered to have paid or authorized the payment of a bribe is unlikely to change his behavior if he believes that the worst that will happen is that his company will pay a large financial penalty.

- *Not transparent enough:* Settlements provide less transparency than public trials, and settlements carried out by civil or administrative means tend to be even less transparent than those resolved under criminal law.

- *Absence of the victim in the settlement:* Civil society organizations (CSOs) that are part of the UNCAC Coalition consistently alert the international bodies working on anticorruption on the misrepresentation (or absence) of victims in the settlements of foreign bribery cases. According to them, the implementation of the current international instruments, such as UNCAC, does not take into account victims rights appropriately, despite the UNCAC provisions and the emergence of the victims' voice during recent political events like the Arab Spring. As publicly expressed by the UNCAC Coalition, "To recognize the costs of corruption, G20 governments should promote compensation to victims, including countries and companies, in the context of foreign bribery cases and set up robust legal mechanisms in this regard."[33] CSOs point out that settlements are not designed to allow third parties to be represented as the victims.

Debate around the notion of the "victim" in foreign corruption cases is increasing. CSOs have expressed concerns that some public authorities concluding settlements in foreign bribery cases argue that the victims are the people of the country in which the foreign bribery provisions have been breached, that is, the country of settlement. The notion of

---

30. See, for example, OECD, *Phase 3 Report: Germany*, 34, 38 (level of imprisonment and fines not high enough).

31. See, for example, OECD, *Phase 3 Report: Germany*, 4 (fines limited under certain German code provisions); OECD, *Phase 3 Report: Italy*, 4, 19–22 (monetary sanctions should be higher).

32. It is interesting to note that certain jurisdictions, such as the United States, have recently made prosecuting more individuals a priority. Critics cited a lack of past efforts. See J. Stewart, "Bribes Without Jail Time," *New York Times*, April 28, 2012, which cites academic research stating that, between 2005 and 2010, 37 of 57 companies faulted for bribery by the DOJ entered settlements and no related individuals were charged. More on the same is available at Richard L. Cassin, "Corporate Enforcement Countdown," FCPA Blog, http://www.fcpablog.com/blog/2010/9/16/corporate-enforcement-countdown.html.

33. UNCAC Coalition, Civil society Recommendations in Reaction to New G20 Anti-Corruption Plan 2013–14, December 10, 2012, http://www.uncaccoalition.org/learn-more/articles/190-civil-society-recommendations-in-reaction-to-new-g20-anti-corruption-action-plan-2013-2014.

victim is, however, in constant evolution, and because of the absence of an international legal definition, the notion of victims remains mostly based on case law. For instance, in the United States, the Second Circuit has recently developed a theory for restitution to countries that are victims of wildlife smuggling based on the Mandatory Victims Restitution Act, imposing restitution to South Africa of more than $54 million as part of a settlement.[34] That shows, if needed, that the fact of the settlement is not an impediment *per se* for taking into consideration of the victims. Settlements allow flexibility with regard to the nature of the monetary sanctions imposed, and thus there is potential for restitution to victims.[35]

Not withstanding these various considerations, on balance, the recourse to settlements has led to measurable progress in terms of resolving foreign bribery cases.

5. Trends and Developments

The use of settlements to address foreign bribery is evolving. This section begins with a discussion of a number of general trends and then focuses specifically on proceedings conducted by countries whose own officials have been bribed, a special category in which a number of innovations are nascent. In reflecting on these observations, it is important to keep in mind that in most countries the number of settlements so far is small. Thus, the analysis and conclusions remain preliminary pending a larger set of data in the future.

5.1 General Trends

The following specific observations flow from this study:

- Over the past decade, the frequency of settlements has increased worldwide.
- The monetary sanctions imposed have grown larger.
- The number of countries that have successfully prosecuted legal persons has risen, with countries frequently resolving those cases through settlements.
- Settlements are predominantly found in countries that are major financial centers (where the type of large companies likely to supply the bribe money are located). Settlements are less often found in developing countries (although, as discussed in other parts of the study, certain developing countries have started to make use of settlements). Where the increase in enforcement is most notable, in certain OECD countries, some of those countries recently have begun to bring more cases against natural persons, in the hope that prison sentences for individual offenders will have stronger deterrent effect than monetary sanctions for companies. There can be little doubt that hearing that a person of the same job title is

---

34. US v. Arnold Maurice Bengis, Jeffry Noll & David Bengis, Case No. 03-cr-308 (SDNY), Report and Recommendation filed August 16, 2012, http://imcsnet.org/wp-content/uploads/2012/08/Bengis-AJP -report-and-recommendation.pdf.
35. See discussion chapter 4.

going to jail would deter a person far more effectively than hearing that a person's employer is paying large monetary sanctions.

Broader, more conceptual trends have also been noted:

More varied enforcement through use of administrative and civil tools: As noted, countries are using, not only the criminal law, but also civil and administrative enforcement powers to great effect. Settlements appear to offer flexibility of legal tools, enhancing overall enforcement.

Emerging parallel enforcement: A small number of prosecuting jurisdictions are starting to work together to conduct parallel investigations of the same or related misconduct, and thus parallel settlements. For example:

- *Johnson & Johnson:* The Johnson & Johnson cases (mid-2011) illustrate synergies that resulted from timely cooperation among authorities in at least four countries: Greece, Poland, the United Kingdom, and the United States. This led to substantial settlements in the United States and the United Kingdom, an asset freeze in Greece, and ongoing proceedings in Poland.[36]
- *Innospec:* The 2010 cases against Innospec show that global settlements are a trend. The company settled allegations of bribery (committed with respect to several countries) in a coordinated way with the U.S. and U.K. authorities.[37]
- *Siemens:* A further example is the jointly orchestrated settlement of the major Siemens investigations by the United States and Germany, announced on the same day.[38] Other Siemens actions were settled by Greece, Italy, and the World Bank. Figure 2.1 illustrates the timing of some of the overlapping cases, which occurred over a six-year period.

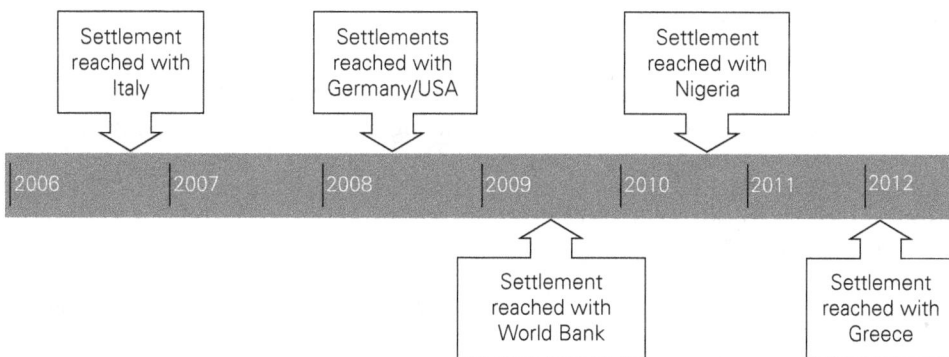

FIGURE 2.1 Timeline of Settlements in Various Cases against Siemens

---

36. For a summary of the case, see chapter 6, case 7.
37. For a summary of the BAE case, see chapter 6, case 3; for Innospec see chapter 6, case 6.
38. For a summary of the case, see chapter 6, case 12.

Offsetting of financial sanctions: A number of jurisdictions are also taking into account financial penalties paid elsewhere in setting the financial sanctions in their own cases.

- *Innospec:* In setting the fines in the Innospec case, the U.K. courts had to take into account the fines and disgorgement ordered against the company in the U.S. courts, as translated into the settlement presented by the prosecutors.
- *Statoil:* In parallel proceedings, Statoil settled with the U.S. Department of Justice and U.S. Securities and Exchange Commission, who both took into account the financial penalties Statoil had already paid in Norway.[39]
- *Siemens:* In the Siemens Power Turbines case, Italy prosecuted Siemens for bribery relating to two turbine contracts, and Siemens agreed to forfeit the profits. When the German authorities also prosecuted that bribery, the German court offset confiscation already paid in Italy.[40] The law of at least one country (Germany) explicitly provides that a punitive fine can be reduced if the company has been or will be punished in another jurisdiction for the same offense.[41]

Reduced role of the courts: The more cases are concluded by means of a settlement rather than proceeding to trial, the more the role of the courts is reduced. In common law systems, in particular, the greater involvement of the courts usually leads to greater clarification of what the law means. But as greater use is made of settlements and guilty pleas, this clarifying role is diminished. In a trial, issues are litigated with full arguments made on each side, permitting a judge to weigh the merits of the legal issues in light of the facts. In common law jurisdictions, such case law plays a large role, and its effect on the development of the law is considered desirable.[42] Moreover, in such systems, legal precedent is often binding on future cases.

A similar effect may exist in civil law systems, where past decisions are not binding but are nonetheless consulted as a source of authority. Thus, if cases are settled at an early stage through an agreement and summary punishment order, the finer points of law may never be reached; and what the laws mean in practice may remain unclear. Some commentators have remarked that this increases the power of prosecutors and deprives the law of an evolution that would otherwise occur.

Self-reporting and self-investigation: An increasing number of foreign bribery cases ending in settlements have involved self-reporting and subsequent self-investigations

---

39. For a summary of the case, see chapter 6, case 13.
40. See analysis in OECD/World Bank, *Identification and Quantification*, 51–53.
41. OECD, *Phase 3 Report: Germany*, 36.
42. For example, commentators mentioned the lack of clarity of the legal contours of the "identification theory" under U.K. law, a doctrine under which a legal person is responsible if its "directing mind" possesses the guilty intent to commit the crime. How far down the corporate structure a "directing mind" might go is an open question. Since the recent cases of Mabey and Innospec resulted from guilty pleas rather than full trials, the legal issues of concern were not argued by the litigants and settled by a court. The OECD noted this issue in its *Phase 3 Report: United Kingdom*. While this particular point is likely to become less relevant as new antibribery legislation has come into effect in the United Kingdom, other legal issues will remain unsettled if few or no cases proceed to full trial.

by companies.[43] Self-reporting means that the companies voluntarily disclose their own misconduct. The practice has contributed to an increase in the detection and enforcement of foreign bribery cases. In the United States and the United Kingdom, for example, the level of cooperation of the company with the authorities is taken into account in reaching the settlement agreements. Given budget constraints for law enforcement agencies, relying on self-investigation by companies as long as it meets the agreed upon standards is also a way for these agencies to reduce the costs of their activities.

However, while self-reporting certainly improves the detection of foreign bribery cases, some commentators have raised concerns about the prosecution's reliance on internal investigations performed by the defendant. That process may not encourage the enforcement agencies to cast a broad net in the investigations of bribery schemes at play, notably with regard to all the participants and intermediaries. Self-investigation presents a particular challenge in terms of following a money trail.[44] Private investigators, acting on behalf of the company, even in good faith, might not be able to access financial documentation or information on beneficial ownership located overseas or in the hands of other entities than the company itself. In such instances, the asset recovery process may be impaired by a too narrow picture of the bribery scheme, and countries through which the money was channeled or where the bribery took place may miss relevant information.

5.2 Developments in Countries Whose Officials Have Been the Object of Alleged Bribes

While exact statistics are not readily available, anecdotal sources and our research suggest very few countries have taken enforcement action against foreign companies or individuals who have bribed their public officials (or committed similar offenses). Nonetheless, a small number of countries—Nigeria, Costa Rica, Greece, and Lesotho, for instance—have successfully adopted a variety of innovative methods for concluding cases against legal persons.

Nigeria: Nigeria has settled several matters, negotiating significant restitution payments in exchange for ceasing its investigations of foreign bribery. These cases have been against both legal persons (Halliburton, Siemens, Saipem, and Technip) and natural persons. The total fines and disgorgement amounted to $170.8 million.[45]

- In the settlement with Siemens, for instance, the company agreed to pay a large sum in exchange for the Nigerian government's dismissing criminal charges and refraining from initiating any other criminal, civil, or administrative actions.
- In 2010, Nigeria entered into settlements with Halliburton Corporation, Snamprogetti Netherlands BV, JGC, and Technip, all of which held an interest in a joint venture known as TSKJ. The Attorney General of the Federation of Nigeria

---

43. See, for example, OECD, *Phase 3 Report: United Kingdom*, 31; and OECD, *Phase 3 Report: United States*, 11, 17.
44. For example, the extent to which intermediaries and/or corporate legal entities located in offshore jurisdictions and ultimate recipients of the illicit payments will be identified is not clear.
45. See chapter 6, case 14.

had investigated alleged improper payments to government officials in Nigeria in connection with the construction and subsequent expansion by TSKJ of a natural gas liquefaction project on Bonny Island, Nigeria. Under the settlement agreements, the Economic and Financial Crimes Commission agreed to dismiss all lawsuits and charges against KBR, Halliburton, Snamprogetti, JCG, and Technip corporate entities and associated persons and agreed not to bring any further criminal charges or civil claims against those entities or persons. Halliburton, Snamprogetti, JGC and Technip agreed to pay a total restitution of $127.5 million, mostly in penalties.[46] Notably, the agreement contained a cooperation provision, under which Halliburton agreed to provide reasonable assistance to Nigeria in its effort to recover amounts frozen in a Swiss bank account of a former TSKJ agent.[47]

Costa Rica: Costa Rica's Procuraduría de la Ética Pública brought a civil suit against a subsidiary of the French company Alcatel-Lucent SA on the legal theory that the company's involvement in the corruption of public officials had resulted in significant *daño social* (social damages) to the nation.[48] In 2010, Costa Rica reached a civil settlement with the French company, agreeing out of court voluntarily to dismiss its criminal and civil investigations in exchange for a payment of roughly $10 million.

Greece: Using another novel mechanism, in April 2012, Greece concluded a settlement of foreign bribery allegations against Siemens by multiple public entities that had contracts with the company by means of parliamentary action.[49] Siemens agreed to waive €80 million in obligations owed by the Greek government to Siemens (explicitly acknowledging that this write-off could not constitute a donation for the purposes of Greek tax law). It also agreed to provide €90 million to finance various entities and endeavors advancing the Greek public interest (including supporting the country's anticorruption platform); to invest €100 million in Siemens' activities within Greece; and to carry out a structured plan to consider and develop further investment opportunities within Greece.[50]

---

46. See Halliburton Company, "Halliburton Confirms Agreement to Settle with Federal Government of Nigeria," press release, December 21, 2010, http://www.halliburton.com/public/news/pubsdata/press _release/2010/corpnws_12212010.html; Saipem, "Snamprogetti Netherlands BV Enters Agreement with Federal Government of Nigeria," press release, December 20, 2010, http://www.saipem.com/site/Home /Press/Byyear/articolo6034.html; JGC Co., "Consolidated Financial Statements Summary for the Period Ending March 31, 2011," disclosure, May 13, 2011, 2, http://www.jgc.co.jp/en/06ir/pdf/financial _statements-summary/FY10/fy10_yem.pdf; and Technip SA, "Reference Document 2010 Including the Annual Financial Report," Autorité des marchés financiers filing, March 24, 2011, 175, http://www.technip .com/sites/default/files/technip/publications/attachments/DRF_Technip2010_VA_web_interactif.pdf.
47. While the settlement agreement is not public, the foregoing information was announced by Halliburton. For a summary of the case, see chapter 6, case 14.
48. For a summary of the case, see chapter 6, case 1. See also chapter 3. A Costa Rican state-owned entity did not succeed in its effort to claim restitution in United States courts in a related matter. See J. Olaya, K. Attisso, and A. Roth, "Repairing Social Damage Out of Corruption Cases: Opportunities and Challenges As Illustrated in the Alcatel Case in Costa Rica" (2010), http://ssrn.com/abstract=1779834 or http://dx.doi .org/10.2139/ssrn.1779834.
49. Specifically, the Greek parliament ratified a draft agreement and authorized the Minister of Finance to sign that agreement on behalf of Greece. For a summary of the case, see chapter 6, case 12.
50. For a summary of the case, see chapter 6, case 12.

Lesotho: Lesotho successfully prosecuted multinational companies (Schneider Electric SA and its related entities) as well as Lesotho officials. The company had made illegal payments to secure contracts for the Lesotho Highlands Water Project. After having requested and obtained mutual legal assistance from France and Switzerland, Lesotho prosecutors filed charges that ended in Schneider pleading guilty to 16 counts of bribery in 2004 and being ordered to pay a penalty of approximately $1.4 million.[51]

In order to supplement the publicly available data, the study team reached out to 28 countries seeking further information on efforts that had been taken by countries whose public officials allegedly had been bribed—whether such action had been taken in parallel to a case prosecuted in or as a follow-up action to the settlement concluded in a foreign jurisdiction. Of the 28, only 3 countries responded to this request for information with substantive feedback: Latvia, Serbia, and Turkey.

Latvia: The Latvian Corruption Prevention and Combatting Bureau (KNAB) initiated criminal proceedings against 17 persons in relation to the bribery of Latvenergo public officials. The KNAB also initiated criminal proceedings against several suspected municipality officers who had allegedly accepted bribes from a subsidiary of Daimler AG's company—EvoBus Gmb. Latvia noted that they had sent 34 mutual legal assistance requests (MLAs) to 14 countries during the course of their investigations, which were ongoing at the time of the study's research.

Serbia: Out of three cases concluded by settlements in a foreign jurisdiction that had ties with Serbia, two in the hands of local prosecutions were still ongoing at the time of research. The extent of the international cooperation received by Serbia for these cases is not known.

Turkey: It appears that two attempts were made by Turkish prosecutors to follow up on settlements concluded in the United States and in Germany.[52] The Turkish authorities sent an MLA request to Germany after learning of bribery cases through press articles. However, the German authorities refused the request, on the basis that there was insufficient information as to the particulars of the offence, details of the criminal actions (such as the facts pertaining to place and time), or the relevant legal basis. It is not clear if any MLA request was sent to the United States on the Daimler Benz case or if any information was obtained on the Delta & Pine Land case. The Turkish courts issued a judgment of no grounds for prosecution concerning the bribery of Turkish officials in these cases.

The preceding examples show how some jurisdictions are developing ways to enforce law against foreign legal persons who have bribed their own officials. The question now arises as to whether settlements in one jurisdiction affect cases in other jurisdictions. We have already noted in this study that in some cases off-setting monetary sanctions have been practiced based on sums previously paid in another jurisdiction. In the next chapter, we explore whether and how legal principles addressing duplicative or overlapping cases may affect future foreign bribery cases elsewhere.

---

51. For a summary of the case, see chapter 6, case 11.
52. Delta & Pine Land case in the United States; Siemens case in Germany.

3. The Impact of Settlements on Pending and Future Cases in Other Jurisdictions

With settlements becoming ever more prominent as a method of prosecuting foreign bribery cases, a question has increasingly arisen: how does a settlement in one jurisdiction affect legal actions in other jurisdictions? Uncertainty is exacerbated by the fact that settlements are often reached (or are being negotiated) in one jurisdiction without the input, or even knowledge, of another affected jurisdiction. It is not uncommon that affected jurisdictions become aware of a settlement only after it has been concluded. Settlement negotiations take place in private and away from the public eye, as opposed to trials, which take place in public courtrooms. Hence, the need to consider how settlements by one jurisdiction impact other affected jurisdictions is of great concern.

The following concerns were raised during the course of this study:

- The principle of *ne bis in idem*, or double jeopardy, is common in both civil and common law systems. It dictates that no criminal legal action can be instituted twice for the same cause of action against the same party. In the case of foreign bribery and related offenses, there is concern that this principle could mean that the settlement of a case in one jurisdiction could prevent subsequent prosecutions of the same case in another jurisdiction.
- There is also a practical concern that the law enforcement and judicial authorities of a country that has reached a settlement might be reluctant to provide mutual legal assistance (MLA) or any other form of cooperation to another jurisdiction investigating the same or similar facts. Practitioners consulted during this study raised concerns about the hurdles to obtaining evidence of even the predicate offence from jurisdictions that had already concluded a settlement.[1] In particular, the practitioners from developing countries felt this as a very real concern, especially if the authorities of the country from whom help is requested regarded the offense as having already been sufficiently addressed through the penalties imposed by their own courts or as part of a settlement.

---

1. Switzerland reported to the Organisation for Economic Co-operation and Development (OECD) negative effects from settlements elsewhere about which they had never been consulted. See, e.g., OECD, *Phase 3 Report on Implementing the OECD Anti-Bribery Convention in Switzerland* (Paris: OECD, 2011), http://www.oecd.org/daf/anti-bribery/anti-briberyconvention/Switzerlandphase3reportEN.pdf. Paragraph 12 notes that prosecutors reported that in several cases actions by foreign law enforcement authorities, especially following agreement with the parties, left the Swiss authorities unable to pursue the crime because of principles of *ne bis in idem* under Swiss law. Paragraph 15 notes that unnamed investigation based on the same facts was dismissed. Swiss authorities emphasized these concerns to the team during the course of this study.

- Finally, some cases suggest a tendency on the part of prosecutors, when setting monetary sanctions, to take any monetary sanctions incurred in prior settlements into account.[2] The implications of this are not yet clear.

Given the difficulties of gathering data, we cannot discount the possibility of some negative influence from settlements. Nonetheless, the study finds that despite these legal and practical concerns, settlements have actually had little impact on the ability of a country to pursue a foreign bribery case or related domestic bribery, money-laundering, or fraud cases. Furthermore, good practices in drafting settlement documents, highlighted later in this chapter, can help reduce negative impacts of settlements.

1. The Principles of *Ne Bis in Idem* and Double Jeopardy

In most legal systems, subjecting a suspect to criminal prosecution more than once for the same behavior or offense is considered contrary to the principles of fairness and proportionality. In common law countries, this is known as the principle of double jeopardy; in civil law countries, it is known as the doctrine of *ne bis in idem*. These principles are typically limited to prosecutions of the same parties for the same acts.

For offenses that are transnational in nature, the principles may apply when one country has judged and punished a suspect for an offense and another country wishes to prosecute the offender for the same, or a similar, underlying conduct.[3] For instance, in Europe, Articles 54–58 of the Convention Implementing the Schengen Agreement require contracting parties to refrain from multiple prosecutions for the same act(s).[4] Until a fully international treaty is in force, however, the only limitations that exist are those that countries have committed to voluntarily, either through domestic legislation or as part of their basic legal principles.

Most jurisdictions apply the principle of double jeopardy or *ne bis in idem* primarily to domestic cases (i.e., those prosecuted by their own authorities). This study did not find

---

2. Jurisdictions including the United Kingdom, United States, and Germany have demonstrably offset financial penalties paid elsewhere against their own imposed financial penalties. See "Trends and Developments" in chapter 2.

3. Note that these principles would not apply to a country prosecuting a corrupt foreign official for receiving a bribe after another country had settled allegations against the company that paid the bribe, because receiving a bribe and paying a bribe are two distinct offenses against two distinct defendants (the first being the bribe payer and the second being the bribe taker). Similarly, the principles would not prevent a country from seeking the assets obtained by a corrupt foreign official, even if the bribe-paying company had been pursued by a different country.

4. The European Court of Justice has provided guidance on the interpretation and applicability of the *ne bis in idem* principle under EU law, including Gözutök und Brügge, ECJ/ Judgment of 11.2. 2003, C-187 + 385/01 (NJW 2003, 1172), on the concept of *mutual recognition*, which is the "necessary implication that the Member States have mutual trust in their criminal justice systems and that each of them recognizes the criminal law in force in the other Member States even when the outcome would be different if its own national law were applied." See "*ne bis in idem*," excerpted from Schomburg et al., *Internationale Rechtshilfe in Strafsachen* [International cooperation in criminal matters], 5th ed., (Munich 2012), http://www.ejtn .net/PageFiles/3103/ne_bis_in_idem.pdf, posted by the European Judicial Training Network.

any jurisprudence applying the principle in cases where prosecutions were pursued in multiple jurisdictions. Furthermore, from a technical-legal perspective, the principle usually bars only subsequent criminal prosecutions, not subsequent civil or administrative prosecutions. This means that, when another country pursues foreign bribery through the application of civil or administrative sanctions, that activity falls outside the scope of the doctrines as understood by most jurisdictions.

There are examples of subsequent prosecutions of the same companies in different jurisdictions for closely related offenses, including the cases discussed earlier in this study. For example, the cases of BAE, Innospec, Siemens, and Statoil all illustrate enforcement action by multiple jurisdictions.

In addition, the TSKJ cases provide a good example.[5] In this set of cases, the United States prosecuted four companies for the foreign bribery of public officials in Nigeria, resulting in a guilty plea by Kellogg, Brown & Root LLC and deferred prosecution agreements (DPAs) with other companies forming part of the corrupt consortium. It is important to note that the United States does not apply double jeopardy in the international context. Meanwhile, Nigeria carried out an investigation of the same bribery scheme, also filing charges against the consortium members. Nigeria entered into a settlement with the four companies, accepting restitution and agreeing to dismiss all pending charges.[6] The United Kingdom opted for a civil as opposed to criminal resolution (because of concerns of double jeopardy), with the U.K. High Court issuing to Kellogg a civil recovery order for over £7 million, the amount representing the "share dividend income attributable to the illicit venture."[7] Figure 3.1 illustrates the various proceedings.

While not barring further legal action, a country may opt to pursue a different form of action based on legal actions elsewhere. The United Kingdom is the only jurisdiction identified in this study where it would appear that the double jeopardy principle has caused the authorities to pursue a different remedy: a non-conviction-based asset forfeiture procedure, rather than a criminal prosecution, in view of a settlement reached in another jurisdiction. In the Johnson & Johnson case,[8] an investigation conducted by the United States into acts of corruption committed by a subsidiary of Johnson & Johnson resulted in a DPA, in which the company admitted having paid bribes in Greece, Poland, and Romania. The same day as the DPA was entered in the United States, the U.K. authorities imposed a civil recovery order on another subsidiary of Johnson & Johnson as part of a settlement agreement for the same underlying offenses. Acknowledging that the underlying facts had been identical to those under criminal investigation in the United States, the U.K. authorities opted to pursue civil recovery with a view to avoiding any possible violation of the double jeopardy principle.[9]

---

5. See the summary of the case at chapter 6, case 14.
6. See the summary of the case at chapter 6, case 14.
7. U.K. SFO, "MW Kellogg Ltd. to pay 7m pounds in SFO High Court Action," February 16, 2011.
8. For a summary of the case, see chapter 6, case 7.
9. For a summary of the case, see chapter 6, case 7.

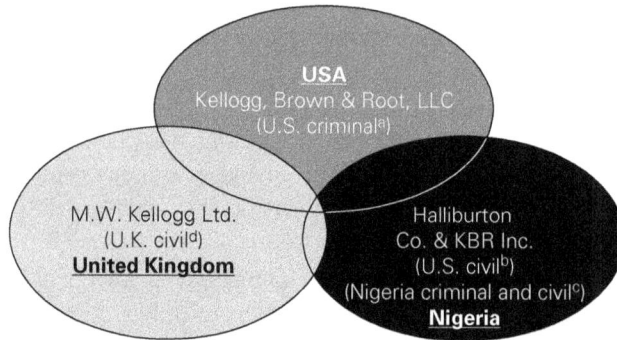

| FIGURE 3.1 | Settlements in Multiple Jurisdictions by a Multinational Corporation Involved in a Bribery Scheme Related to the Bonny Island Liquefied Natural Gas Project (Nigeria) |

[a] Resolved by a plea of guilty to foreign bribery and conspiracy charges before the U.S. DOJ. See Judgment, U.S. v. Kellogg Brown & Root LLC, Case No. 09-cr-071 (S.D. Tex.), February 12, 2009, http://www.justice.gov/criminal/fraud/fcpa/cases/kelloggb/02-12-09kbr-judgment.pdf.
[b] Resolved by acceptance of a U.S. SEC civil order. See Consent of Defendant KBR, SEC v. Halliburton & KBR, Case No. 4:09-cv-399 (S.D. Tex.), February 11, 2009; and Consent of Defendant Halliburton and Final Order, SEC v. Halliburton & KBR, Case No. 4:09-cv-399 (S.D. Tex.), February 11, 2009, available on PACER, http://www.pacer.gov.
[c] Resolved by agreement with the Federal Government of Nigeria for the cessation of all civil and criminal proceedings. See Halliburton Company, "Halliburton Confirms Agreement to Settle with Federal Government of Nigeria," press release, Houston, December 21, 2010, http://www.halliburton.com/public/news/pubsdata/press_release/2010/corpnws_12212010.html.
[d] Resolved by a U.K. High Court civil recovery order. See U.K. Serious Fraud Office, "MW Kellogg Ltd to Pay 7m Pounds in SFO High Court Action," press release, February 16, 2011, http://www.sfo.gov.uk/press-room/press-release-archive/press-releases-2011/mw-kellogg-ltd-to-pay-7-million-in-sfo-high-court-action.aspx.
Note: For more details, see the case summary of TSKJ Consortium in chapter 6, case 14.

Experts consulted for the purpose of this study indicated that, in practice, the relevance of these principles is limited by the nature of foreign bribery schemes and the fact that prosecutors often can select the incidents on which to focus. The limiting legal principles apply to prosecutions based on the same conduct at a particular place and time. Foreign bribery by corporate bodies seldom presents itself as an isolated occurrence. Usually, the individual incident which is detected and investigated becomes the entry point to a much larger complex of corruption-related offenses, typically spanning an extended period of time and affecting multiple jurisdictions. Different countries can choose to target their investigations on different aspects in different places or at different times.

The cases summarized in chapter 6 illustrate the often extensive scope of corrupt practices in which corporations engage, frequently extending over several continents for a period of years. Even when the corruption is on a smaller scale, it generally follows a similar pattern, with companies using the same modus operandi. The following examples show how multiple punishable acts may occur in the same scheme or schemes:

- *Innospec:* In the Innospec case, the United Kingdom and the United States each pursued criminal cases but based on different facts in different places constituting both the same and different offenses. The United Kingdom prosecuted foreign bribery (payments to win or continue contracts) with respect to Indonesia, while the United States prosecuted conspiracy, foreign bribery, and books and records violations relating to conduct affecting Iraq.[10]

- *Siemens:* In the Siemens case, several jurisdictions pursued the company for conduct in cases that, in part, overlapped. The United States pursued criminal charges while Germany pursued administrative violations for a similar modus operandi but in different specific instances than those pursued by the United States, while Italy pursued another angle altogether. Nigeria appears to have effected a criminal settlement for conduct overlapping to some extent with that prosecuted in the United States, Germany, and Italy.[11]

Similarly, the following considerations show that, in practice, double jeopardy and *ne bis in idem* need not constitute obstacles to enforcement in more than one jurisdiction.

- *Multiple offenses:* Foreign bribery is, in practice, rarely a one-off offense but is most often a series of transactions. As a result, cases pursued in different jurisdictions are unlikely to cover precisely and exclusively the same acts. Experts consulted for the purposes of this study felt that authorities in different jurisdictions could easily avoid objections of double jeopardy or *ne bis in idem* by focusing on individual offenses not yet covered by parallel or previous prosecutions, judgments, or settlements. As noted earlier, if a subsequent case is not based on the same facts or offenses, it would not be barred.[12]
- *Variety of procedures:* Cases such as Johnson & Johnson show that where jurisdictions have a variety of legal procedures at their disposal (including criminal, administrative, and civil enforcement tools), they will also likely be able to mitigate any objections of double jeopardy or *ne bis in idem* by carefully choosing the legal procedure they use. Noncriminal proceedings, in particular, are unlikely to be barred.
- *Still to be adjudicated:* Where settlements do not include a plea of guilty to a criminal offense, even if they include an admission of guilt, courts may very well consider the matter as not yet adjudicated, and thus the double jeopardy or *ne bis in idem* principle would not apply. For example, in the United States, in the case of a DPA, the defendant may admit that he engaged in the conduct amounting to the offense, but he will not have pleaded guilty and been convicted, since the prosecution is deferred.[13]

---

10. See a summary of the case, see chapter 6, case 6.

11. For a summary of the case, see chapter 6, case 12. Siemens also agreed to a comprehensive settlement with the World Bank on July 2, 2009, to establish a $100 million fund for the creation of a Siemens Integrity Initiative, which will support organizations and projects that fight corruption and fraud. See *Siemens' Integrity Initiative,* http://www.siemens.com/sustainability/en/core-topics/collective-action /integrity-initiative/index.php.

12. As noted, this is not to imply that if a case is based on the same facts it will be barred. Focusing on different specific acts within the same array of misconduct means merely that a case would not fall under the doctrines at all, since the doctrines apply only to cases of the same facts.

13. While the extent to which a Non-Prosecution Agreement would be accorded weight, even in a jurisdiction that takes a broad view of double jeopardy like the United Kingdom, is not clear, it would seem

- *Not necessarily applicable to MLA:* It is unlikely that double jeopardy or *ne bis in idem* would generally preclude providing mutual legal assistance.[14] Although the principles are applicable in the context of repeated sanctioning or prosecution, they do not apply to other procedures, such as MLA. This study was unable to identify any reported case in which countries had refused to provide MLA on the grounds of double jeopardy or *ne bis in idem*.

In sum, it is clear that, although the principles of double jeopardy and *ne bis in idem* deserve careful consideration and could in theory complicate matters, the evidence so far is that, in practice, settlements in one jurisdiction are not—and in general have not been—an obstacle to enforcement in other jurisdictions.

2. International Cooperation and Mutual Legal Assistance

As it is, the overwhelming majority of settlements involve only one jurisdiction. Figure 3.2 shows that out of 395 settlements examined for the purposes of this study, only a small fraction involved multiple jurisdictions. This begs the question, Why aren't there more cases prosecuted in more than one jurisdiction and hence more multijurisdictional settlements? It is possible that these numbers may reflect a temporary or transitional situation. Concluding a foreign bribery case can be time consuming.

| FIGURE 3.2 | Settlements in Foreign Bribery Cases Settled across Multiple Jurisdictions |

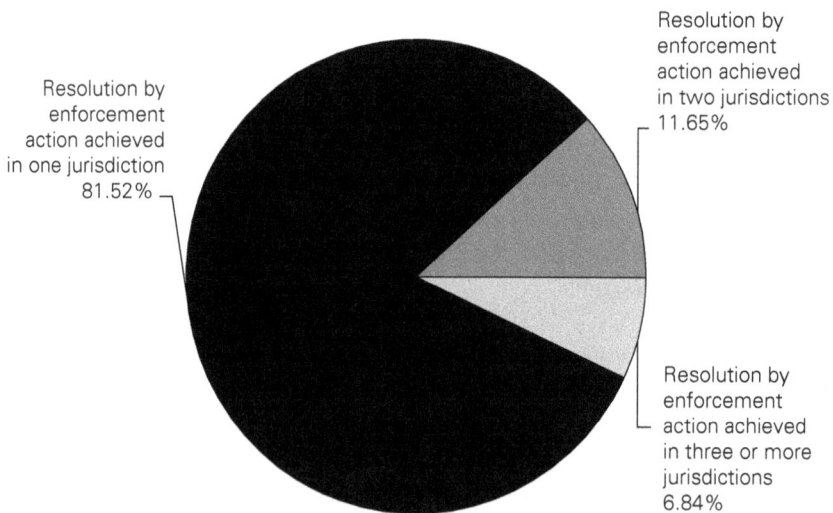

Resolution by enforcement action achieved in one jurisdiction 81.52%

Resolution by enforcement action achieved in two jurisdictions 11.65%

Resolution by enforcement action achieved in three or more jurisdictions 6.84%

safe to say any effect would be less than that of a Deferred Prosecution Agreement. The defendant could use the argument that he has already been punished, so any subsequent punishment would be unfair.
14. Note that in matters of extradition, additional or different constraints may apply.

Based on interviews with experienced practitioners, the average length of a case from the start of the investigation to conclusion probably exceeds three years. Since the figures collected for this study give no indication of how many multijurisdictional cases are currently in the pipeline, it is possible that the proportion of successful subsequent or parallel prosecutions may rise.

A possible reason for the low number of multijurisdictional cases is the practical and operational challenges encountered by jurisdictions when seeking assistance from other countries (either one that has concluded a settlement or a third country following a settlement elsewhere).[15] Gathering data on this question is difficult, not least because most requests for international cooperation and MLA occur in the context of criminal investigations and are therefore highly confidential. As a result, much of the information available for this study is anecdotal.

In some instances the study found that depending on how the settlement is structured, a settlement in another jurisdiction could actually improve the likelihood of international cooperation (see box 3.1). In light of the lack of certainty on this point, it may be useful to review how the basic forms of international cooperation and MLA—both informal and formal—work in practice.

Formal MLA is best accomplished within the context of an established legal framework, since that is what creates an obligation on the part of one country to assist another. Relevant sources of legal authority here include bilateral treaties, multilateral treaties, domestic legislation, and promises of reciprocity (such as in letters rogatory).[16] Such laws set out and define what one country needs to do in order to gain assistance from another. The country from which assistance has been requested must comply with the request if these requirements are met or if it is has a treaty obligation to do so. Having been ratified by 168 countries, the United Nations Convention against Corruption (UNCAC) is the most widely applicable international instrument addressing international cooperation in the context of corruption. UNCAC is the only multilateral convention that specifically addresses for the recovery of proceeds of corruption.[17] As noted in previous chapters, UNCAC requires member states to afford one another the widest measure of mutual legal assistance (MLA) in investigations, prosecutions, and judicial proceedings in relation to the offenses covered by the convention.[18] It also stresses the proactive nature of the expected international assistance, which includes the unsolicited provision of information.

---

15. This process of seeking assistance and evidence from other countries is commonly referred to as *international cooperation.*

16. See Jean-Pierre Brun, Clive Scott, Kevin M. Stephenson, and Larissa Gray, *Asset Recovery Handbook: A Guide for Practitioners* (Washington, DC: World Bank, 2011), 138–141, http://star.worldbank.org/star /publication/asset-recovery-handbook.

17. It is important to note that UNCAC is not directly applicable in all countries and may require implementing legislation. Many countries have enacted such legislation.

18. UNCAC Articles 43, 46, 47, 48–50, and 56.

An obligation to respond to a formal MLA request from another country is not affected by whether a case has been concluded by means of a settlement or a trial.[19] The requirements are typically defined with respect to international instruments, and there appear to be no exceptions for settlements.[20] While the legal aspect is clear, the practical aspects are less so. Some practitioners have noted that settlements have made it more difficult to obtain MLA.[21] As a general matter, jurisdictions should not be deterred from requesting assistance. Practitioners consulted for the purpose of this study confirmed that it was their understanding that settlements do not affect the duty or readiness of their countries in responding to formal MLA requests.

Thus, settlements are unlikely to hinder formal requests for MLA.[22] They are even less likely to create any legal barriers in the case of less formal international cooperation. Nonetheless, the same legal, institutional, and operational obstacles to cooperation present in any case—especially those affecting the speed of cooperation—may remain. For example, authorities may be reluctant to prioritize a request from another jurisdiction concerning a case that they are currently investigating and for which they are considering settlement, preferring instead to conclude their own settlement before extending any form of informal or formal cooperation to another jurisdiction. Especially when investigative and prosecutorial resources are scarce (as is often the case), authorities are typically more likely to expend resources rapidly to achieve a resolution of the matter in their own jurisdiction before diverting resources to provide international cooperation. Once again, however, these issues are neither directly related to the use of settlements as a legal tool nor unique to situations requiring pre-MLA cooperation.

In any event, we conclude by noting that the way in which a settlement is drafted can reduce any potential negative effects on other enforcement efforts. The material in box 3.1 suggests a number of practices that can help to facilitate international cooperation in the wake of a settlement.

---

19. While the authors of the study note that, in the Asia-Pacific region, some treaties relating to MLA contain provisions that may limit MLA on grounds of double jeopardy or ongoing proceedings in the requested state (Australia is an example), research for this study did not disclose any further information on the actual practice or implementation of these provisions.

20. See Kevin M. Stephenson, Larissa Gray, Ric Power, Jean Pierre Brun, Gabriele Dunker, and Melissa Panjer, *Barriers to Asset Recovery: An Analysis of the Key Barriers and Recommendations for Action* (Washington, DC: World Bank, 2011), app. B, 113 ff., which lists the MLA frameworks and grounds for refusal of MLA for 14 countries. None of these make reference to settlements or to concluded cases. "Prejudice to an ongoing proceeding" is often a listed reason to refuse. See Stephenson et al., *Barriers to Asset Recovery,* 114 (Canada) and 157 (Singapore). When a case is ended by settlement, that reason may disappear, and MLA may become more likely. Entire text of report at http://star.worldbank.org/star /publication/barriers-asset-recovery.

21. As noted, Switzerland reported to the OECD working group on bribery that it had experienced difficulties getting international cooperation after unspecified settlements elsewhere about which Switzerland had not been consulted. See OECD, *Phase 3 Report: Switzerland,* para. 12, para. 15, 90.

22. See Stephenson et al., *Barriers to Asset Recovery,* for information on analysis of legal, institutional, and operational barriers to asset recovery, focusing on MLA and international cooperation.

To facilitate international cooperation in cases ending in settlements, a number of measures can be used to enhance the transparency of the process and assist other affected countries in pursuing their legitimate interests. These measures can also help to increase public confidence in the settlement process.

1. Include as a term of the written settlement an obligation that the offender, under the direction of the settling jurisdiction, cooperate with other countries investigating related matters.

For example, the United States routinely requires that companies agree, under the direction of the U.S. Department of Justice (DOJ), to cooperate with foreign authorities and other institutions investigating the company's conduct.[a] This does not imply that, in the absence of such a provision, companies should not cooperate. The purpose is merely to put on the record that a company must expect that the jurisdiction with which it is settling will provide assistance to other jurisdictions and that the company itself will assist the settling jurisdiction by cooperating with any other prosecuting jurisdictions after settlement.

2. Specifically reserve, in the settlement documents, the right for the prosecuting country to conduct further investigations in the event that it receives any requests for MLA.

The United Kingdom has included this provision in some of its agreements.[b]

3. Make settlement agreements and statements of facts public, so that other affected countries can quickly and easily determine what corrupt conduct led to the settlement and consider how it affects their own investigations.

Some countries, such as the United States, already do this by making all resolution agreements and statements of facts public. For the U.S. DOJ, this even includes posting Deferred Prosecution Agreements (DPAs) and Non-Prosecution Agreements (NPAs) on its website. Some countries post the documents for a limited time after the settlement (for example, 14 days in Switzerland), while others, including the United Kingdom, have public hearings but do not always publish settlement documents after the fact.[c]

4. Require defendants to admit to and sign a complete statement of the facts regarding their foreign bribery, even if the case is resolved on a different offense.[d]

A full admission will limit the ability of a defendant to later deny the essential nature of its foreign bribery and may therefore help other affected countries to

(continued next page)

BOX 3.1   (*continued*)

pursue their respective cases against both the defendant and any other offenders (in particular, bribe recipients).

5. **Make clear that a settlement in one jurisdiction does not purport to
   resolve pending or future cases in other jurisdictions.**

A statement to this effect would erode a defendant's possible claims to have
been under the impression that the settlement resolved all charges for an offense
in all places. On a related note, it is best to avoid granting blanket immunities
from prosecution for undisclosed past and future criminal acts.

6. **Proactively notify countries whose officials have been bribed, or who
   are in any other way affected by the case being settled, of any settlement. This can be by way of spontaneous official declaration to the
   relevant judicial or law enforcement authorities in the affected jurisdiction, as provided for in UNCAC.[e]**

Reports received in the course of research for this study show that often enforcement authorities in the country whose officials were allegedly bribed were not
aware of the case under way against the bribe payer in another jurisdiction.
Formally notifying the relevant judicial authorities would eliminate any risk that an
affected country is not informed.

7. **Take advantage of networks and platforms that can provide useful
   support to multiple jurisdictions working on the same complex case,
   with a view to enhancing coordinated action in multiple jurisdictions.**

[a] The Johnson & Johnson DPA (see chapter 6, case 7) is an example of such a provision in a settlement agreement. The
company "agrees to cooperate fully with the Department, the SEC, and any other authority or agency, domestic or foreign,
designated by the Department, in any investigation of J&J or any subsidiary or operating company thereof, or any of its present
or former directors, officers, employees, agents, consultants, subsidiaries, contractors, or subcontractors, or any other party, in
any and all matters relating to corrupt payments." U.S. Department of Justice, letter to Johnson & Johnson, Case 1:11-cr-
00099-JDB Document 1-1, January 14, 2011, http://www.justice.gov/criminal/fraud/fcpa/cases/depuy-inc/04-08-11depuy-dpa
.pdf.
[b] Examples include provisions in the settlement agreements in M.W. Kellogg (summarized in chapter 6, case 14, with TSKJ
Consortium cases) and Macmillan (chapter 6, case 9). See also OECD, Phase 3 Report on Implementing the OECD Anti-Bribery
Convention in the United Kingdom (Paris: OECD, 2012), 48, http://www.oecd.org/daf/anti-bribery/UnitedKingdomphase3
reportEN.pdf.
[c] In some cases, the United Kingdom has included confidentiality clauses in its settlements, barring it from disclosing further
information.
[d] In the United States, the prosecution normally requires the defendant to admit to a fuller account of its corrupt acts even if it
is pleading guilty to a lesser offense or entering into a DPA or NPA. See, for example, case summaries of BAE Systems and
Siemens AG, chapter 6, case 3 and case 12, respectively.
[e] United Nations Convention against Corruption, Articles 46 (para. 4) and 56.
Note: The OECD Convention on Combating Bribery of Foreign Public Officials in International Business Transactions encourages
its member countries to confer concerning jurisdiction. See Article 4, http://www.oecd.org/corruption/oecdantibribery
convention.htm. Furthermore, reference can be made to the OECD's Working Group on Bribery in International Business
Transactions, *Recommendation of Council for Further Combating Bribery of Foreign Public Officials in International Business
Transactions*, specifically recommendation 13 (International Cooperation), which recommends that member countries "consult
and otherwise co-operate with competent authorities in other countries, and, as appropriate, international and regional law
enforcement networks involving Member and non-Member countries, in investigations and other legal proceedings
concerning specific cases of such bribery, through such means as the sharing of information spontaneously or upon request,
provision of evidence, extradition, and the identification, freezing, seizure, confiscation and recovery of the proceeds of bribery
of foreign public officials." See http://www.oecd.org/investment/anti-bribery/anti-briberyconvention/44176910.pdf.

4. Implications of Settlements on Asset Recovery

In this chapter, we consider the intersection of settlements with the recovery and return of the proceeds of corruption. The United Nations Convention against Corruption (UNCAC) established a highly innovative architecture of legal, institutional, and operational measures that have return of assets as their "fundamental principle." In the context of settlements, defendants agreeing to settlements have paid large fines, had assets confiscated and profits disgorged, and paid other forms of restitution or penalty.

For the most part, the monetary sanctions collected by countries enforcing their foreign bribery laws have stayed within those countries' jurisdictions, with only a very small percentage going to the countries whose officials were bribed or allegedly bribed. At the same time, 83 percent of the cases examined in this study involved misconduct relating to public procurement projects and contracts with state-owned enterprises. Although the extent of harm suffered by the so-called "jurisdiction affected by bribery" is not known, it is clear that these jurisdictions have suffered harm as a result of acts of foreign bribery.

1. Recovering Assets in the Context of Settlements: The Current State of Affairs

Before turning to asset recovery in the context of settlements, it is useful to examine the components of monetary sanctions. The nature of various monetary sanctions may determine who has a legitimate claim under UNCAC.

In most cases, the monetary sanctions are not a lump sum penalty or payment. Depending on the legal system under which sanctions are imposed, sanctions may be "paid" through various methods, including compensation, confiscation, disgorgement, fines, reparations, and/or restitution. Box 4.1 defines the most common components and gives an indication as to whom they may be payable.

In most cases, these sanctions or remedies are not exclusive. In other words, most legal systems permit the combination of a number of remedies in the same case, in both criminal and civil cases.[1] In the Siemens/Enel case in Italy, for example, the company accepted a *patteggiamento*, agreeing to pay a €500,000 fine in addition to the

---

1. However, civil recovery orders in the United Kingdom consist of a single figure. See, for example, the Macmillan case summary, chapter 6, case 9.

BOX 4.1   Components of Monetary Sanctions

FIGURE B4.1.1   Methods for Recovering the Proceeds of Corruption

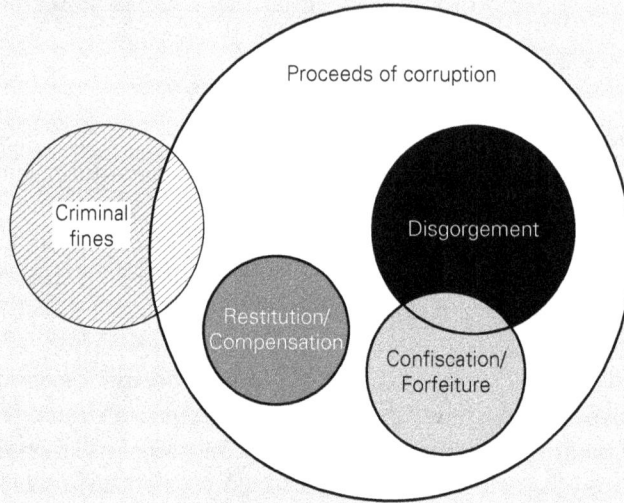

Confiscation is the permanent deprivation of assets by order of a court or other competent authority; also known as *forfeiture*. There are three basic kinds: (1) criminal confiscation, (2) non-conviction-based confiscation, and (3) administrative confiscation. Criminal confiscation requires a criminal conviction; the court can enter a final order of confiscation only when the defendant has been convicted. Under domestic laws, confiscated assets are typically payable to the state, although they can also be used in some jurisdictions for restitution or compensation of victims.

Disgorgement is a civil (as opposed to criminal) remedy in common law jurisdictions. Unlike confiscation, this remedy is derived not from statute but from the courts' equitable power to correct unjust inequality. Similar to confiscation, disgorgement is the forced giving up of illegally obtained profits.

Fines are monetary sanctions meant to punish the wrongdoer. They can be imposed by civil, criminal, or administrative procedures, and they are almost always payable to the state.

Restitution is based on the principle that a person who has suffered loss as a result of a wrong committed against him/her must be restored as nearly as possible to their circumstance before the damage took place. Restitution can be either civil or criminal. In some jurisdictions, the court has the power to order the guilty party to pay restitution to the victim as part of a criminal conviction in an amount equal to the costs incurred by the victim as a result of the guilty party's actions.

Compensation is similar to restitution in that a court may issue a compensation order in a criminal case where a victim has been identified in the proceedings

(continued next page)

confiscation of €6.121 million of profits relating to the Enel contracts.[2] Similarly, in the Alstom Network case in Switzerland, for failure to prevent bribery the company was given a fine of Sw F 2.5 million and a confiscation penalty of Sw F 36.4 million, calculated on the basis of the profits earned by the entire group through the contracts involving bribery, in addition to procedural costs amounting to some Sw F 95,000. In the companion case concerning parent company Alstom SA, the company paid Sw F 1 million in reparations to the International Committee of the Red Cross (ICRC), to be used in its projects in Latvia, Malaysia, and Tunisia.

It is also important to keep in mind that some jurisdictions have maximum pecuniary ceilings on fines as penalties, which can explain the several options taken in settlements.

1.1 Combination and Ratio of Monetary Sanctions: Sample Jurisdictional Comparisons

Just as different jurisdictions employ different types of settlements and different methods for reaching them, they also employ different proportions of various types of monetary sanctions. For example, in the Swiss criminal settlement of the Alstom case, confiscation of profits made up about 91 percent of the overall monetary sanctions, fines made up 6 percent, and indirect reparations to jurisdictions whose officials were allegedly bribed by Alstom made up 3 percent (see figure 4.1). (Reparations were made through an international humanitarian organization.) About 0.2 percent of overall sanctions went to procedural costs.

In the BAE Systems criminal case settlement in the United Kingdom, reparations (in the form of ex gratia payment) made up nearly all of the monetary sanctions, as illustrated in figure 4.2.

---

2. For a summary of the case, see chapter 6, case 12.

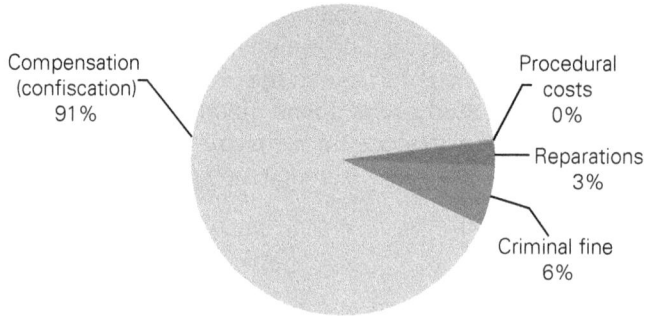

Compensation
(confiscation)
91%

Procedural
costs
0%

Reparations
3%

Criminal fine
6%

Source: Office of the Attorney General of Switzerland, "Criminal Proceedings against Alstom Entities Are Brought to a Close," November 22, 2011, http://www.news.admin.ch/message/?lang=en&msg-id=42300.

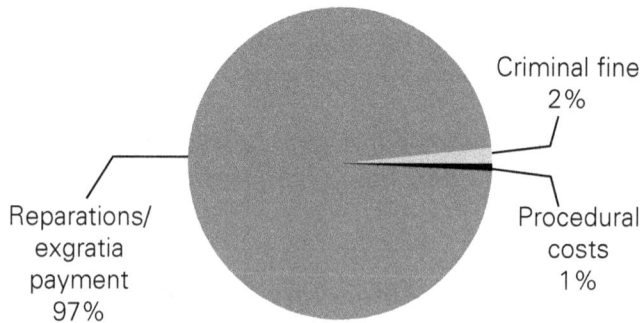

Criminal fine
2%

Reparations/
exgratia
payment
97%

Procedural
costs
1%

Source: Sentencing Remarks made by Mr. Justice Bean in the case of Regina v. BAE Systems PLC, Southwark Crown Court, Case No. S2010565 (December 21, 2010), http://www.judiciary.gov.uk/Resources/JCO/Documents/Judgments/r-v-bae-sentencing-remarks.pdf.

In contrast to the Swiss and U.K. settlements, which involved only criminal enforcement, most foreign bribery settlement cases in the United States comprise a criminal case settlement with the U.S. Department of Justice (DOJ) and, in parallel, a civil or administrative case settlement with the Securities and Exchange Commission (SEC). For example, in the Alcatel-Lucent settlement in the United States, the criminal case concluded with the agreement by the company to pay $92 million in fines, and the civil case ended with the company agreeing to disgorge profits of $45,372,000. In this case, 67 percent of monetary sanctions were in the form of criminal fines and 33 percent were in civil sanctions in the form of disgorgement of profits. (See figure 4.3.)

FIGURE 4.3   Alcatel Lucent: U.S. Settlement

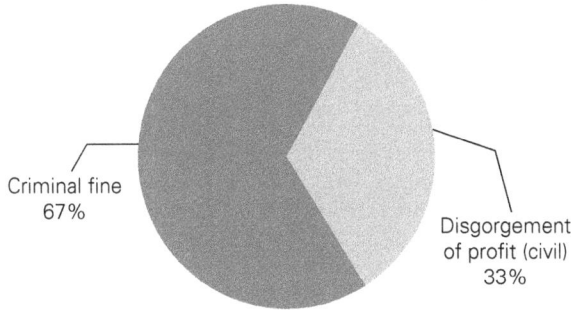

Criminal fine
67%

Disgorgement
of profit (civil)
33%

Source: U.S. Department of Justice, "Alcatel-Lucent S.A. and Three Subsidiaries Agree to Pay $92 Million to Resolve Foreign Corrupt Practices Act Investigation," press release, December 27, 2010, http://www.justice.gov/opa/pr/2010/December/10-crm-1481.html; U.S. Securities and Exchange Commission (SEC), SEC v. Alcatel-Lucent, S.A., Case No. 1:10-cv-24620 (S.D. Fla.), December 27, 2010; U.S. SEC, "SEC Files Settled Foreign Corrupt Practices Act Charges Against Alcatel-Lucent, S.A. with Total Disgorgement and Criminal Fines of Over $137 Million," litigation release no. 21795, December 27, 2010, http://www.sec.gov/litigation/litreleases/2010/lr21795.htm.

1.2 Monetary Sanctions Imposed

Based on their functions, these monetary penalties can be grouped into four main groups:

1. Fines and penalties
2. Confiscation, forfeiture, and disgorgement (payments relating to ill-gotten gains)
3. Restitution[3] and reparations
4. Legal costs (expenses related to the investigation and prosecution).

Figures 4.4, 4.5, and 4.6 indicate the percentage of the monetary sanctions imposed in each of these categories in the foreign bribery cases included in our database, looking first at criminal cases and then at civil and/or administrative cases.

As illustrated in figure 4.4, between 1999 and July 2012, a total of about $4.2 billion was collected in criminal monetary sanctions. About 71 percent of the criminal sanctions were imposed in the form of fines. Confiscations and forfeitures made up about 26.3 percent of the total, with 2.4 percent from restitution or reparations and 0.3 percent imposed in legal or procedural costs.

In civil and administrative case settlements, 9.3 percent of monetary penalties was in the form of fines, 60.2 percent consisted of disgorgement of profits (including prejudgment interest, if any), and 0.7 percent was in the form of restitution. The balance consisted of a variety of other kinds of payments. See figure 4.5.

When combining criminal and civil and/or administrative monetary sanctions in settlements and comparing them with the amounts eventually ordered returned to

---

3. Also called *compensation*, for example in U.K. law.

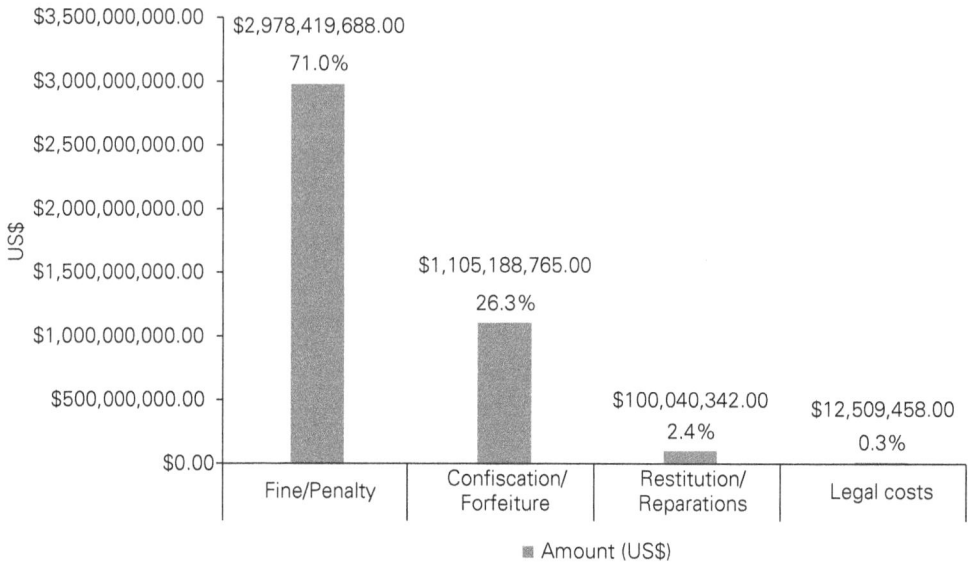

FIGURE 4.4 Monetary Sanctions in Settlements of Criminal Foreign Bribery and Related Cases

Source: Based on StAR Database of Settlements of Foreign Bribery and Related Cases (1999–July 3, 2012), http://star.worldbank.org/corruption-cases/?db=All.

Note: The total amount of monetary sanctions does not include unspecified amounts ordered by Germany against 34 individual defendants, as only a range of sanctions imposed was given in the OECD's *Phase 3 Report on Implementing the OECD Anti-Bribery Convention in Germany* (Paris: OECD, 2011), http://www.oecd.org/germany/Germanyphase3reportEN.pdf; and the OECD's *Recommendation of the Council for Further Combating Bribery of Foreign Officials in International Business Transactions* (Paris: OECD, 2011), http://www.oecd.org/investment/anti-bribery/anti-briberyconvention/44176910.pdf. Included in the criminal fines total are $19.5 million in civil damages assessed in U.S. criminal enforcement actions against AMEC plc/AMEC Construction Management Inc. and Oily Rock/Omega Advisors, Inc. Restitutions/reparations include the ex gratia (voluntary) payment in the BAE Plc case in the United Kingdom. Not included in the figure for legal costs are nominal costs imposed in the United States in the form of court assessments, which generally ranged from $100 to $200 per criminal count adjudicated (i.e., those who admitted guilt) but included are special assessments imposed by the enforcement agency.

other affected countries (in particular, those countries whose public officials were allegedly bribed) and entities,[4] it is clear that the amount of assets ordered returned is only a tiny fraction of the overall volume of monetary sanctions imposed in settlements. Figure 4.6 and table 4.2 illustrate this finding. Table 4.1 lists cases where the jurisdiction of enforcement and jurisdiction of involved foreign public officials were the same; in table 4.3 are cases in which asset returns have taken place.

For context, only 4 of the 30 countries reviewed in the OECD/StAR progress report *Tracking Anti-Corruption and Asset Recovery Commitments* with regard to the commitments they had made at the Third High Level Forum on Aid Effectiveness in Accra, Ghana, in 2008, had returned assets to a foreign jurisdiction between 2006 and 2009. These countries are Australia, Switzerland, the United Kingdom, and the United States (map 4.1). They have repatriated a total of $227 million to foreign jurisdictions.

---

4. For example, the Development Fund for Iraq and the World Bank.

FIGURE 4.5

Monetary Sanctions in Civil and Administrative Settlements of Foreign Bribery and Related Cases

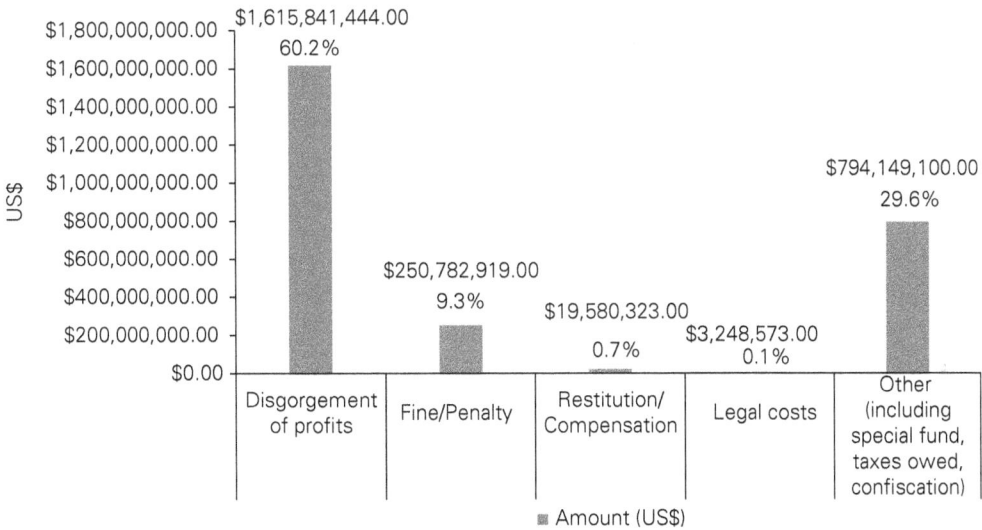

Source: Based on StAR Database of Settlements of Foreign Bribery and Related Cases.
Note: Amounts in "Other" included the following: $100 million in the Siemens settlement with the World Bank and the creation of the Integrity Initiative Fund (see press release at http://web.worldbank.org/WBSITE/EXTERNAL/NEWS/0,,cont entMDK:22412179~pagePK:64257043~piPK:437376~theSitePK:4607,00.html); $253.4 million in the Siemens AG tax settlement with German authorities (see Siemens AG, Annual Report 2007, http://www.siemens.com/investor/pool/en /investor_relations/financial_publications/annual_reports/2007/e07_00_gb2007.pdf; $355.7 million in the Siemens-Greece settlement; and $84 million in the Kazakh-Swiss-U.S. settlement resulting in establishment of the BOTA Foundation.

FIGURE 4.6

Total Monetary Sanctions and Assets Returned or Ordered Returned Where Jurisdiction of Settlement Differed from Jurisdiction of Foreign Public Officials

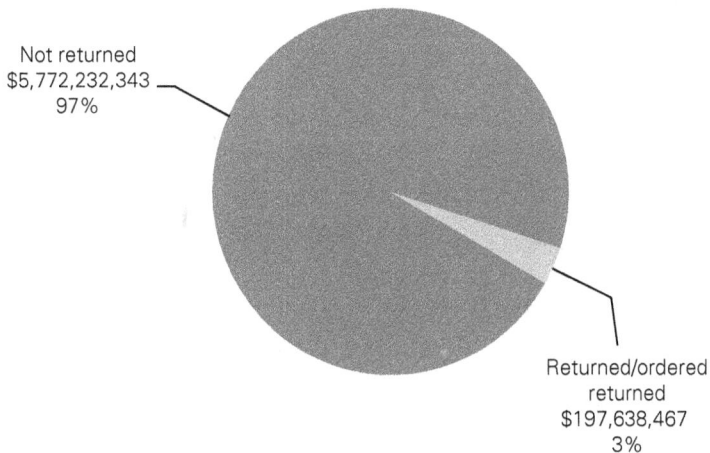

Source: Based on StAR Database of Settlements of Foreign Bribery and Related Cases.
Note: The total amount of monetary sanctions amount do not include unspecified amounts collected by Germany from 34 individual defendants, as only a range of sanctions imposed was given in OECD, Phase 3 Report: Germany, and OECD, Recommendation of the Council. Also not included are legal costs imposed in the United States in the form of court assessments, which generally ranged from $100 to $200 per criminal count adjudicated (i.e., who admitted guilt), but special assessments imposed by the enforcement agency are included.

TABLE 4.1 Assets Returned/Ordered Returned Where the Jurisdiction of Enforcement and the Jurisdiction of Allegedly Bribed Foreign Public Officials Were the Same

Case name	Jurisdiction of settlement	Jurisdiction of settlement/ enforcement agency	Year of settlement	Legal form of settlement	Monetary sanctions (types)	Total monetary sanctions/ returned (US$)
Alcatel-Lucent S.A./ Costa Rica attorney general civil suit[a]	Costa Rica	Office of the Attorney General; Fiscalía [Prosecutor] de Delitos Económicos, Corrupción y Tribu- tarios; Office of the Public Ethics Prosecutor	2010	Settlement agreement	Civil restitution	$10,000,000.00
Siemens AG/ Siemens S.A.[b]	Greece	Parliament	2012	Parliamentary decree	Other	$355,703,000.00
Siemens AG[c]	Italy	Milan Prosecutors Office	2006	Patteggiamento	Criminal fine, disgorgement of profits	$8,373,905.00
Lesotho Highlands Water Project/ Jacobus Michiel Du Plooy[d]	Lesotho	Director of Public Prosecutions	2003	Guilty plea	Criminal fine	$62,266.50

Lesotho Highlands Water Project/ Schneider Electric S.A.[a]	Lesotho	Director of Public Prosecutions	2004	Guilty plea	Criminal fine	$1,504,530.00
Nigeria settlements (multiple companies)[f]	Nigeria	Attorney General, Economic and Financial Crimes Commission	2010–11	Non-Prosecution Agreement	Criminal fine, disgorgement	$180,800,000.00
					Total:	$556,443,701.50

Source: Based on StAR Database of Settlements of Foreign Bribery and Related Cases, http://star.worldbank.org/corruption-cases/?db=All.

a. U.S. v. Alcatel-Lucent France, S.A., et al., Case No. 1:10-cr-20906-MGC and U.S. v. Alcatel-Lucent S.A., Case No. 1:10-cr-20907-MGC (S.D. Fla.), Office of the Attorney General of the Republic, Request for Recognition of Settlement Agreement, filed in Case No. 04-6835-647-PE, Criminal Court of the Second Judicial Circuit of San Jose (signed January 20, 2010), which was attached as Exhibit 1 of Government's Response to Instituto Constaricense de Electricidad's Petition for Victim Status and Restitution filed May 23, 2011. See also Alcatel-Lucent S.A., U.S. Securities and Exchange Commission (SEC) Form 20-F, *Annual Report 2011*, chap. 6, sect. 10, "Legal Matters," http://www3.alcatel-lucent.com/sustainability/pdf/Contingencies-2011-280212p.pdf.

b. Waiver of €80 million in obligations owed by Greek government to Siemens; payment of €90 million to finance anticorruption platform; and investment of €100 million to Siemens' activities within Greece. Siemens AG, "Siemens and the Hellenic Republic Reach a Settlement Agreement and Mark a New Beginning," press release, April 5, 2012, http://www.siemens.com/press/pool/de/pressemitteilungen/2012/corporate/AXX20120420e.pdf. See also Organisation for Economic Co-operation and Development (OECD), *Phase 3 Report on Implementing the OECD Anti-Bribery Convention in Greece* (Paris: OECD, 2012), http://www.oecd.org/daf/anti-bribery/Greecephase3reportEN.pdf.

c. Sentence against Siemens AG and individual defendants issued by the Second Tribunale Ordinario di Milano (25 July 2006), http://www.penalecontemporaneo.it/upload/Trib.%20Milano,%2025.7.2006%20_sent._,%20GUP%20Varanelli%20_Confisca_.pdf; text of Legislative Decree No. 231 of 8 June 2001—Administrative Liability of Legal Persons, excerpted in OECD, *Phase 3 Report: Italy* (2011), http://www.oecd.org/daf/anti-bribery/anti-briberyconvention/Italyphase3reportEN.pdf.

d. R v. DuPlooy, High Court of Lesotho (CRI/T/111/1999), October 17, 2003, sentencing date, http://www.lesotholii.org/ls/judgment/high-court/2003/122; *Combating Multilateral Development Bank Corruption: U.S. Treasury Role and Internal Efforts, Hearing Before the Senate Committee on Foreign Relations*, 108th Cong. (204) (testimony of Guido Penzhorn SC, "Comments on the current Lesotho Bribery Prosecutions," July 21, 2004), http://www.gpo.gov/fdsys/pkg/CHRG-108shrg97666/html/CHRG-108shrg97666.htm.

e. L.L. Thesane and GH Penzhorn SC, "Case Study: The Lesotho Bribery Prosecutions," presented at the Conference on the Protection and Optimization of Public Funds: The Cooperation between National and International Authorities, Rabat, 14–16 May 2007, http://star.worldbank.org/corruption-cases/sites/corruption-cases/files/documents/arw/Lesotho_Highlands_EU_Anti_Fraud_Case_Study_Thetsane_Penzhorn_May_2007.pdf. See also, Schneider Electric SA v. Director of Public Prosecutions (CRI/APN/751/2003), accessed at http://www.lesotholii.org/ls/judgment/high-court/2003/150.

f. Mr. Mohammed Bello Adoke, SAN, Attorney General and Minister of Justice, "2010 Ministerial Media Briefing on the Activities of the Federal Ministry of Justice," 22 December 2010, provided to the study by the Nigerian Economic and Financial Crimes Commission; ENI Company, "Snamprogetti Netherlands BV Enters Agreement with Federal Government of Nigeria," press release, December 20, 2010, http://www.saipem.com/site/download.jsp?idDocument=2013&instance=2; JGC Corporation, "Notice of Loss and Revisions of Earnings Forecasts for Fiscal Year Ending March 31, 2011," January 31, 2011, http://www.jgc.co.jp/en/06ir/pdf/financial_statements_summary/fy10/fy10_3rdqtr_revision.pdf; Halliburton Company, "Halliburton Confirms Agreement to Settle with Federal Government of Nigeria," press release, December 21, 2010, www.halliburton.com/public/news/pubsdata/press_release/2010/corpnws_12212010.html; Noble Corporation, U.S. SEC Form 8-K, filed January 31, 2011, www.sec.gov/Archives/edgar/data/1169055/000095012311006909/h79316e8vk.htm; Tidewater, Inc., U.S. SEC Form 8-K, filed March 3, 2011, http://www.sec.gov/Archives/edgar/data/98222/000119312511055141/d8k.htm; Siemens, "Legal Proceedings," May 4, 2011, http://www.siemens.com/press/pool/de/events/2011/corporate/2011-q2/2011-q2-legal-proceedings-e.pdf.

TABLE 4.2	Assets Returned/Ordered Returned Where the Jurisdiction of Enforcement and Jurisdiction of Foreign Public Officials Were Different					
Case name	Jurisdiction of settlement	Jurisdiction of settlement/ enforcement agency	Year of settlement	Legal form of settlement	Monetary sanctions (types)	Total monetary sanctions returned or ordered returned (US$)
Alstom S.A.[a]	Switzerland	Office of the Attorney General	2011	Payment of reparations (Art. 53 Swiss Criminal Code)	Reparations	$1,089,510.00
BAE Systems plc[b]	United Kingdom	Serious Fraud Office	2010	Guilty plea	Criminal fine, criminal reparations, legal costs	$45,788,700.00
Bayoil (USA), Inc. and Bayoil Supply & Trading Limited/ David Chalmers[c]	United States	United States Attorney for the Southern District of New York	2007	Guilty plea	Criminal restitution	$9,016,151.00
Bribery of and by World Bank Officials/ Gautam Sengupta[d]	United States	Department of Justice	2002	Guilty plea	Criminal fine, criminal restitution	$127,000.00
Bribery of Officials at Telecommunications D'Haiti (Haiti Telecol)/ Juan Diaz[e]	United States	Department of Justice	2009	Guilty plea	Criminal restitution, criminal forfeiture	$73,824.00
CBRN Ltd./Ananias Tumukunde[f]	United Kingdom	Crown Prosecution Service	2008	Guilty plea	Criminal restitution	$73,242.00

Chevron Corporation (UN Oil-for-Food)[g]	United States	United States Attorney for the Southern District of New York	2007	Non-Prosecution Agreement	Criminal penalties, criminal forfeiture	$20,000,000.00
El Paso Corporation[h]	United States	United States Attorney for the Southern District of New York	2007	Non-Prosecution Agreement	Criminal forfeiture	$5,482,363.00
El Paso Corporation/ Oscar J. Wyatt, Jr.[i]	United States	United States Attorney for the Southern District of New York	2007	Guilty plea	Criminal restitution	$11,023,245.91
Julian Messent (PWS International Ltd.)[j]	United Kingdom	Serious Fraud Office	2010	Guilty plea	Criminal restitution	$157,399.00
Kazakh Oil Mining/US Settlement (BOTA Foundation)[k]	United States	Department of Justice	2007	Memorandum of understanding	Civil confiscation	$84,000,000.00
Mabey & Johnson Ltd.[l]	United Kingdom	Serious Fraud Office	2009	Guilty plea	Criminal fine, criminal restitution, criminal confiscation, legal costs, monitoring costs	$2,296,021.00
Oxford University Press[m]	United Kingdom	Serious Fraud Office	2012	Civil recovery order (Proceeds of Crime Act)	Civil recovery order, legal costs, voluntary payment	$3,135,220.00

(continued next page)

TABLE 4.2 Assets Returned/Ordered Returned Where the Jurisdiction of Enforcement and Jurisdiction of Foreign Public Officials Were Different (continued)

Case name	Jurisdiction of settlement	Jurisdiction of settlement/ enforcement agency	Year of settlement	Legal form of settlement	Monetary sanctions (types)	Total monetary sanctions returned or ordered returned (US$)
Vitol SA (UN Oil-for-Food)[n]	United States	New York County District Attorney's Office	2007	Guilty plea	Restitution, legal costs	$13,000,000.00
Weir Group plc	United Kingdom	Crown Office (Scotland), Procurator Fiscal Service (Scotland)	2010	Guilty plea	Restitution	$2,375,790.00
Total						**$197,638,465.91**

Source: Based on StAR Database of Settlements of Foreign Bribery and Related Cases, http://star.worldbank.org/corruption-cases/?db=All.

[a] OECD, *Phase 3 Report: Switzerland* (2011), para. 40, http://www.oecd.org/dataoecd/59/53/49377354.pdf; Office of the Attorney General of Switzerland, "Criminal Proceedings against Alstom Entities Are Brought to a Close," press release, November 22, 2011, http://www.news.admin.ch/message/index.html?lang=en&msg-id=42300.

[b] U.K. Department for Business, Innovation, and Skills (BIS), *Steps Taken to Implement and Enforce the OECD Convention on Combating Bribery of Foreign Public Officials in International Business Transactions* (London: U.K. BIS, August 16, 2011), http://www.oecd.org/dataoecd/17/30/48362318.pdf; U.K. Serious Fraud Office (SFO), "BAE Fined in Tanzania Defence Contract Case," press release, December 21, 2010, http://www.sfo.gov.uk/press-room/press-release-archive/press-releases-2010/bae-fined-in-tanzania-defence-contract-case.aspx; Between: R and BAE SYSTEMS PLC, Case No. S2010565, Crown Court at Southwark, December 21, 2010, http://www.judiciary.gov.uk/Resources/JCO/Documents/Judgments/r-v-bae-sentencing-remarks .pdf; Victor Temple QC, Timothy Cray, and Louis Mably, "Prosecution Note for Opening," Crown Court at Southwark, 22 November 2010, http://www.sfo.gov.uk/media/133543/bae%20 opening%20statement%2020.12.10.pdf; Settlement Agreement between the U.K. SFO and BAE Systems plc, February 2010, at http://www.sfo.gov.uk/media/133535/bae%20-%20 settlement%20agreement%20and%20basis%20of%20plea.pdf.

[c] U.S. v. David B. Chalmers, Jr., Bayoil (USA) Inc., and Bayoil Supply & Trading Limited, Case No. 1:05-cr-00059 (SDNY), Order of Restitution filed on March 25, 2008; and U.S. Attorney, Southern District of New York, "U.S. Announces Four Guilty Pleas in Oil-for-Food Case," press release, August 17, 2007, http://www.justice.gov/usao/nys/pressreleases/August07 /chalmersdionissievbayoiloilforfoodpleaspr.pdf.

[d] U.S. Department of Justice (DOJ), "Bribery of and by World Bank Officials Case Summary," in *Steps Taken to Implement and Enforce the OECD Convention on Combating Bribery of Foreign Public Officials in International Business Transactions* (Washington, DC: U.S. DOJ, May 31, 2011), 125–126, http://www.oecd.org/dataoecd/18/8/42103833.pdf; U.S. DOJ, "Former World Bank Employee Sentenced for Taking Kickbacks and Assisting in the Bribery of a Foreign Official," press release, April 25, 2008, http://www.justice.gov/opa/pr/2008/April/08-crm-341 .html; U.S. v. Gautam Sengupta, Case No. 1:02-cr-040-RWR (D.D.C.), Plea Agreement filed January 30, 2002, http://www.justice.gov/criminal/fraud/fcpa/cases/senguptag/01-30-02sengupta -plea-agree.pdf, and judgment filed February 15, 2006, http://www.justice.gov/criminal/fraud/fcpa/cases/senguptag/02-15-06sengupta-judgment.pdf.

e U.S. DOJ, "Bribery of Officials at Telecommunications D'Haiti (Haiti Teleco) Case Summary," in *Steps Taken to Implement and Enforce the OECD Convention*, 51–52; U.S. v. Diaz, Case No. 1:09-cr-20346-JEM (S.D. Fla.), filed April 22, 2009, http://www.justice.gov/criminal/fraud/fcpa/cases/diazj/04-22-09diaz-info.pdf; U.S. v. Diaz, Plea Agreement filed May 18, 2009, http://www .justice.gov/criminal/fraud/fcpa/cases/diazj/05-18-09diaz-plea-agree.pdf; U.S. v. Diaz, Factual Agreement filed May 18, 2009, http://www.justice.gov/criminal/fraud/fcpa/cases/diazj/05 -18-09diaz-fatual-agree.pdf; U.S. v. Diaz, Judgment filed August 5, 2010, http://www.justice.gov/criminal/fraud/fcpa/cases/diazj/08-05-10diaz-judgment.pdf; and U.S. v. Diaz, Sentencing Hearing (July 30, 2010) transcript filed August 5, 2010, accessed via Pacer.gov. See also U.S. DOJ, "Florida Businessman Sentenced to 57 Months in Prison for Role in Foreign Bribery Scheme," press release, July 30, 2010, http://www.justice.gov/opa/pr/2010/July/10-crm-883.html.

f U.K. Department for International Development, *Self-assessment Checklist on the Implementation of the United Nations Convention against Corruption*, September 2008, at www.dfid .gov.uk; Paul Lewis and Rob Evans, "Ugandan Is Jailed in UK Bribery Crackdown," *Guardian*, September 22, 2008, http://www.guardian.co.uk/uk/2008/sep/23/ukcrime.law; U.K. BIS, *Steps Taken to Implement and Enforce the OECD Convention*, (London: BIS, August 16, 2011), http://www.oecd.org/dataoecd/17/30/48362318.pdf.

g U.S. Attorney, Southern District of New York (SDNY), "Chevron Corporation Agrees to Pay $30 Million in Oil-for-Food Settlement," press release, November 14, 2007, http://www.justice .gov/usao/nys/pressreleases/November07/chevronagreementpr.pdf; U.S. DOJ SDNY, Chevron Corporation Non-Prosecution Agreement, letter dated November 8, 2007, http://judiciary.house .gov/hearings/pdf/deferredprosecution/Chevron071108.pdf.

h U.S. Attorney, SDNY, El Paso Corporation Non-Prosecution Agreement, letter dated February 5, 2007, http://fcpa.shearman.com/files/82c/82c7a6a47d469bdfa8a7c6d82bf03737.pdf?i=dfef6 d9305307bf27b828e9290194bef; U.S. Attorney SDNY, "Texas Oil Executive and Two Corporations Sentenced on Charges Involving a Scheme to Pay Secret Kickbacks to the Former Government of Saddam Hussein," press release, March 7, 2008, http://www.justice.gov/usao/nys/pressreleases/March08/chalmersetalsentencingpr.pdf.

i U.S. Attorney, SDNY, "U.S. Announces Four Guilty Pleas in Oil-for-Food Case," press release, August 17, 2007, http://www.justice.gov/usao/nys/pressreleases/November07 /wyattsentencingpr.pdf; U.S. v. Wyatt, Case No. 1:05-cr-00059-DC (SDNY), Court Docket Report as of January 4, 2012 and Government Sentencing Memorandum filed November 26, 2007, accessed via Pacer.gov.

j U.K. BIS, *Steps Taken to Implement and Enforce the OECD Convention*, http://www.oecd.org/dataoecd/17/30/48362318.pdf; U.K. SFO, "Insurance Broker Jailed for Bribing Costa Rican Officials," press release, October 26, 2010, http://www.sfo.gov.uk/press-room/press-release-archive/press-releases-2010/insurance-broker-jailed-for-bribing-costa-rican-officials.aspx.

k *Memorandum of Understanding by the Swiss Confederation, United States, and the Republic of Kazakhstan* (May 2007), Annex 2, "Service Agreement for TDB BOTA Foundation among the International Bank for Reconstruction and Development and the Governments of the United States of America, the Swiss Confederation, and the Republic of Kazakhstan," http://www .state.gov/documents/organization/108887.pdf; U.S. DOJ, *Steps Taken to Implement and Enforce the OECD Convention*, Mercator Corporation case summary, 104–5, http://www.oecd.org /dataoecd/18/8/42103833.pdf.

l U.K. BIS, *Steps Taken to Implement and Enforce the OECD Convention*, http://www.oecd.org/dataoecd/17/30/48362318.pdf; U.K. SFO, "Mabey & Johnson Ltd Sentencing," press release, September 25, 2009, http://www.sfo.gov.uk/press-room/press-release-archive/press-releases-2009/mabey–johnson-ltd-sentencing-.aspx; U.K. House of Commons, International Develop-ment Committee, *Eleventh Report of Session 2010–12, Vol. I* (London: November 30, 2011), appendix B, "Notes on Other Cases by the Serious Fraud Office," http://www.publications .parliament.uk/pa/cm201012/cmselect/cmintdev/847/84702.htm.

m U.K. SFO, "Oxford Publishing Ltd to Pay Almost £1.9 Million as Settlement after Admitting Unlawful Conduct in Its East African Operations," press release, July 3, 2012, http://www.sfo .gov.uk/press-room/latest-press-releases/press-releases-2012/oxford-publishing-ltd-to-pay-almost-19-million-as-settlement-after-admitting-unlawful-conduct-in-its-east-african-operations.aspx; U.K. SFO and Oxford Publishing Ltd. Consent Order, July 2, 2012, http://www.sfo.gov.uk/media/215466/sealed_consent_order.pdf; U.K. SFO and Oxford Publishing Ltd. Claim Form, http:// www.sfo.gov.uk/media/215458/part_8_claim_form_n208.pdf; U.K. SFO and Oxford Publishing Ltd. Application Notice Form, http://www.sfo.gov.uk/media/215462/application_notice_form _n244.pdf.

n U.S. DOJ, Vitol S.A. case summary, in *Steps Taken to Implement and Enforce of the OECD Convention*, 90–91, http://www.oecd.org/dataoecd/18/8/42103833.pdf; New York County District Attorney's Office, news release on Vitol SA Plea, November 20, 2007, http://manhattanda.client.tagonline.com/whatsnew/press/2007-11-20.shtml, last accessed January 6, 2012.

TABLE 4.3 Other Asset Returns

Case name	Jurisdiction of settlement	Jurisdiction of settlement/ enforcement agency	Year of settlement	Legal form of settlement	Monetary sanctions (types)	Total monetary sanctions (US$)
Siemens AG/Former Com Group (tax settlement relating to 2007 Munich case)[a]	Germany	Tax authorities	2007	Tax settlement	Tax settlement	$253,446,100
Siemens AG[b]	World Bank	Integrity Vice Presidency	2009	Administrative	Establishment of special fund (Integrity Initiative Fund)	$100,000,000
Total						**$353,446,100**

Source: Based on StAR Database of Settlements of Foreign Bribery and Related Cases, http://star.worldbank.org/corruption-cases/?db=All.

[a] Siemens AG, *Annual Report 2007*, http://www.siemens.com/investor/pool/en/investor_relations/financial_publications/annual_reports/2007/e07_00_gb2007.pdf.

[b] World Bank, "Siemens Settlement Agreement Fact Sheet," n.d., http://siteresources.worldbank.org/INTDOII/Resources/Siemens_Fact_Sheet_Nov_11.pdf; World Bank, "Siemens to Pay $100m to Fight Corruption as Part of World Bank Group Settlement," press release 2009/001/EXT, July 2, 2009, http://web.worldbank.org/WBSITE/EXTERNAL/NEWS/0,,contentMDK:22234573~pagePK:34370~piPK:34424~theSitePK:4607,00.html. See also *Siemens Integrity Initiative*, http://www.siemens.com/sustainability/en/core-topics/collective-action/integrity-initiative/index.php.

MAP 4.1 Assets Returned by 30 OECD Countries (2006–09)

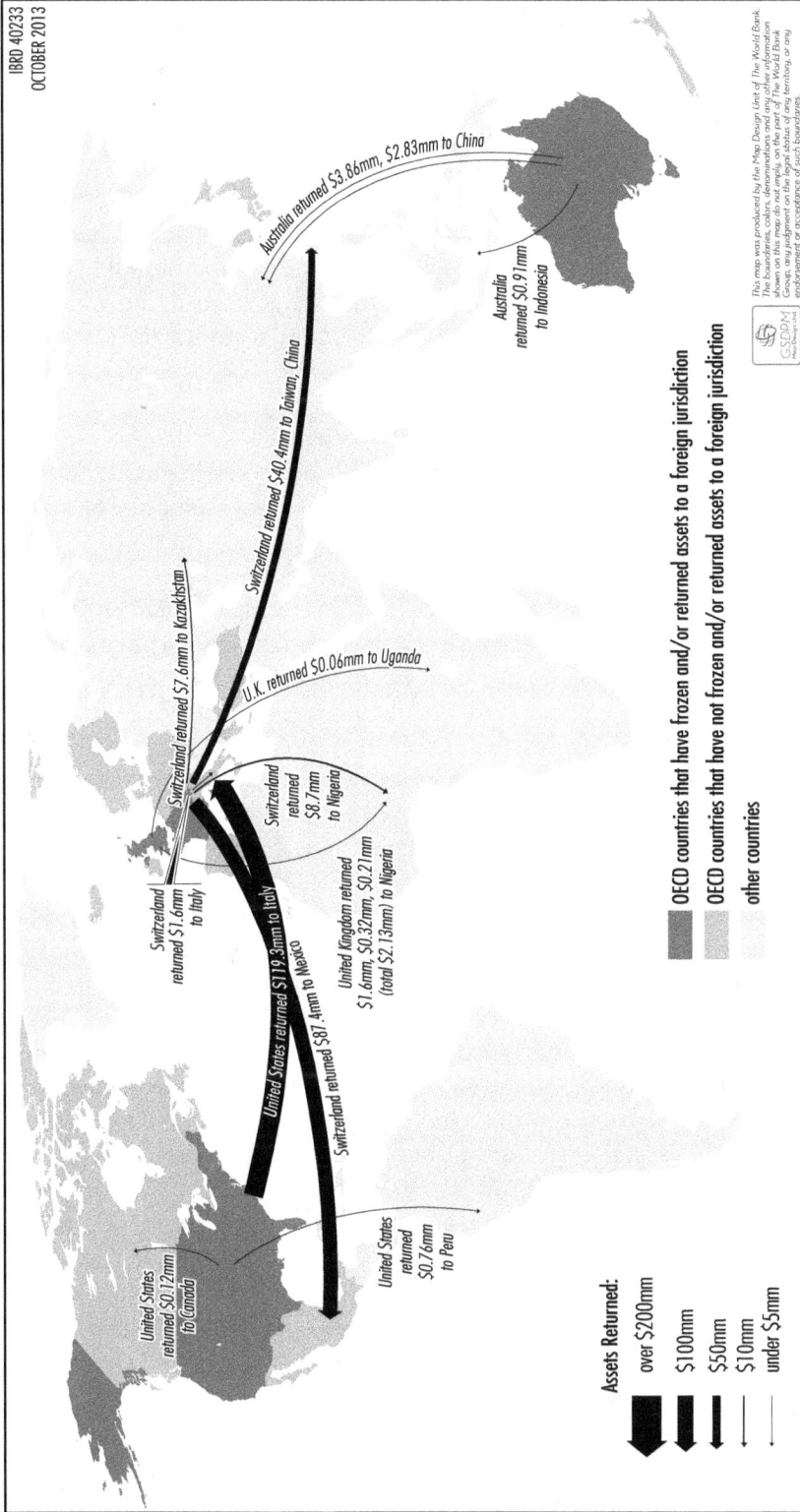

IBRD 40233
OCTOBER 2013

Australia returned $3.86mm, $2.83mm to China

Switzerland returned $40.4mm to Taiwan, China

Switzerland returned $7.6mm to Kazakhstan

U.K. returned $0.06mm to Uganda

Switzerland
returned
$8.7mm
to Nigeria

Switzerland
returned $1.6mm
to Italy

United Kingdom returned
$1.6mm, $0.32mm, $0.21mm
(total $2.13mm) to Nigeria

United States returned $119.3mm to Italy

Switzerland returned $87.4mm to Mexico

United States
returned $0.12mm
To Canada

United States
returned
$0.76mm
to Peru

Australia
returned $0.91mm
to Indonesia

Assets Returned:

over $200mm
$100mm
$50mm
$10mm
under $5mm

OECD countries that have frozen and/or returned assets to a foreign jurisdiction

OECD countries that have not frozen and/or returned assets to a foreign jurisdiction

other countries

This map was produced by the Map Design Unit of The World Bank.
The boundaries, colors, denominations and any other information
shown on this map do not imply, on the part of The World Bank
Group, any judgment on the legal status of any territory, or any
endorsement or acceptance of such boundaries.

GSDPM
Map Design Unit

Source: Figure 1.4. Assets returned by 30 OECD Countries, 2006–2009, OECD and StAR, *Tracking Anti-Corruption and Asset Recovery Commitments: A Progress Report and Recommendations for Action,* 32, http://www.oecd.org/dac/governance-development/49263968.pdf.

Note: The map was updated in October 2013 by the World Bank map office (original producer of the map) to reflect the establishment of the newly independent South Sudan, but the information about the flow of funds was not changed.

Moreover, France and Luxemburg have frozen assets of more than $1.2 billion pending court decisions. In the remaining countries that were examined, there were no such activities.[5] Only a few developing countries have had assets frozen or returned.[6]

1.3 Involvement of Public Procurement Contracts and State-Owned Enterprises

The negative association between corruption and development has become widely accepted. And while the full extent of economic distortion and overall harm resulting from foreign bribery has yet to be analyzed in full and quantified, the settlement cases compiled for this study by definition involve the public sector, as the underlying conduct concerns the bribery of foreign public officials.

As shown in figure 4.7, a very large majority—83 percent—of the cases in the study's database of foreign bribery and related settlements cases concern misconduct related to public procurement contracts and/or (alleged) bribery of officials of state-owned enterprises.[7]

As quoted in the study's executive summary, the U.S. acting assistant attorney general, in announcing the U.S. Department of Justice's settlement with Siemens, stressed that "corruption is not a gentlemen's agreement where no one gets hurt. People do get hurt. And the people who are hurt the worst are often residents of the poorest countries on the face of the earth, especially where it occurs in the context of government infrastructure projects, contracts in which crucial development decisions are made, in which a country will live by those decisions for good or for bad for years down the road, and where those decisions are made using precious and scarce national resources."[8] The extent to which the development decisions were affected by the bribery is beyond the scope of this study, but the cases involve a wide range of economic sectors, including oil and gas, infrastructure, telecommunications, health care, information technology, mining, and others. The cases also ranged from those involving relatively small procurement contracts to large-scale projects involving hundreds of millions of dollars or, for example in the Bonny Island Liquefied Natural Gas project, billions of dollars. More data would be needed to understand the extent to which these cases have resulted in economic harm to the countries that paid for the involved public procurement contracts and operate the state-owned enterprises whose officials were allegedly bribed.

---

5. OECD and StAR, *Tracking Anti-Corruption and Asset Recovery Commitments: A Progress Report and Recommendations for Action* (Paris and Washington, DC: OECD and World Bank, 2011), 5, http://www.oecd.org/dac/governance-development/49263968.pdf.
6. OECD and StAR, 27.
7. Of the remaining cases, 12.7 percent involved other public sector officials, such as customs and tax authorities. In 4.3 percent of cases, the recipients and/or alleged recipients of the bribes were not specified.
8. U.S. Department of Justice (DOJ), "Transcript of Press Conference Announcing Siemens AG and Three Subsidiaries Plead Guilty to Foreign Corrupt Practices Act Violations," December 15, 2008, http://www.justice.gov/opa/pr/2008/December/08-opa-1112.html.

FIGURE 4.7   Sector Involvement in Foreign Bribery and Related Cases

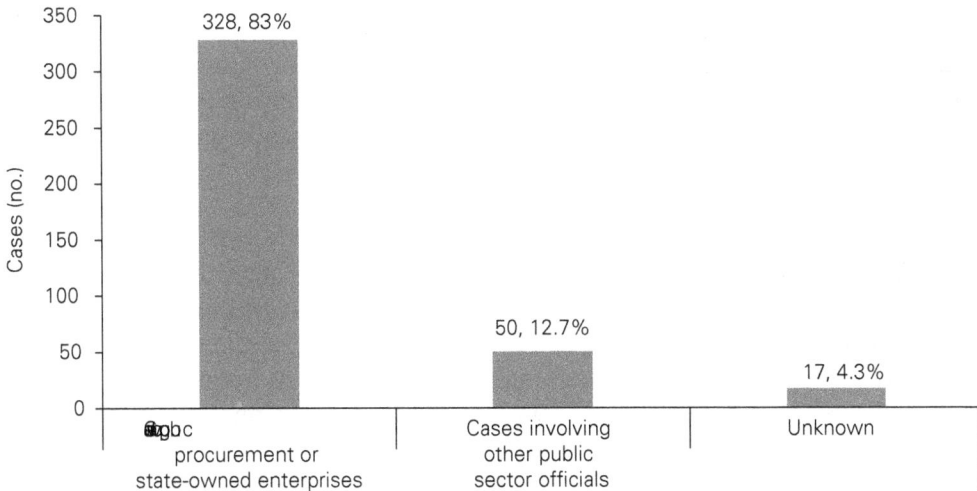

Source: Based on StAR Database of Settlements of Foreign Bribery and Related Settlement Cases.

2. Barriers to Asset Recovery in the Context of Settlements

In general, the recovery of assets in the context of foreign bribery is a challenging process. There are numerous legal, institutional, and operational challenges, elaborated on in the StAR study on *Barriers to Asset Recovery*[9] in corruption cases. These include a lack of political will, antiquated legislation, immunity granted to high level officials, difficulties in international cooperation, and insufficient enforcement capacity, to name just a few.[10] For the most part, these barriers exist independently of whether a case does or does not conclude in settlement.

Settlements, however, may create specific challenges for the asset recovery process. As previously noted, where a settlement occurs during the pretrial phase (which is almost always the case), other affected countries often remain unaware of the case until it

---

9. Kevin M. Stephenson, Larissa Gray, Ric Power, Jean Pierre Brun, Gabriele Dunker, and Melissa Panjer, *Barriers to Asset Recovery: An Analysis of the Key Barriers and Recommendations for Action* (Washington, DC: World Bank and StAR, 2011). To highlight just a few challenges, the reasons why the process of asset return is complicated and challenging include the following: (i) the coordination and collaboration with domestic agencies in multiple jurisdictions with different legal systems and procedures, (ii) the need for special investigative techniques and skills to follow the money beyond borders, and (iii) the ability to move quickly to avoid dissipation of the assets. See also generally Jean Pierre Brun, Clive Scott, Kevin M. Stephenson, and Larissa Gray, *Asset Recovery Handbook: A Guide for Practitioners* (Washington, DC: World Bank, 2011).

10. Stephenson et al., *Barriers to Asset Recovery,* grouped these into three main categories: (i) general (such as the lack of political will and absence of policy to identify asset recovery as a priority); (ii) legal (such as onerous requirements for the provision of mutual legal assistance (MLA) and international cooperation); and (iii) operational (such as lack of clear focal points and processes).

is over.[11] Unless the authorities of the country pursuing the settlement case make a conscious effort to involve or inform other affected countries, the latter stand little, if any, chance of effectively claiming any assets recovered in the enforcement action taken in another country. Generally, cases that settle tend to be less transparent than cases that proceed to full trial, in terms of both the agreements or decisions released and amount of proceedings open to the public. Thus, it is more difficult for other countries whose officials have been allegedly bribed to obtain information on the content and underlying facts of a concluded settlement.[12]

Where there *is* an opportunity for other affected countries formally to participate in the investigation or prosecution—as may occur in civil law countries which allow for the victims of crime to take part in the criminal procedure as *partie civile*[13]—the time in which to do so may be limited by law. In cases concluded by settlement, this window of opportunity may close even faster, since the negotiations typically require less time than a full trial. In addition, when the prosecuting country is aiming at a settlement, it might be more reluctant to allow another affected country to be part of the process, fearing that the addition of a third party might make it more difficult to reach an agreement.

It is also true that some jurisdictions may not consider that the country whose officials were allegedly bribed to have been harmed in such a way as to justify monetary compensation.[14] Anticorruption laws in some countries do not recognize individuals or states as victims but rather wish to protect the integrity of the public administration, the public's trust in the state and its institutions, and/or the rule of law. They may view bribery, whether domestic or foreign, as a crime committed against society as a whole rather than against individual persons, entities, and foreign countries. The latter would therefore not be defined as victims and would therefore not be considered justified, within the context of the criminal proceeding, to pursue damages.[15] When enforcing their own foreign bribery laws, some countries also consider themselves as the primary victims of the offence and thus are less inclined to recognize the potential claims of other countries.

Most of the experts consulted for the purpose of this study indicated that settlements provide the prosecuting authorities with wider discretion to choose the form(s) of monetary sanctions imposed than they would have if the case went to a full trial.

---

11. Even if a case is in the foreign media, it may not come to the attention of affected countries. Not every country has the resources to monitor all news that may be relevant to corruption by its officials.

12. Much of the negotiation of the terms of settlement agreements, for example, take place in private between the prosecutors and other enforcement authorities and the defendant companies and individuals. Once agreement is reached on the terms of the settlement, usually a court approves the agreement, although, this is not a universal practice. In addition, while nearly all settlement agreements are published and publicly available, again this is not a universal practice. In contrast, most court proceedings and resulting hearing records or transcripts are nearly always accessible to the public (with some exceptions regarding publication of names, for example, in countries with strict privacy laws vis-à-vis individual defendants), affording them greater transparency than the practice of settlements.

13. *Partie civile* is French for *civil party*.

14. A party may need to show that harm is "direct" and "proximate." See also chapter 4, section 3.3.

15. This legal barrier, however, leaves unaffected the option of pursuing damages in a private civil lawsuit.

Their choices on the form(s) of monetary sanctions have direct implications for the designation of beneficiary and for the recoverability of assets. Confiscated or disgorged assets that represent proceeds of crime may more directly fit UNCAC's description of recoverable assets than other forms of monetary sanctions. By giving prosecuting authorities this discretion to set the form of monetary sanctions, therefore, settlements give them considerable power to influence, for better or for worse, the ability of other affected countries to claim and recover assets.

Taking into account these settlement-related barriers, there are a number of strategies that settling countries could use to aid the recovery of assets and their return to other affected jurisdictions.

1. *The authorities in jurisdictions pursuing settlements could become more proactive in sharing information in accordance with Articles 46 (para. 4) and 56 of UNCAC. If provided with information about ongoing settlement negotiations—and about the terms and content of settlements once concluded—other affected countries could weigh their alternatives more fully. Settling countries could also proactively share information on other ways that affected nations could be involved in the asset recovery process—for example by joining the criminal proceedings as a partie civile or by pursuing compensation for damages through private civil litigation.*
2. *In recognition of Article 53 (c) of UNCAC,[16] it would be beneficial if settling countries would permit their courts and other competent authorities to recognize another State Party's claims of ownership or damages when deciding on a confiscation or other monetary sanction relating to a settlement.*
3. *Consideration might also be given to changes in law and practice to permit the formal inclusion of third parties in settlement agreements in foreign bribery cases.*

Meanwhile, other affected countries, especially those whose officials have allegedly been bribed, could make better use of the various legal avenues provided by UNCAC and the legal mechanisms described below.

1. *Most important, they could pursue damages and recovery of the proceeds of corruption through private civil lawsuits in the home country of the wrongdoer or a country where the assets are located, in accordance with Article 53(a) of UNCAC.[17]* This route, unfortunately, carries the disadvantages of costly legal fees and long delays due to congested civil courts.
2. *They could explore the mechanisms by which they could become involved in criminal/enforcement actions mounted in other jurisdictions.* Such participation may be possible in cases concluded by settlement. There have been a few promising examples of countries whose officials were allegedly bribed participating in the

---

16. Article 53(c) states that States Parties "shall…take such measures as may be necessary to permit its courts or competent authorities…to recognize another State Party's claim as a legitimate owner of property acquired through the commission of an offense established in accordance with this Convention."
17. The World Bank is producing a study on this topic of civil remedies for asset recovery, due for release in 2014.

settlement process of another jurisdiction and thereby obtaining some monetary damages. A number of such cases are studied in detail in the next section.

3. *By adding the tool of non-conviction–based forfeiture to their arsenal of anticorruption weapons, countries could avoid many of the difficulties of obtaining seizure and confiscation orders through the criminal route to asset recovery.*[18]

On the positive side, in almost all cases, if a settlement has occurred, monetary sanctions have been imposed, and thus some groundwork has been laid for asset recovery efforts by countries seeking such remedies.

3. Modes of Participation in Criminal Enforcement Actions for the Purpose of Asset Recovery

3.1 Participation of Affected Countries through Formal Legal Avenues

Legal systems across jurisdictions offer a variety of options for affected countries to seek compensation for damages suffered as a result of bribery of their officials by foreign entities or persons who are the subject of ongoing criminal or enforcement actions. Some of these options involve formal participation and are available when authorities pursue a settlement. In several civil law jurisdictions, those who suffered damages as a result of the bribery have the opportunity to join the proceedings as a *partie civile,* either at the investigative stage or once the matter has gone to trial. While common law jurisdictions do not provide for this option, they do allow affected entities or persons to apply to the court for a restitution order. These two avenues merit consideration in an overall asset recovery strategy.

The availability of either of these avenues, however, will depend on a number of factors. First, the affected country must be aware of the ongoing investigation, which is by no means guaranteed, even though some investigations are reported in the news media or other forms of public information prior to settlement. What is at stake is not necessarily the availability of the information *per se* but the proactive sharing of that information by the settling country with the other affected countries. The expert consultations conducted during this study seem to suggest that lack of notice is one of the main reasons that, despite the available legal avenues, only in a very small number of cases have affected countries even attempted to obtain compensation for damages in the context of criminal proceedings.

Second, scarce resources, weak institutional capacity, and insufficient knowledge about other legal systems on all sides tend to diminish the chances of successful participation in the prosecution or enforcement actions of other jurisdictions.

Third, as noted earlier, the laws of some countries position bribery as an offense committed against society as a whole, thereby excluding individual persons, entities, and foreign countries from the general definition of *victim.*[19] In some countries, unless

---

18. UNCAC, Articles 55 and 57.
19. This tends to be the case with Canada, Germany, Italy, and the United States, for example.

the affected country is able to specifically demonstrate that it suffered harm as a direct result of the offense, it may not be considered a "victim" eligible for compensation. In others, notably in some of the U.K. cases and a Swiss case, the prosecuting authorities and the courts have made the determination on their own and provided for reparations for the country harmed by the bribery.

While these barriers may sound insurmountable, this study shows that there are several examples of affected countries participating in criminal cases and successfully pursuing compensation for damages outside of their own jurisdiction. This has occurred in France, Switzerland, the United Kingdom, and the United States. In addition, Costa Rica and Haiti have received damage awards in the context of criminal corruption cases, and Iraq has succeeded in obtaining a restitution order for the benefit of its citizens. As noted previously, the procedural mechanisms for participation differ based on whether the legal system of the prosecuting country is based in civil law or common law. Examples from both systems are explored below.

3.2 Participation in Criminal Enforcement Action in Civil Law Jurisdictions

In many civil law jurisdictions, the criminal procedure provides a way for those claiming harm from an offense to participate in a criminal case, either at the stage of the investigation or at the pretrial stage, with a view to becoming a party to the case. Thus, in addition to pursuing damages in the context of a separate and self-standing civil litigation, in these jurisdictions countries affected by corruption can consider joining the criminal proceedings as a *partie civile*.

If an affected country can convince the court that it has suffered harm as a consequence of the foreign bribery of their public officials, it will be granted access to the case file and related evidence and permitted to pursue damages through the medium of settlement. The affected country's claim for damages will be adjudicated during the criminal proceedings, avoiding the need to bring a separate private civil lawsuit. In some jurisdictions, even in the event of an acquittal, the criminal court has authority to reach a decision on damages if the facts have been sufficiently established.[20]

Becoming a *partie civile* to a criminal proceeding has a number of advantages over pursuit of a private civil lawsuit:

- It is usually faster, simpler and less expensive.[21]
- A *partie civile* enjoys extensive rights to participate in the criminal action. Indeed, in several civil law jurisdictions these rights are equal to those of the defendant.

---

20. This is the case in France, even though it is not a frequent practice of the French criminal courts.
21. Depending on the particular legal system, application may need to be made early. Time limits may apply, to ensure that an ongoing proceeding is not disrupted by a party joining too late in the process. For example, in one case in Switzerland, the Czech Republic attempted to qualify as a civil party but was rejected because its application was made too late in the process. See BB.2012.2 (decision of 1 March 2012) (rejecting appeal).

They include access to the examining magistrate's or prosecutor's investigative file, participation in the interrogation of witnesses and suspects, and the right to request certain measures, including the sending of a mutual legal assistance (MLA) request, the freezing of assets, the execution of house searches, and the seizing of documents both at home and abroad. These latter rights are of particular significance, of course, in cases of financial crime such as bribery.

- A *partie civile* is in a position to establish and maintain frequent contact with the investigating magistrate or prosecutor, which can be useful both for transmitting additional evidence and for requesting timely follow-up actions. Often, an affected country acting as a *partie civile* in another jurisdiction will hire a local lawyer—knowledgeable about local procedures and well positioned to monitor developments—to perform this liaison function on its behalf.

The benefits of participation in a criminal prosecution as a *partie civile* are therefore considerable; indeed, in most cases they may go beyond those that can be obtained through a request for MLA.[22]

While the number of countries being granted *partie civile* status is on the increase, with several success stories of obtaining damage awards for corruption-related offenses, there are as yet still only a few examples relating to cases of foreign bribery. The discussion below details how Nigeria, Tunisia, and Brazil have become civil parties to criminal actions in Switzerland or France.

Although these cases did not conclude with settlements but entailed full criminal proceedings, they still constitute excellent examples of *partie civile* participation from as early as the start of an investigation.[23]

The Abacha case, prosecuted by Swiss authorities with Nigeria as a *partie civile*, is one such case. Nigeria had itself initiated a criminal investigation into corruption by the former Nigerian president Sani Abacha's family and associates and had filed a request for MLA in Switzerland that included requests to freeze several accounts holding hundreds of millions of U.S. dollars. Without Nigeria's knowledge, however, those accounts had already been emptied, with the assets transferred to other jurisdictions such as Luxembourg, Liechtenstein, the United Kingdom, and Jersey. If Nigeria had

---

22. However, becoming a civil party is not a substitute for MLA requests, as demonstrated by the Abacha case and subsequent Swiss litigation. See, e.g., Mark Pieth, ed., *Recovering Stolen Assets* (Bern: Peter Lang, 2008), 49–50. It is important to note that, in the course of the proceedings, the Swiss court clarified that Nigeria could not make use of its access as a civil party simply to use all evidence in the Swiss file for its legal proceedings in Nigeria. See ATF 1.A.157/2001 and 1A.158/2001, December 7, 2001, published on http://www.bger.ch/. Nigeria had to agree not to use the evidence until the end of the MLA proceedings. Thus, civil party status is unlikely to replace a request for MLA. Moreover, the civil party to the criminal action will usually be bound by confidentiality requirements and other limits on the use of the information to which it becomes privy.

23. As noted above, France has just introduced expanded possibilities for settlements, and Switzerland has been making more frequent use of its summary procedures (as in, for example, the Alstom cases, for a summary, see chapter 6, case 2).

waited to receive that information through the formal channel of MLA, it would have received only the information necessary to file additional requests in those jurisdictions.[24] It is likely that the process of being one step behind the funds would have repeated itself, resulting in no effective freezes of the proceeds of corruption.[25]

Meanwhile, however, the Swiss authorities were themselves looking into the Abacha family and its cronies for alleged money laundering and participation in an organized criminal group. Perceiving an opportunity to reduce the risk of Abacha's associates moving funds out of Switzerland, the Swiss lawyer representing Nigeria lodged a criminal complaint with the Swiss authorities and made a formal request to join the investigation as a *partie civile* on the grounds that Nigeria had an interest in the laundered funds.[26] Within a short time, the request was granted, and Swiss authorities swiftly obtained freezing orders for the accounts of Abacha's family members and cronies, securing many millions of dollars' worth of the proceeds of corruption.[27] Nigeria was also able to have further influence on the litigation, to its considerable benefit.

In a more recent case, the Swiss authorities had been investigating suspected money laundering and participation in a criminal organization by the former Tunisian president Zine El Abidine Ben Ali and his associates. After opening their own investigation in Tunisia, the Tunisian authorities requested to join the Swiss proceedings as a *partie civile*. This request was granted and affirmed on appeal in March 2012.[28] Status as a *partie civile* will now enable Tunisia to work closely with Swiss examining magistrates, advance its own investigations through access to bank records and other key evidence, and assert claims on various assets within the framework of the Swiss prosecution.

These two cases illustrate the benefits of *partie civile* status in the investigative stage. There are also examples, however, of how the right to claim damages imparted by *partie civile* status can be utilized in the later stages of prosecution. In another Swiss case, for example, Brazil was able to qualify as *partie civile* in a money laundering case against several Brazilian tax inspectors, who had extracted bribes in exchange for ending inspections and/or reducing fines and consequently deposited some of the proceeds in Swiss accounts. While Brazil was ultimately not awarded any damages upon the facts of the case, the reasoning of the court is nonetheless instructive. The defendants argued that since the crime of corruption was one committed against "the collective interest," rather than specifically against the Brazilian state, Brazil could not claim to have been

---

24. The fact that parties had challenged the MLA requests and that Swiss prosecutors were bound by secrecy exacerbated delays. See Pieth, *Recovering Stolen Assets*, 48.

25. See T. Daniel and J. Maton, "The Kleptocrats' Portfolio Decisions, or Realities in State Asset Recovery Cases," in P. Reuter, ed., *Draining Development: Controlling Flows of Illicit Funds from Developing Countries* (Washington, DC: World Bank, 2012), 423; and E. Monfrini and Y. Klein, "L'État requérant lésé par l'organisation criminelle: L'exemple des cas Abacha et Duvalier," *Criminal Law Updates* (October 1, 2010), http://www.jdsupra.com/post/documentViewer.aspx?fid=db81bee9-95ab-4e62-85c5-f0bb65438f26.

26. See Pieth, *Recovering Stolen Assets*, 49.

27. Daniel and Maton, "The Kleptocrats' Portfolio," 423; Pieth, *Recovering Stolen Assets*, 49–50.

28. See BB.2011.130 TPF, Swiss decision of March, 20, 2012, Federal Criminal Court.

immediately and directly harmed by it. In November 2010, however, the Swiss court rejected that argument, finding that the laundered proceeds of domestic bribery now held in Switzerland did include funds due to the state of Brazil. Brazil could therefore contend that it had suffered damage as a result of a crime and could thus lay legitimate claim to recompense.[29]

The principle that the state can be a victim of corrupt schemes, and therefore can qualify as a *partie civile* with the right to claim damages, was reinforced in the recent Swiss ruling on the Tunisia case just discussed. The court stated that "the State can be harmed by corrupt schemes" and that "if the corrupt acts harm the State directly, the money laundering which follows also harms the State."[30]

In another example, in 2007 Nigeria became a *partie civile* to a French-prosecuted money laundering case against former Nigerian energy minister Dan Etété. He was convicted and sentenced to three years in jail, and as a civil party to the criminal action, Nigeria was awarded €150,000 as recompense for *prejudice moral* (nonpecuniary damages).[31] Even though Nigeria reportedly failed to pursue an appeal, and so did not ultimately receive the damages owed, the reasoning remains valid as a precedent for future claims by states harmed through the bribery of their officials.[32] These cases all serve to reinforce the idea that the *partie civile* route merits serious consideration by countries harmed by corruption. For a variation on this theme—nongovernmental organizations (NGOs) as *parties civiles,* see box 4.2.

BOX 4.2   **NGOs as** *Parties Civiles*

Nongovernmental organizations whose purpose is to fight corruption may also possibly qualify as civil parties to criminal prosecutions of corruption, insofar as they represent the interests of parties/countries harmed by corruption. In France, the NGO Transparency International France (TI France) filed a criminal complaint against three African heads of state for suspected money laundering. One was Equatorial Guinea President Obiang, whose associates were known to be in possession of luxury cars and residences suspected to have been acquired with assets stolen from the national treasury. In November 2010, after lengthy court proceedings, French courts approved the complaint and opened a criminal investigation. Finding that TI France had demonstrated legitimate and direct damage to the collective interests it represented, the NGO was admitted as a civil party.[33] TI France announced that it hopes the investigation will eventually lead to an effective exercise of the right to restitution. The case is ongoing.

---

29. See BB_901/2009, Swiss decision of November 3, 2010, Federal Criminal Court.

30. See BB.2011.130, p. 5.

31. Nonpecuniary damages are damages such as pain and suffering that cannot be quantified in precise monetary terms.

32. Tribunal de Grand Instance (TGI) de Paris, 11eme chambre, 7 novembre 2007.

33. Transparency International, "Clamping Down on Kleptocrats," November 8, 2011, http://www .transparency.org/news/feature/clamping_down_on_kleptocrats.

3.3 Restitution and Compensation in Common Law Jurisdictions

In common law countries, as in civil law jurisdictions, there is a right to ask for restitution if a party can show itself to have suffered direct and proximate damage as a result of a crime.[34] In the case of financial crimes, parties must supply the prosecution with proof of such damage (e.g., records or receipts demonstrating the economic loss or expenses resulting from the crime). Under some systems, the injured party must file a declaration with the court.[35] This is, however, the limit of their participation in the criminal proceedings; in common law countries, the role of those pursuing restitution is generally confined to submitting proof of damages to the prosecution, which then acts on their behalf.[36]

As in the civil law system, under the common law system an affected party may possibly obtain a judgment without the need to bring a separate private lawsuit. However, their interests are funneled through the prosecution for the most part. It is possible that the party may also be granted *priority creditor* status. In most common law systems, the payment of restitution has priority over orders to pay fines, forfeitures, or costs.[37] Depending on the legal framework of the jurisdiction, if an order for restitution is granted, the prosecutor's office may assist in enforcing the judgment, and/or the injured party may be entitled to undertake its own civil enforcement action.

Despite the more limited legal rights of injured parties in common law systems, countries have managed to obtain compensation in certain corruption-related cases, including a number of cases ending in settlements. The study has found examples of Costa Rica, Haiti, and Iraq receiving compensation in the courts of United Kingdom and/or the United States, indicating that participation in this way may be a viable avenue to pursue damages in certain cases.[38]

---

34. For example, U.S. federal law provides that a crime victim is a person "directly or proximately harmed" as a result of the commission of a federal crime. See 18 United States Code § 3771(e).

35. This is the case under U.K. law. If an injured party does not properly register, the court will lack the authority to grant it an order of compensation. To qualify, the party must establish *locus standi*, or standing. In an example, Zambia provided a witness statement in the Frederick Chiluba case resulting in the U.K. court issuing an order freezing millions of dollars of his assets. See Attorney General of Zambia v. Meer Care & Desai (A Firm) & Ors [2007] EWHC 952, [2008] EWCA Civ 1007 (31 July 2008). In another example, Nigeria provided a statement as part of its efforts to recoup frozen assets in the case of Nigerian former state governor James Ibori, who pleaded guilty on February, 27, 2012, to money laundering and conspiracy to defraud. Under U.K. law, parties can register and apply for compensation orders in the context of civil recovery orders (CROs) as well as criminal judgments—a relevant consideration, in light of the fact that a number of foreign bribery cases in the United Kingdom have been resolved by CROs. For more information on how various United Kingdom remedies interact, and how compensation fits in, see appendix 2 (United Kingdom Remedies).

36. The experts consulted for this study revealed that prosecutors are often reluctant to have the injured party play much of a role in the proceedings, especially in complex cases. Even in civil law systems, the judge may have the option of deferring matters of relevance to the *partie civile* until later in the proceeding, or of leaving their concerns unresolved, such that the *partie civile* still needs to bring a civil suit to obtain full compensation. This may be the case with complicated damage claims.

37. The United States and the United Kingdom are examples.

38. As for timing, unlike the requirement of entry near the start of a case that exists in some civil law countries, in common law countries, entry could occur much later. For example, in the United States, as long as the claim for restitution is presented before sentencing, it may be considered.

In a prosecution for corruption and insurance fraud in the United Kingdom, for example, Costa Rica qualified as an injured party and was awarded compensation.[39] Julian Messent was a director of the London-based insurance broker PWS International Ltd. In 2010, under a plea agreement, Messent pleaded guilty to two counts of corruption.[40] Messent admitted that he had supervised corrupt payments to Costa Rican officials at the Instituto Nacional de Seguros (INS) and the Instituto Costarricense de Electricidad (ICE) and their associates, as inducements or rewards to appoint or retain PWS as the broker of a lucrative reinsurance policy for INS. Messent was not only sentenced to 21 months in jail but also ordered to pay £100,000 in compensation to Costa Rica.[41]

Similarly, in the United States there have been several criminal corruption cases where restitution was ordered to, or paid for the benefit of, a country. Most significantly, in 2010 Haiti was awarded restitution in the Haiti Teleco cases. These cases dealt with wide-ranging bribery of Haitian officials of the state-owned telecommunications company in exchange for various business advantages.[42] A large number of individuals and companies were found guilty, including Juan Diaz, the president of a company that facilitated the laundering of bribe money. In 2009, Diaz pleaded guilty to money laundering and conspiracy to violate the Foreign Corrupt Practices Act, confessing that his company was set up as a front for the scheme to bribe Haitian officials. At the sentencing of Diaz, the court referred to the Government of Haiti as the "victim" of the scheme and ordered Diaz to pay restitution to Haiti in the amount of $73,824.20.[43]

A number of other examples arose in the context of U.S. investigations into corrupt abuse of the UN Oil-for-Food Programme (OFFP), wherein pricing on oil purchase agreements was inflated to disguise kickbacks to Iraqi government officials. In 2007, several defendants pleaded guilty to various charges pertaining to this misconduct.[44] The following defendants were required to pay the sums indicated: the El Paso Corporation and its subsidiary (restitution of $5,482,363); American businessman David Chalmers and two corporations he operated, Bayoil (USA), Inc. and Bayoil Supply & Trading Ltd (restitution of approximately $9,000,000); businessman Oscar Wyatt (restitution of $11,023,245.91); and Chevron Corporation (forfeited $20,000,000

39. The United States uses the term *restitution* while the United Kingdom uses the term *compensation*.
40. U.K. SFO, "Insurance Broker Jailed for Bribing Costa Rican Officials," press release, October 25, 2010, http://www.sfo.gov.uk/press-room/press-release-archive/press-releases-2010/insurance-broker-jailed-for-bribing-costa-rican-officials.aspx. The previous law is the Prevention of Corruption Act of 1906. It has since been replaced with the Bribery Act of 2010.
41. Messent was ordered to pay £100,000 compensation within 28 days to the Republic of Costa Rica or serve an additional 12 months imprisonment. See "Written Evidence from Transparency International UK (TI-UK)," para. 10, in House of Commons, International Development Committee (IDC), *Financial Crime and Development, Eleventh Report of Session 2010–12, Vol. 2* (London: November 15, 2011), http://www.publications.parliament.uk/pa/cm201012/cmselect/cmintdev/847/847vw11.htm.
42. For a summary of the case, see chapter 6, case 5.
43. Transcript of sentencing hearing, U.S. v. Juan Diaz, Case No. 09-cr-20346 (S.D. Fla.) July 30, 2010, 22–24, accessed via Pacer.gov. The funds were "payable to the clerk of courts, who shall upon receipt forward the money to the victims."
44. U.S. Attorney SDNY, *Fact Sheet: U.S. Attorney's Office SDNY Efforts to Combat Corruption at the United Nations*, May 8, 2008, http://www.justice.gov/usao/nys/pressreleases/factsheets/factsheetuncases.pdf.

as a condition of a Non-Prosecution Agreement). Vitol, SA, a Swiss oil-trading company, also pleaded guilty to charges related to its participation in OFFP and was ordered to pay $13 million in restitution to the Iraqi people.[45] As part of their plea agreements, the defendants agreed to forfeit their proceeds of crime; in turn, the monies were forwarded to the Development Fund for Iraq "for the benefit of the people of Iraq," who were recognized as victims of the schemes.[46] These cases alone garnered nearly $60 million in restitution orders for the benefit of the Iraqi people through the fund.

Nevertheless, restitution claims by parties whose officials have been bribed do not always succeed in U.S. courts. In 2010, Alcatel-Lucent SA admitted that it had engaged in the bribery of Costa Rican public officials, including those of the state-owned enterprise ICE, previously mentioned in connection with the Messent matter. Alcatel-Lucent SA entered into both a DPA with the U.S. DOJ and a settlement with the U.S. SEC, obligating it to pay fines and disgorge illegal profits.[47] ICE filed an action attempting to block the plea agreements, claiming that the U.S. government had violated ICE's rights.[48] ICE attempted to claim victim status under two U.S. laws providing for restitution in the context of criminal cases.[49] The U.S. DOJ opposed ICE's claim for victim status, arguing that ICE board members and senior managers had been directly involved in the criminal conduct and therefore the company had actually functioned as the offenders' coconspirator.[50] The U.S. courts identified the pervasive, constant, and consistent illegal conduct by the "principals" (i.e., members of the board of directors and management) of ICE and concluded that ICE could not overcome the argument made by the U.S. prosecution that a participant in a crime cannot claim restitution.[51]

Nonetheless, for countries or other entities able to demonstrate direct damage suffered as a result of corrupt acts (to which they were in no way party), the avenues for formal participation in a criminal case under both civil and common law systems should certainly be considered as a means to pursuing restitution.

---

45. See U.S. DOJ, *Response of the United States: Questions Concerning Phase 3, OECD Working Group on Bribery* (Washington, DC: U.S. DOJ, 3 May 2010), "Appendix C: Summaries of Foreign Corrupt Practices Act Enforcement Actions by the United States January 1, 1998–September 30, 2010," case 44, Vitol SA, 73, http://www.justice.gov/criminal/fraud/fcpa/docs/response3.pdf.

46. U.S. Attorney SDNY, *Fact Sheet*, see supra n. 44.

47. For a summary of the case, see chapter 6, case 1.

48. Petition for Relief Pursuant to 18 U.S.C. §3771(d)(3) and Objection to Plea Agreements and Deferred Prosecution Agreement, May 2, 2011, http://www.mediafire.com/?g768l1tg66lcla8; and Victim Instituto Costarricense de Electricidad's Reply to the United States of America's Opposition to its Petition for Relief Pursuant to 18 U.S.C. §3771(d)(3) and Objection to Plea Agreements and Deferred Prosecution Agreement, May 27, 2011, http://www.mediafire.com/?91coio43f8feuby.

49. The laws were the Crime Victims' Rights Act (CVRA), 8 U.S.C. 3771, and the Mandatory Victims Restitution Act (MVRA), 18 USC 3663A.

50. *Government's Response to ICE's Petition for Victim Status and Restitution*, May 23, 2011, http://www.mediafire.com/?v14224s4d4s6dkc.

51. U.S. Court of Appeals for the 11th Circuit, "In re: Instituto Costarricense de Electricidad," Case No. 11-12708-G, denial, June 17, 2011, http://www.mediafire.com/?turaenl2l0ppdz6.

3.4 Participation of Affected Countries in Settlements through Other Avenues

In addition to avenues for formal participation in a criminal action described above, countries whose officials have been bribed may be able to seek monetary compensation through *informal* participation in cases headed for settlement. There are a number of cases where defendants have been persuaded to include voluntary monetary compensation for affected countries in their settlements, either as part of their guilty plea or other forms of settlement. In some cases, this has taken the form of voluntary reparations paid directly to the affected country. In others, monetary restitution has been effected by voluntary payment to a charitable or development agency for programs in the affected country or by the establishment of dedicated foundation with a neutral administrator.

3.4.1 Reparations and/or Voluntary Payments to Countries Directly

In two examples in the United Kingdom, settlements have involved reparations and voluntary payments made directly to the countries whose officials were allegedly bribed.

- *Mabey & Johnson:* In 2009, Mabey & Johnson was investigated for participation in a kickback and bribery scheme. The company negotiated an agreement with the U.K.'s Serious Fraud Office (SFO) in which it agreed to plead guilty to two counts of conspiracy to corrupt and to accept financial penalties to be assessed by the court. [52] The court ordered the company to pay reparations in the amount of £1,415,000 to the three countries to whose officials it had made payments: Ghana (£658,000), Jamaica (£139,000), and Iraq (£618,000).[53] Since the Development Fund for Iraq had been in place since 2003, transfer of the funds to Iraq occurred expeditiously. With respect to Jamaica, however, much time elapsed before the funds were eventually transferred in early 2012. With respect to Ghana, no transfer of funds has yet taken place, reportedly at Ghana's own request.[54]

- *BAE Systems:* The BAE case, which concerned the sale of a military radar system to Tanzania, provides another illuminating example of voluntary reparations as part of a settlement agreement.[55] At the time, the court acknowledged that "the victims of this way of obtaining business … are not the people of the UK, but the people of Tanzania. The airport at Dar es Salaam could no doubt have had a new radar system for a good deal less than $40 million if $12 million had not been

---

52. Prosecution Opening Note [Iraq], Regina v. Mabey & Johnson Ltd., Reference No. T2009 7513, Crown Court at Southwark, September 25, 2009, para. 102.

53. U.K. SFO, "Mabey & Johnson Ltd, Sentencing," press release, September 25, 2009, http://www.sfo.gov.uk/press-room/press-release-archive/press-releases-2009/mabey--johnson-ltd-sentencing-.aspx.

54. See House of Commons, IDC, *Financial Crime and Development, Eleventh Report of Session 2010–12, Vol. 1* (London, November 30, 2011). SFO reported that the company was unsuccessful in transferring funds to Ghana and "it is understood that the issue here concerns the reluctance of the Ghanaian authorities to accept that any corruption was involved."

55. Settlement in this case was reached in Regina v. BAE Systems Plc, Case No. S2010565, EW Misc 16. Crown Court Southwark (2010). See also House of Commons, IDC, *Financial Crime and Development, Vol. 2*, Ev w1 (evidence, witness 1), http://www.publications.parliament.uk/pa/cm201012/cmselect/cmintdev/847/847vw01.htm, para. 3–5. For a summary of the case, see chapter 6, case 3.

paid to" the intermediary.[56] The court also noted that it had no power to order compensation or restitution and expressed displeasure with the SFO for not having charged a more serious corruption offense and for dropping all further investigations.[57] Instead, the court reached a settlement with BAE, wherein the latter agreed to make an *ex gratia* payment of £30 million (less any fine imposed by the court) "for the benefit of the people of Tanzania in a manner to be agreed upon between the SFO" and BAE.[58] At sentencing, the judge imposed a fine payable to the UK Treasury of £500,000 and directed the company to "voluntarily" remit £29,500,000 for the benefit of the citizens of Tanzania. In addition the judge imposed prosecution costs of £225,000.[59] Tanzania did not play a role in the settlement of the case or the determination of the restitution payment. Nonetheless, the outcome was positive for Tanzania.

3.4.2 Reparations/Voluntary Payments to Charitable/Development Agency

Another practice of recovery for countries is through a payment to a third party for the benefit of the citizens rather than to the country itself. In the context of a settlement, a charitable, developmental, or other NGO may be identified as an appropriate vehicle through which a corrupt company can make amends to countries whose officials it bribed.

This was the case in the Alstom affair, which, as previously noted, was resolved with the issuing of a *summary punishment order* to the Alstom subsidiary that had failed to prevent bribery.[60] The Swiss Office of the Attorney General formally declined to prosecute parent company, Alstom SA, because, not only had it had made efforts to improve its antibribery measures, but it had also paid as voluntary reparations the sum of Sw F 1 million to the ICRC for its projects in the countries in which the company had made suspect payments (Latvia, Malaysia, and Tunisia). It is not clear, however, if these affected countries played any role in arranging or determining the reparations paid through the ICRC.

A third example of innovative arrangements for the return of proceeds of corruption to a country whose officials were allegedly bribed is found in the Mercator/James Giffen case.[61] The return was effected to benefit Kazakhstan with funds located in Switzerland, using a financial vehicle supervised and monitored by the World Bank.[62] In 2007, Switzerland, Kazakhstan, and the United States executed a trilateral memorandum of

---

56. Regina v. BAE Systems Plc; see chapter 6, case 3.

57. The court noted that a civil society organization, Campaign Against the Arms Trade, tried to challenge the settlement on the ground that the authorities should have charged corruption, and that the effort had been rejected by a previous court. Regina v. BAE Systems Plc; see also chapter 6, case 3.

58. Settlement Agreement between the SFO and BAE Systems plc, dated February 2010, http://www .thecornerhouse.org.uk/sites/thecornerhouse.org.uk/files/bae%20-%20settlement%20agreement%20 and%20basis%20of%20plea.pdf.

59. Sentencing Remarks of Justice Bean in Regina v. BAE Systems Plc (2010), EW Misc 16 (CC), December 21, 2010, Crown Court Southwark, case no. S2010565.

60. For a summary of the case, see chapter 6, case 2.

61. For a summary of the case, see chapter 6, case 10.

62. See chapter 6, case 10.

understanding (MOU) concerning $84 million that had been frozen and seized by the Swiss at the request of the United States in a forfeiture action.[63] Under the MOU, the funds were earmarked to establish the BOTA Foundation, an independent not-for-profit agency created in May 2008 to improve the lives of children and youth suffering from poverty in Kazakhstan.[64] The BOTA board of trustees and program manager, with the oversight of the World Bank, supervise financial management of these funds.[65]

4. Conclusion

As of October 2013, 168 States Parties have ratified UNCAC, giving it near universal reach. This convention has established an innovative architecture for the recovery and return of assets that is built on a foundation of shared responsibility among developed and developing countries. As outlined in this chapter, various avenues exist for countries harmed by corrupt acts of foreign bribery to seek redress, under national legal frameworks and UNCAC.

At the same time, countries on their own cognizance and through their respective national legal frameworks have recognized harm done by their companies that paid bribes to win public infrastructure projects or procurement contracts, for example, and provided restitution to the countries where those projects and contracts originated. In the Kazakh Oil Mining case, three countries came together to craft a political solution to best use proceeds of bribery for the benefit of the people who were most affected by the corrupt acts at issue in the case. Other innovative examples also exist. However, given the very wide gap between the monetary sanctions collected by the countries of settlement—which include disgorgement of profits and forfeited criminal proceeds—and the amounts returned to countries most directly affected by the foreign bribery acts, there is still much work to be done to fulfill the promise of UNCAC.

---

63. See chapter 6, case 10.
64. "Amended Memorandum of Understanding Among the Governments of the United States of America, the Swiss Confederation, and the Republic of Kazakhstan," May 2008, bota.kz/en/uploads/4cbe8cabc70d3.pdf.
65. World Bank, "Kazakhstan BOTA Foundation Established," news release no: 2008/07/KZ, June 4, 2008, http://siteresources.worldbank.org/INTKAZAKHSTAN/News%20and%20Events/21790077/Bota_Establishment_June08_eng.pdf. Finally, in 2010 the United States concluded its prosecution of Giffen through his plea to one count of failing to disclose control of a Swiss bank account. For a summary of the case, see chapter 6, case 10.

5. Conclusions

While several conclusions emerge from this study, some knowledge gaps remain regarding the nexus between settlements and asset recovery. This is largely due to the fact that, in many countries, settlements in cases of foreign bribery are still a relatively recent phenomenon, and there is an ongoing debate concerning the obligations of the settling jurisdiction to consider the return of monetary sanctions to the jurisdictions whose officials have been bribed. We can however, note the following:

1. Over the past decade, enforcement actions against foreign bribery have increased. This is a positive and welcome trend, especially since improvements in enforcement also improve the climate for asset recovery. This progress in enforcement has largely been due to the effective use of settlements in a steadily increasing number of jurisdictions.

2. It is also clear that settlements are increasingly being used to resolve cases of foreign bribery and related offenses, both in developed and, to a lesser extent, in developing countries. From a domestic enforcement perspective, law enforcement and judicial authorities consider settlements an efficient and effective tool to handle complex cases of foreign bribery, in particular when companies are involved.

3. The United Nations Convention against Corruption (UNCAC) and other relevant international legal instruments do not explicitly deal with settlements.[1] However, chapter 5 of UNCAC established as a fundamental principle the recovery and return of assets to prior legitimate owners and those harmed. It provides countries with a comprehensive set of legal avenues for successful cooperation in the tracing, seizing, confiscating, and recovering the proceeds of corruption.

4. Settlements have been concluded, for the most part, without the involvement or cooperation of the jurisdictions whose officials were allegedly bribed.

5. At the same time, there is very limited information on law enforcement action taken in the jurisdictions whose officials were allegedly bribed, against those officials as well as the payers of bribes, even when the authorities in the jurisdictions concerned became aware of such cases. The available data suggest weak enforcement and few results.

6. Monetary sanctions imposed as part of these settlements are very significant, exceeding $6.9 billion between 1999 and July 2012.

7. Out of the $6.9 billion, $5.9 billion was imposed in the settling jurisdictions against companies or individuals for bribes paid in other jurisdictions, mostly in

---

1. While UNCAC does not contain any explicit provisions dealing with settlements it does in Article 37, para. 2, oblige States Parties to "consider providing for the possibility, in appropriate cases, of mitigating punishment of an accused person who provides substantial cooperation in the investigation or prosecution of an offence established in accordance with the Convention."

developing countries. At the same time, only $197 million, or 3.3 percent of the $5.9 billion, was ordered returned to the latter countries.

8. About $556 million in monetary sanctions were imposed by countries whose officials were allegedly bribed and from which the related contracts or projects originated.

9. In view of the legal framework provided by UNCAC, this very small share of monetary sanctions ultimately returned to the countries whose officials were allegedly bribed raises questions: notably, whether settlements in practice hinder the effective application of the relevant provisions of UNCAC.

10. Key concerns that were voiced by experts contacted for this study include (i) the lack of participation by or coordination with other affected jurisdictions in the settlement process, (ii) the opacity of the terms and content of settlements, and (iii) the limited judicial oversight in many cases.

11. This study suggests a range of options to address these settlement-specific challenges to asset recovery, including the following:

   • Countries should develop a clear legal framework regulating the conditions and process of settlements.

   • Countries pursuing settlements should, wherever possible, seek to transmit information proactively to other affected countries concerning basic facts of the case, in line with Articles 46, paras. 4 and 56 of UNCAC.

   • Where applicable, countries pursuing corruption cases could inform other potentially affected countries of the legal avenues available under their legal system to participate in the investigation and/or claim damages suffered as a result of the corruption.

   • Countries should consider permitting their courts or other competent authorities to recognize the claims of other affected countries when deciding on confiscations in the context of settlements, consistent with Article 53 (c) of UNCAC.

   • While some countries publish settlement agreements widely, the study found that this did not necessarily result in other affected countries learning about the cases before, during, or after the settlements were conducted. Concerns were raised that countries often did not find out about settlements until after they were concluded, and that they sometimes did learn about them all. Therefore, countries could further proactively share information pertaining to concluded settlements with other potentially affected countries. Such information could include the exact terms of the settlement, the underlying facts of the case, the content of any self-disclosure, and any evidence gathered by the investigation. This information could enable other affected countries to undertake the following:

     ○ Initiate law enforcement actions within their own jurisdiction against the payers and recipients of bribes as well as any intermediaries

     ○ Seek mutual legal assistance from countries pursuing cases

     ○ Pursue the recovery of assets through international cooperation in criminal matters

     ○ Pursue the recovery of assets through private civil litigation

- Participate formally in the initiating jurisdiction's investigation and/or prosecution, with a view to pursuing compensation for damages suffered
- Seek to annul or rescind any public contracts that were concluded in the context of bribery cases
- Initiate actions for the debarment of companies as well as withdrawal of concessions and permits that have been granted as a result of the corruption
- Where applicable, monitor the compliance of companies with any resolutions of the settlement, obligating them to establish or reinforce their respective internal anticorruption measures when conducting business transactions within the country's jurisdiction.

The authors of this study believe that by adopting these measures, countries are likely to take a common approach to tackling settlements in foreign bribery, particularly approaches leading to asset recovery, and will move closer to fulfilling their commitments to the United Nations Convention against Corruption—commitments both to tackle corruption and to promote asset recovery.

6. Case Summaries

This chapter presents summaries of 14 key cases involving foreign bribery.

1. Alcatel-Lucent (Costa Rica and United States)

In December 2009, the French company Alcatel-Lucent SA (Alcatel) reached an agreement in principle with prosecuting authorities in the United States that resulted in the settlement of alleged corruption charges by means of a deferred prosecution agreement (DPA).[1]

The U.S. government had charged the company with misconduct that included improper payments to foreign officials in Costa Rica; Honduras; Malaysia; and Taiwan, China, as well as falsification of books and records and internal controls violations concerning the suspect hiring of third-party agents in Kenya, Nigeria, Bangladesh, Ecuador, Nicaragua, Angola, Côte d'Ivoire, Uganda, and Mali.[2] This study focuses only on the charges related to the alleged bribery activity in Costa Rica, which involved the parent company Alcatel and three of its subsidiaries.[3]

The U.S. government alleged that, in or around 2001, two high-level executives of the Alcatel group, Edgar Valverde, the president of Alcatel CR and country senior officer in Costa Rica, and his superior Christian Sapsizian, the director for Latin America of Alcatel CIT, arranged for Alcatel AG to enter into numerous "sham consulting agreements" with two Costa Rican consulting firms: Servicios Notariales, Q.C. SA, and Intelmar Costa Rica, SA.[4] The purpose of these agreements was to help Alcatel CIT obtain mobile telephone contracts from the Instituto Costarricense de Electricidad SA (ICE), Costa Rica's state-owned telecom authority. Sapsizian admitted in court that from "February 2000 through September 2004, he conspired with Valverde and others to make millions of dollars in bribe payments to Costa Rican officials." More than

---

1. Alcatel-Lucent S.A., U.S. Securities and Exchange Commission (SEC) Form 20-F, *Annual Report*, for the fiscal year ended December 31, 2009, chap. 6, sect. 10, "Legal Matters," 72–74, http://www.alcatel-lucent .com/investors/annual-reports (link to March 23, 2010, 2009 Annual Report on Form 20-F).
2. U.S. Department of Justice (DOJ), "Alcatel-Lucent S.A. and Three Subsidiaries Agree to Pay $92m to Resolve Foreign Corrupt Practices Act Investigation," press release, Washington, DC, December 27, 2010, http://www.justice.gov/opa/pr/2010/December/10-crm-1481.html.
3. The subsidiaries were Alcatel CIT S.A. (Alcatel CIT), now known as Alcatel-Lucent France S.A; Alcatel Standard A.G. (Alcatel AG), now known as Alcatel-Lucent Trade International A.G.; and Alcatel de Costa Rica S.A. (Alcatel CR), now known as Alcatel Centroamerica S.A. See U.S. DOJ, "Alcatel-Lucent S.A. and Three Subsidiaries Agree to Pay."
4. Deferred Prosecution Agreement (DPA), U.S. v. Alcatel-Lucent, S.A., Case No. 10-cr-20907 (December 27, 2010), Attachment A: "Statement of Facts," paras. 9–15.

$14 million went to sham consultancy arrangements, and at least $2.5 million in bribes were transferred to senior Costa Rican officials. As a result, Alcatel obtained contracts worth $149 million.[5]

The U.S. government commented on the deficient nature of the Alcatel group's compliance practices, noting that Alcatel "pursued many of its business opportunities around the world through the use of third-party agents and consultants. This business model was shown to be prone to corruption, as consultants were repeatedly used as conduits for bribe payments to foreign officials (and business executives of private customers) to obtain or retain business in many countries."[6]

Investigations were pursued in Costa Rica by the Office of the Attorney General, the Fiscalía de Delitos Económicos, and the Corrupción y Tributarios; in the United States by the Department of Justice (DOJ) Criminal Division's Fraud Section, the U.S. Securities and Exchange Commission (SEC), the Federal Bureau of Investigation (FBI), and Immigration and Customs Enforcement; and in France by the French Ministry of Justice, Tribunal de Grande Instance de Paris, and the Service Central de Prévention de la Corruption.[7]

According to an SEC disclosure by Alcatel, upon learning of the Costa Rican investigation in October of 2004 the company began an internal inquiry, and Valverde and Sapsizian were fired within the same month.[8] According to the same filing, there were pending criminal charges in Costa Rica against Valverde, Sapsizian, "and certain local consultants, based on their complicity in a bribery scheme and misappropriation of funds" as well as charges against Sapsizian alone in France.[9]

In the United States, Sapsizian and Valverde were indicted on multiple charges under the Foreign Corrupt Practices Act (FCPA). Sapsizian entered a plea of guilty on June 6, 2007, and was sentenced on September 23, 2008.[10] His plea agreement, which reduced the total number of charges from five to two, required the forfeiture of $261,500, three years of supervised release, a $200 special assessment, and continued cooperation with the broader government investigation.[11] Valverde, on the other hand, has yet to face prosecution for the offense; he is unable to appear in court due to imprisonment by the Costa Rican authorities on related charges.[12]

---

5. U.S. DOJ, "Former Alcatel Executive Pleads Guilty to Participation in Payment of $2.5m in Bribes to Senior Costa Rican Officials to Obtain a Mobile Telephone Contract," press release, September 23, 2008.
6. DPA, U.S. v. Alcatel-Lucent, para. 29.
7. U.S. DOJ, "Alcatel-Lucent S.A. and Three Subsidiaries Agree to Pay."
8. Alcatel-Lucent S.A., SEC Form 20-F, 72–74.
9. Alcatel-Lucent S.A., SEC Form 20-F, 72–74.
10. Judgment [as to Christian Sapsizian], U.S. v. Christian Sapsizian, et al., Case No. 06-cr-20797 (S.D. Fla.), September 26, 2008.
11. Judgment [as to Christian Sapsizian], U.S. v. Christian Sapsizian, et al.
12. U.S. DOJ, "Former Alcatel Executive Pleads Guilty."

In late 2010, Alcatel-Lucent entered into a DPA with the DOJ.[13] As part of the deal, the DOJ filed charges of conspiracy to violate the antibribery provisions, books and records provisions, and internal controls provisions of the FCPA and received guilty pleas from three involved subsidiaries: Alcatel CIT, Alcatel AG, and Alcatel CR. A concurrently negotiated civil agreement between Alcatel and the SEC was filed on December 27, 2010, bringing the total monetary sanctions of the Alcatel group to U.S. authorities up to $137,372,000.[14] The SEC complaint alleged that "from December 2001 to October 2004, Alcatel's agents and/or subsidiaries paid at least $47 million in bribes to government officials in Costa Rica to obtain or retain three contracts to provide telephone services in Costa Rica totaling approximately $303 million." The complaint did not specify how much profit Alcatel earned from the Costa Rican contracts. It should be noted that at least some of the $92 million in criminal fines and $45.372 million disgorgement surrendered to the SEC represent criminal penalties and illicit profits related to Alcatel misconduct in nations outside of Costa Rica.[15]

Costa Rica successfully prosecuted 11 alleged participants of the scheme, including the country's former president Miguel Ángel Rodríguez and high-level collaborators within ICE. However, media accounts suggest that some if not all of the convicted persons will appeal their convictions, and final outcomes remain unknown as of July 2012.[16] The outcomes of related criminal investigations in France are similarly unknown.

Costa Rica's Office of the Public Ethics Prosecutor of the Office of the Attorney General of the Republic (Procuraduría de la Ética Pública, Procuraduría General de la República) also brought a civil suit against Alcatel CIT based on the legal theory that the company's involvement in the corruption of public officials had resulted in significant *daño social*

---

13. U.S. DOJ, "Alcatel-Lucent S.A. and Three Subsidiaries Agree to Pay."

14. U.S. SEC v. Alcatel-Lucent, S.A., Case No. 10-cv-24620 (S.D. Fla.), December 27, 2010.

15. U.S. SEC, "SEC Files Settled Foreign Corrupt Practices Act Charges Against Alcatel-Lucent, S.A. With Total Disgorgement and Criminal Fines of Over $137m," litigation release no. 21795, Washington, DC, December 27, 2010.

16. The convictions are confirmed by reference in U.S. Government's Response to ICE's Petition for Victim Status and Restitution, in U.S. v. Alcatel-Lucent France S.A., et al., Case No. 1:10-cr-20906 (S.D. Fla., May 23, 2011), 3: "In fact, within the past few weeks a court in Costa Rica convicted the former president of Costa Rica, Miguel Angel Rodriguez, and a number of now-former ICE officials for the same bribery that forms the basis of the instant cases." The case in Costa Rica is Causa Penal por peculado número: 04-6835-647-PE, contra Miguel Ángel Rodríguez Echeverría y otros (Tribunal de Hacienda del segundo circuito penal de San José en Goicoechea). An unverified copy of the charging document, Acusacion Formal y Solicitud de Apertura a Juicio en la Causa: 04-06835-647-PE Contra Miguel Angel Rodriguez Echeverria y Otros en Perjuicio del Instituto Costarricense de Electricidad (ICE). 04-6835-647-PE, contra Miguel Ángel Rodríguez Echeverría y otros en perjuicio del Instituto Costarricense de Electricidad (July 27, 2007), www.nacion.com/CustomerFiles/nacioncom/Generales/Subsitios/Sucesos/2010/ICEALCATEL/acusacion.pdf (subscription needed), and http://star.worldbank.org/corruption-cases/sites/corruption-cases/files/documents/arw/Acusacion_Rodriguez.pdf.

(social damages) to the nation.[17] The suit was settled out of court, being voluntarily dismissed in exchange for a payment of roughly $10 million in 2010.[18]

The telecommunications authority ICE worked closely with domestic prosecutors during the investigation and prosecution phase of Costa Rica's inquiry into the Alcatel bribery scheme, and it also unsuccessfully attempted to assert several claims within the United States. In El Instituto Costarricense de Electricidad v. Alcatel-Lucent SA et al., ICE attempted to bring Racketeer Influenced and Corrupt Organizations Act (RICO) charges against Alcatel and its subsidiaries and agents, but a Florida court dismissed ICE's suit on nonsubstantive grounds.[19] ICE's U.S. counsel, the law firm Wiand, Guerrera, King, announced plans to appeal the ruling but stated that a resulting stipulation by all parties to consent to Costa Rica as jurisdiction and to waive statute of limitations would be beneficial to ICE should the case eventually be tried in Costa Rica.[20]

In mid-2011, ICE also petitioned the District Court for the Southern District of Florida to object to Alcatel-Lucent's plea agreement and DPA with the U.S. government in the Alcatel-Lucent SA criminal cases. ICE sought to be recognized as a victim and be entitled to restitution, pursuant to the Crime Victims' Rights Act (18 USC Section 1651), U.S. Federal Rules on Criminal Procedure, and the Mandatory Victim Restitution Act (18 USC Section 3663A).[21]

---

17. For more on the concept of *daño social* as articulated by the government of Costa Rica, see CAC /COSP/2011/CRP.6 *Corrupción y daño social*, a presentation by the government of Costa Rica to the Conference of States Parties to UNCAC, October 13, 2011, www.unodc.org/documents/treaties/UNCAC /COSP/session4/V1186372s.pdf.

18. Procuradora General de la República, *Informe de Gestión 2004–2010* (San José: Procuradora General de la República, 2011), 32–33.

19. The dismissal order was signed January 18, 2011, by the 11th Judicial Circuit Court for Miami-Dade County, Florida. Factors for the dismissal included the following: (i) ICE, as a foreign plaintiff as well as an arm of the Costa Rican government, weighed heavily in favor of dismissal on *forum non conveniens* grounds; (ii) Costa Rica provides an adequate alternative forum (the court noted ICE's concurrent pursuit of a claim in Costa Rica based on the same facts alleged); (ii) private interest—the vast majority of witnesses and documents in the case are located in Costa Rica, the laws of which would also apply to plaintiff's claims, and civil RICO claims do not apply extraterritorially to a foreign plaintiff's injury for bribes made abroad to foreign officials; (iv) public interest—Florida taxpayers should not bear the cost of a case brought by an arm of the Costa Rican, government whose property was allegedly injured in Costa Rica; and (v) ability to reinstate suit—in Costa Rica, without undue inconvenience or prejudice, as Florida's *forum non conveniens* statute provides that each defendant will be deemed "to automatically stipulate that the action will be treated in the new forum as though it had been filed in that forum on the date it was filed in Florida" (if action is filed within 120 days of the dismissal). See Order of Dismissal, El Instituto Costariccense de Electricidad v. Alcatel-Lucent, S.A., et al., Case No. 10-25859 CA 13, Circuit Court of the 11th Judicial Circuit, in and for Miami-Dade County, FL, Order signed January 18, 2011, and filed as Exhibit 17 of U.S. Government's Response to ICE's Petition for Victim Status and Restitution, in U.S. v. Alcatel-Lucent France S.A., et al., Case No. 1:10-cr-20906 (S.D. Fla., May 23, 2011).

20. Wiand, Guerra, King, "ICE to Appeal Transfer Order," press release, January 20, 2011, www.wiandlaw .com/ice-to-appeal-transfer-order.

21. U.S. v. Alcatel-Lucent S.A., Case No. 1:10-cr-20907 (S.D. Fla.); Petition for Relief Pursuant to 18 U.S.C. Section 3771(d)(3); Objection to Plea Agreements and Deferred Prosecution Agreement filed May 3, 2011; and Petition for Writ of Mandamus Pursuant to the Crime Victims' Rights Act, 18 USC Section 3771(d) (3) filed June 15, 2011.

Citing ICE's complicity in the Alcatel scheme as legal basis,[22] the U.S. government's response to ICE's petition for victim status and restitution, filed May 23, 2011, argued that, "Under the facts and circumstances in the instant matter, which reflect profound and pervasive corruption at the highest levels of ICE, the government does not believe it is appropriate to consider ICE a victim in these cases. ... Moreover, regardless of whether ICE is considered a victim, the government does not believe that restitution should be ordered in this matter, because, under the facts and circumstances present in this case, any restitution calculation would be entirely speculative and would unduly prolong and complicate the sentencing process—something that the law does not support."[23] This argument was accepted by the district court and upheld on appeal.[24] The court also cited the inability to show direct and proximate harm and the complexities of the case as additional reasons why ICE was not entitled to the relief it sought.

ICE appealed to the U.S. Supreme Court that the district court had violated its rights under the Crime Victims' Rights Act. However, in December 2012, the U.S. Supreme Court denied ICE's petition.[25]

2. Alstom (Switzerland, Tunisia, Latvia, Malaysia, and World Bank)

On 22 November 2011, the Swiss Office of the Attorney General (OAG) issued a summary punishment order against Alstom Network Schweiz AG, acting for the Alstom Group. The company was charged with not having taken all reasonable and necessary organizational measures required to prevent the payment of bribes to foreign public officials in Latvia, Malaysia, and Tunisia.[26] Alstom was sentenced to a fine of Sw F 2.5 million and a compensatory penalty of Sw F 36.4 million. The amount of the penalty was calculated on the basis of the profits earned by the entire group through the contracts involving bribery.[27] The company was also ordered to pay procedural costs amounting to some Sw F 95,000. In a decision issued the same day, Swiss authorities concluded a matter against the parent company, Alstom SA, using

---

22. U.S. v. Lazarenko, 624 F.3d 1247, 1250-52 (9th Cir. 2010): "An individual who is both a victim and a participant in a money-laundering scheme who profited from the conspiracy cannot recover restitution for crimes in which s/he participated."
23. U.S. Government's Response to ICE's Petition for Victim Status and Restitution, in U.S. v. Alcatel-Lucent France S.A., et al., Case No. 1:10-cr-20906 (S.D. Fla., May 23, 2011).
24. In re: Instituto Costarricense de Electricidad, No. 11-12707-G and No. 11-12708-G (11th Cir.), On Petition for Writ of Mandamus to the United States District Court for the Southern District of Florida filed June 17, 2011, and September 2, 2011, Denial of ICE's Motion for Petition for Rehearing En Banc; see also Consolidated Opposition of Alcatel-Lucent, S.A., Alcatel-Lucent France, S.A., Alcatel-Lucent Trade International, A.G. and Alcatel Centroamerica, S.A. to Petitions for Writs of Mandamus Pursuant to the Crime Victims Rights Act, 18 U.S.C. Section 3771, filed June 17, 2011.
25. Instituto Costarricense de Electricidad v. U.S. and Alcatel-Lucent SA et al., Case Number 12-586, in the U.S. Supreme Court.
26. This was in relation to conduct that took place following the entry into force of Article 102 of the Swiss Criminal Code in October 2003.
27. The Swiss used earnings before interest and tax as the basis for calculating profit.

the reparations provision of Swiss law to hold Alstom SA responsible without prosecution. Switzerland considered that a conviction of the parent company, Alstom SA, in addition to that of Alstom Network Schweiz AG, was not justified because of the following:

- The investigation showed that the Alstom Group had made considerable efforts to develop regulations to prevent the payment of illegal amounts, in particular bribes, in the context of its operations (though the Group was criticized for not having enforced these regulations with the requisite vigor).
- Alstom Network Schweiz AG had been created with the aim of centralizing payments to consultants and ensuring better adherence to compliance obligations. No systematic use of slush funds could be established.
- The Alstom Group, after having recognized the organizational deficiencies in question, had rectified these by reinforcing the role of its ethics and compliance office, which now reports to the group's board of directors.
- Alstom SA paid, as voluntary reparations, a sum of Sw F 1 million to the International Committee of the Red Cross (ICRC) for its projects in Latvia, Malaysia, and Tunisia. This amount was paid by Alstom SA as reparations under Article 53 of the Swiss Criminal Code (SCC). The funds will be equally distributed among ICRC projects in the three countries.

In addition, the Swiss authorities considered that the public interest in prosecuting was insignificant, given that Alstom Network Schweiz AG had already been convicted and fined. Despite the order to dismiss proceedings, the two companies were ordered to pay procedural costs of Sw F 90,000. The decisions handed down on 22 November 2011 did not, however, conclude Swiss proceedings against Alstom; proceedings are still under way against consultants and individuals suspected of passive bribery (for example, those who accept bribes or who overlook company practices that promote corrupt activities).

The criminal investigation by the Swiss authorities between 2008 and 2011 involved 15 countries, many of which were the subject of mutual legal assistance (MLA) requests. The Swiss authorities also used a mechanism for proactively exchanging information with eight countries, including France, the United Kingdom, and the United States. This sharing of information revealed that consultants engaged by Alstom as part of contracts in Latvia, Malaysia, and Tunisia had paid a considerable part of their fees to decision makers in these countries, thereby influencing them in favor of Alstom.

During the proceedings against Alstom Network Schweiz AG and Alstom SA, Swiss authorities examined numerous electric power plant projects around the world. They noted other violations of internal compliance regulations, but despite extensive investigations they were unable to prove that any bribery had occurred after the entry into force of Article 102 SCC. Since the OAG could not establish an offense that would justify prosecution (Article 319(1)(a) Civil Procedure Code [CPC]), and could not hold the companies liable for acts occurring before October 2003 (Article 319(1)(b) CPC), the proceedings against these two Alstom companies were therefore dismissed without fine, and the companies were ordered only to pay procedural costs.

On February 22, 2010, the World Bank announced the sanctioning of Alstom.[28] The Bank debarred Alstom Hydro France and Alstom Network Schweiz AG (Switzerland) for a period of three years following Alstom's acknowledgement of misconduct in relation to a World Bank–financed hydropower project. The debarment came under a negotiated resolution agreement between the World Bank and Alstom, which included a restitution payment by the two companies totaling approximately $9.5 million. The facts underlying the settlement were that, in 2002, Alstom made an improper payment of €110,000 to an entity controlled by a former senior government official for consultancy services in relation to the World Bank–financed Zambia Power Rehabilitation Project. The debarment of the two Alstom companies qualified them for cross-debarment by the other multilateral development banks (MDBs) under the Agreement of Mutual Recognition of Debarment that was signed by the major MDBs in 2010. That agreement means that a company debarred by one MDB can no longer seek business from other MDBs during the period of debarment. The rest of the Alstom entities have been conditionally nondebarred for the same time period.

3. BAE Systems (Tanzania, United Kingdom, and United States)

The BAE Systems Plc case from 2010 illustrates several important points. First, BAE settled allegations of bribery (committed in several countries) in a coordinated way with U.S. and U.K. authorities, reflecting the emerging trend toward multijurisdictional settlements. Second, it illustrates an example of asset return. The settlement between the U.K. Serious Fraud Office (SFO) and BAE was approved by the U.K. courts. The company was ordered to make a £29.5 million payment for the benefit of the people of Tanzania, the country adversely affected by BAE's conduct. (Whether Tanzania had a role in reaching the U.K., however, is unknown, as no such role has been reported.) Third, the BAE case shows that *ne bis in idem* (double jeopardy) need not be a barrier to prosecution and settlement in two jurisdictions, especially when investigations focused on different (though related) offenses, facts, or places. The facts show that the United Kingdom prosecuted record-keeping violations with respect to Tanzania, while the United States prosecuted false statements concerning efforts to prevent bribery and violations of arms regulations relating to countries other than Tanzania.

BAE is one of the world's largest multinational companies, primarily engaged in the manufacture, export, service, and brokering of military defense systems.[29] The United Kingdom-registered company has been investigated in connection with its widespread

---

28. See World Bank, "Enforcing Accountability: World Bank Debars Alstom Hydro France, Alstom Network Schweiz AG, and their Affiliates," press release 2012/282/INT, Washington, DC, February 22, 2012, http://web.worldbank.org/WBSITE/EXTERNAL/NEWS/0,,contentMDK:23123315~menuPK:3446 3~pagePK:34370~piPK:34424~theSitePK:4607,00.html.

29. Proposed Charging Letter, In the Matter of BAE Systems PLC, U.S. Department of State (May 16, 2010), 3.

use of third-party consultancy agreements and payments from shell companies owned by BAE.[30] Such consultancy arrangements have been implicated in BAE's efforts to gain contracts to sell military hardware and vehicles to the governments of Austria, Chile, the Czech Republic, Hungary, Qatar, Romania, Saudi Arabia, and South Africa[31] as well as in a $39,970,000 contract concerning the sale of radar equipment to the government of Tanzania, a nation without an air force (which became the object of the U.K.-settled case).[32] Most relevant for our purposes is the settlement BAE reached with the SFO of the United Kingdom over the Tanzania case, under the terms of which BAE agreed to make an *ex gratia* payment of £29.5 million for the benefit of the people of Tanzania.[33]

A number of other countries had previously run investigations into BAE's activities, but none had resulted in a conviction. On December 14, 2006, under mounting domestic and foreign pressure, the SFO director announced an end to an investigation, citing national security as the only factor relevant to his decision.[34] Though legally contested by civil society groups, the validity of this decision was eventually affirmed by the Lords of Appeal in 2008.[35]

From at least 2007 onward,[36] members of the U.S. FBI's specialized FCPA squad and the Immigration and Customs Enforcement Counter Proliferation Unit (concerned with arms control) also pursued a parallel investigation of BAE,[37] while the SFO continued to look into other potentially corrupt offenses not related to Saudi Arabia.

---

30. Information, United States of America v. BAE Systems PLC, Case No. 1:10-cr-0035 (D.D.C., February 2, 2010), para. 27.

31. See, for instance, Information, United States of America v. BAE Systems PLC, Case No. 1:10-cr-0035, paras. 33–47; "Commission Appointed to Probe Arms Deal Allegations," South Africa Government News Agency, September 15, 2011, http://www.sanews.gov.za/south-africa/commission-appointed-probe-arms -deal-allegations; and House of Commons International Development Committee (IDC), *Financial Crime and Development: Eleventh Report of Session 2010–12, Vol. 2, Additional (Unprinted) Written Evidence* (London: 30 November 30, 2011), Ev [evidence] 18, n.12, http://www.publications.parliament.uk/pa /cm201012/cmselect/cmintdev/847/847vw01.htm.

32. Sentencing Remarks of Justice Bean in Regina v. BAE Systems Plc, 2010, EW Misc 16 (CC) 21 December 2010, Crown Court Southwark, Case No. S2010565, para. 3, citing the plea agreement reached between BAE and the U.K. Serious Fraud Office (SFO), http://www.bailii.org/ew/cases/Misc/2010/16.html.

33. This agreement was reached in Regina v. BAE Systems Plc, Case No. S2010565, EW Misc 16, Crown Court Southwark, 2010; see also U.K. House of Commons IDC, *Financial Crime and Development: Eleventh Report of Session 2010–12, Vol. 2*, Ev w1 [evidence, witness 1], paras. 3–5.

34. U.K. SFO, "BAE Systems Plc/Saudi Arabia," press release, London, December 14, 2006.

35. Opinions of the Lords of Appeal for Judgment in the Cause (on the application of Corner House Research and others) (Respondents) v. Director of the Serious Fraud Office (Appellant) (Criminal Appeal from Her Majesty's High Court of Justice), 2008, UKHL 60 on appeal from (2008) EWHC 246 (Admin), 30 July 2008.

36. Statement of Facts and Grounds in the Matter of an Application for Judicial Review, Campaign against Arms Trade v. Director of the Serious Fraud Office, Reference: CO/2734/2010, EWHC (QB) Admin. 26 February 2010, para. 3.

37. U.S. DOJ, "BAE Systems PLC Pleads Guilty and Ordered to Pay $400m Criminal Fine," press release, March 1, 2010.

In February 2010, the U.S. DOJ and the SFO announced that they had reached settlements with BAE.[38] Neither settlement involved the direct admission of foreign corruption by BAE. In the United States, BAE pleaded guilty to one count of conspiracy (under Title 18, USC $371) on March 1, 2010. The objects of the conspiracy were (i) to defraud the United States, (ii) to make false statements to the United States about BAE's compliance mechanisms to prevent and detect foreign bribery, and (iii) to violate the Arms Export Control Act and International Traffic in Arms Regulations.[39] The conduct concerned Saudi Arabia, the British Virgin Islands, and other locations.[40] BAE was ordered to improve its compliance practices, and paid a fine of $400 million to the U.S. Treasury (at that time, the largest fine ever imposed). The admission of conspiracy to violate the Arms Control Export Act and International Traffic in Arms Regulations further exposed BAE to an administrative penalty of $79 million, ordered by the U.S. State Department.[41] The U.S. settlement did not relate to Tanzania, a fact taken into account by the U.K. court in approving that settlement.[42]

In the United Kingdom, BAE pleaded guilty to one count of record-keeping violations (under Section 221 of the Companies Act 1985,[43] related to the sale of the radar system to Tanzania in 1999. Noting the coordination with the United States, the director of the SFO stated shortly after the settlements that this "team effort by the [DOJ] and the SFO" proved that "global settlements can be achieved."[44]

As part of the U.K. settlement agreement, BAE agreed to make an *ex gratia* payment of £30 million (less any fine imposed by the court) "for the benefit of the people of Tanzania in a manner to be agreed upon between the SFO" and BAE.[45] At sentencing, Justice Bean apportioned £29,500,000 to be voluntarily remitted for the benefit of the citizens of Tanzania, a fine of £500,000 to be payable to the U.K. Treasury, and £225,000 for prosecution costs.[46] The court noted that it had no power to order compensation or restitution and expressed displeasure with the SFO for not having charged a more serious corruption offense and for dropping all further investigations.[47] The court

---

38. U.S. DOJ, "BAE Systems PLC Pleads Guilty"; and U.K. SFO, "BAE Systems Plc," press release, February 5, 2010.
39. Sentencing Memorandum, United States of America v. BAE Systems PLC, Case No. 1:10-cr-0035 (D.D.C.), February 22, 2010, 5.
40. U.S. DOJ, "BAE Systems PLC Pleads Guilty."
41. U.S. Department of State, Bureau of Political-Military Affairs, *The Admission of Conspiracy to Violate the AETA Order, in the Matter of BAE Systems PLC. (Respondent)*, May 16, 2010.
42. Sentencing Remarks of Justice Bean, Regina v. BAE Systems Plc.
43. Sentencing Remarks of Justice Bean, Regina v. BAE Systems Plc, para. 3.
44. Speech by Richard Alderman, director of the SFO, given at the Corporate Investigations Group Seminar, February 16, 2010, http://webarchive.nationalarchives.gov.uk/20121105164358/http://www.sfo.gov.uk/about -us/our-views/director's-speeches/speeches-2010/the--corporate-investigations-group-seminar.aspx, accessed September 9, 2013)
45. Settlement Agreement between the SFO and BAE Systems Plc, dated February 2010.
46. Sentencing Remarks of Justice Bean in Regina v. BAE Systems Plc.
47. The court noted that a civil society organization, Campaign Against the Arms Trade, tried to challenge the settlement on the ground that the authorities should have charged corruption, and that the effort had been rejected by a previous court.

acknowledged that "the victims of this way of obtaining business … are not the people of the UK, but the people of Tanzania."[48] As noted, the U.K. record does not reflect what role, if any, Tanzania played in the settlement of the case or the determination of the restitution payment. Reportedly, Tanzania has had an ongoing investigation of the BAE matter.

With respect to the payment to Tanzania, though BAE originally intended to set up a commission to disburse these funds, the extensive delays caused by this plan led to an inquiry by the U.K. Parliament. Ultimately, in September 2011, BAE committed to paying the funds directly to the Tanzanian Treasury.[49] As of March 2012, it was published that the SFO, the government of Tanzania, BAE Systems, and the U.K. Department for International Development had signed a memorandum of understanding enabling the payment of £29.5 million (plus accrued interest) by BAE Systems for educational projects in Tanzania.

BAE is still the subject of ongoing investigations, with the latest developments arising in Sweden and South Africa.[50]

4. Daimler (More than 22 Countries)

Daimler Aktiengesellschaft (Daimler AG) is a German-based global manufacturer of luxury and commercial vehicles.[51] In a report of 31 May 2011 to the OECD, the U.S. DOJ reported that simultaneous DOJ and SEC settlements had been reached on 22 March 2010 with Daimler AG and three of its international subsidiaries: DaimlerChrysler Automotive Russia SAO (Daimler Russia), Export and Trade Finance GmbH (Daimler ETF), and DaimlerChrysler China Ltd. (Daimler China).[52] The United States alleged that the Daimler group systematically made "hundreds of improper payments worth tens of millions of dollars to foreign officials in at least 22 countries—including China, Côte d'Ivoire, Croatia, Egypt, Greece, Hungary, Indonesia, Iraq, Latvia, Nigeria, Russia, Serbia and Montenegro, Thailand, Turkey, Turkmenistan, Uzbekistan, Vietnam and others" between 1998 and 2008.[53] The criminal information filed against Daimler AG

---

48. Sentencing Remarks of Justice Bean in Regina v. BAE Systems Plc.

49. U.K. Parliament, "BAE Bows to Pressure to Pay People of Tanzania After Delay," news release (London: U.K. Parliament, September 9, 2011); House of Commons IDC, *Financial Crime and Development: Eleventh Report of Session 2010–12, Vol. I, Report, Together with Formal Minutes, Oral and Written Evidence* (London: 30 November 2011), Ev [evidence], 40–41, http://www.publications.parliament.uk/pa/cm201012 /cmselect/cmintdev/847/847.pdf.

50. Saab, "Saab Completes Internal Investigation Regarding Consultant Contract in South Africa," press release, Stockholm, June 16, 2011; "Commission Appointed to Probe Arms Deal Allegations," BuaNews Online.

51. Information, US v. DaimlerChrysler Automotive Russia SAO, Case No. 10-cr-064 (D.D.C., March 22, 2010), para. 3.

52. U.S. DOJ, *Steps Taken to Implement and Enforce the OECD Convention on Combating Bribery of Foreign Public Officials in International Business Transactions* (Washington, DC: U.S. DOJ, May 31, 2011), 49–50, http://www.oecd.org/daf/anti-bribery/anti-briberyconvention/42103833.pdf.

53. U.S. DOJ, United States. *Steps Taken to Implement and Enforce the OECD Convention*, para. 7.

also names Ghana[54] and Liberia[55] as jurisdictions where officials allegedly received bribes from the Daimler group. The offenses in Iraq were a part of the broader United Nations Oil-for-Food-Programme (OFFP) kickback scheme.[56]

Available documents seem to indicate that the earliest allegations of improper practices by the Daimler group occurred in the second half of 2004, when two separate whistle-blower lawsuits were filed by former employees.[57] Additionally, the company was notified of an FCPA investigation by the SEC in August of the same year.[58] Though Daimler announced its cooperation with the SEC investigation in its 2004 annual filing, the criminal information filed against the company states that "only in 2005, sometime after the inception of the SEC and DOJ investigations of Daimler, did Daimler eliminate the use of TPAs [third-party accounts, a corporate ledger system by which illicit payments were transmitted by the company] entirely and impose the controls necessary to prevent, deter, and detect the making of improper payments to foreign government officials."

Resolution of the DOJ and SEC investigations was announced on April 1, 2010.[59] Daimler AG entered a deferred prosecution agreement wherein it accepted responsibility for conspiring to violate and violating the books and records provisions of the FCPA.[60] Daimler AG, without accepting or denying guilt, also accepted a civil judgment in the SEC case enjoining the company from future violations.[61] Daimler China entered a deferred prosecution agreement wherein it accepted responsibility for conspiring to violate and violating the antibribery provisions of the FCPA,[62] while Daimler Russia and Daimler ETF pled guilty to the same offenses.[63] In total, the Daimler group paid $93.6 million in criminal fines and $91,432,967 in disgorgement of illicit profits.[64]

In June 2010 Nigeria's Economic and Financial Crimes Commission announced the launch of an investigation into Daimler's bribery of Nigeria officials and complicit

54. Information, United States v. DaimlerChrysler Automotive Russia SAO, para. 100.
55. Information, United States v. DaimlerChrysler Automotive Russia SAO, paras. 101–102.
56. Information, United States v. DaimlerChrysler Automotive Russia SAO, paras. 136–143.
57. The only one available for review was the complaint filed in David Bazzetta v. DaimlerChrysler Corp, Case No. 2:04-cv-73806 (E.D.Mich., September 28, 2004).
58. Daimler AG, Form 10-K, *Annual Report 2004*, April 6, 2005, 154.
59. U.S. DOJ, "Daimler AG and Three Subsidiaries Resolve Foreign Corrupt Practices Act Investigation and Agree to Pay $93.6m in Criminal Penalties," press release, April 1, 2010.
60. Deferred Prosecution Agreement, US v. Daimler AG, Case No. 10-cr-063 (D.D.C., March 24, 2010).
61. U.S. DOJ, "Daimler AG and Three Subsidiaries Resolve Foreign Corrupt Practices Act Investigation."
62. Deferred Prosecution Agreement, US v. DaimlerChrysler China Ltc., Case No. 10-cr-066 (D.D.C., March 24, 2010).
63. See Plea Agreements in US v. DaimlerChrysler Automotive Russia SAO; and US v. Daimler Export and Trade Finance GmbH, Case No. 10-cr-065-RJL (D.D.C., March 24, 2010).
64. U.S. DOJ, "Daimler AG and Three Subsidiaries Resolve Foreign Corrupt Practices Act Investigation."

parties in a domestic joint venture between Daimler and the Nigerian government called Anambra Motor Manufacturing Company (ANAMMCO).[65]

Latvia's Corruption Prevention and Combating Bureau (KNAB) issued a press release on February 15, 2011, announcing the arrest of one suspect in an investigation begun the previous year into "criminal offenses committed in state authority service" in violation of Chapter 24 of the criminal law of that nation. The allegations related to bribery of Riga officials by EvoBus GmbH, a Daimler subsidiary that had been exposed in the U.S. investigation.[66]

5. Haiti Teleco (Haiti and United States)

This case concerns the money laundering and bribery activities of businessmen operating out of the United States who sought to obtain unjust advantages from senior officials of the state-owned entity Telecommunications D'Haiti SAM (Haiti Teleco) in the early 2000s.[67] Numerous people and business entities have been linked to this scandal.

The Haitian officials suspected of receiving bribes are primarily Haiti Teleco officers, including the company's former director general Patrick Joseph, its director of international affairs Robert Antoine, and Antoine's immediate predecessor in that position, Jean Rene Duperval.[68] (Patrick Joseph is also the son of a Politically Exposed Person, Vénel Joseph, governor of the national Banque de la République d'Haiti at the time of the case.[69])

Three persons and their personal companies are alleged to have facilitated the laundering of bribe money to these officials, including Duperval's sister Marguerite Grandison, then-president of Telecom Consulting Services Corp;[70] Jean Fourcand, president and director of Fourcand Enterprises Inc.;[71] and Juan Diaz, president of J.D. Locator

65. Nigeria Economic and Financial Crime Commission, "EFCC Probes $15m Daimler, ANAMMCO Bribery Scam," press release, June 7, 2010.

66. Latvia Corruption Prevention and Combating Bureau, "KNAB Investigates bribery Case of 4.3m Euro," press release, February 15, 2011. The details of the bribery scheme, which Daimler AG conceded were true, can be found in the Information filed in US v. DaimlerChrysler Automotive Russia SAO, paras. 103–107.

67. Indictment, U.S. v. Joel Esquenazi, Carlos Rodriguez, Robert Antoine, Jean Rene Duperval, and Marguerite Grandison, Case No. 09-cr-21010 (S.D. Fla, December 4, 2009), para. 3.

68. U.S. DOJ, "Two Telecommunications Executives Convicted by Miami Jury on All Counts for Their Involvement in Scheme to Bribe Officials at State-Owned Telecommunications Company in Haiti," press release, August 5, 2011.

69. Superseding Indictment, U.S. v. Washington Vasconez Cruz, Amadeus Richers, Cinergy Telecommunications Inc., Patrick Joseph, Jean Rene Duperval, and Marguerite Grandison, Case No. 09-cr-21010 (S.D. Fla.), 4.

70. U.S. DOJ, "Two Telecommunications Executives Convicted."

71. U.S. DOJ, "Florida Businessman Pleads Guilty to Money Laundering in Foreign Bribery Scheme," press release, February 19, 2010.

Services Inc.[72] Fourcand has admitted that he used his company to conceal the corrupt origin of funds by submitting false invoices and conducting real-estate transactions for the benefit of Antoine,[73] while Diaz confessed that J.D. Locator Services was a front set up entirely for this bribery scheme.[74] It must be noted that many of the individuals charged were accused of money laundering and fraud, including the Haitian public officials who are defendants in the case.

On the side of the companies supplying the bribes, there are three implicated telecom concerns, including the closely related U.S. companies Cinergy Telecommunications Inc. and the now-defunct Uniplex Telecom Technologies Inc.[75] These two companies shared an address and several employees, including their president, Washington Vasconez Cruz (also implicated)[76] and then-director Amadeus Richers.[77] Senior figures from Telecommunications Corp. were also involved, including president Joel Esquenazi, executive vice president Carlos Rodriguez,[78] and former financial employee Antonio Perez.[79]

The first arrests in the case occurred in mid-2009. Haiti, the natural pursuer of such allegations, was dependent in large part on assistance offered by the U.S. federal prosecutors who coordinated the case. The World Bank's *World Development Report* wholeheartedly endorsed this bilateral cooperation: "Proving it in a Haitian court would have been a challenge, given the absence of police and prosecutors with experience handling cases of sophisticated financial crime, and once the earthquake hit in January 2010 it would have been nigh impossible."[80] To complement Haiti's Ministry of Justice and Public Security, financial intelligence unit (Unité Centrale de Renseignements Financiers), and the economic crimes division of its national police (Bureau des Affaires Financières et Economiques), the U.S. DOJ brought the skill sets of its Fraud Section and its Asset Forfeiture and Money Laundering Sections. U.S. Internal Revenue Service criminal investigation specialists were also involved.[81]

---

72. U.S. DOJ, "Two Florida Businessmen Plead Guilty to Participating in a Conspiracy to Bribe Foreign Government Officials and Money Laundering," press release, May 15, 2009.

73. U.S. DOJ, "Florida Businessman Pleads Guilty."

74. U.S., DOJ, "Two Florida Businessmen Plead Guilty."

75. Superseding Indictment, U.S. v. Washington Vasconez Cruz, Amadeus Richers, Cinergy Telecommunications Inc., Patrick Joseph, Jean Rene Duperval, and Marguerite Grandison, Case No. 09-cr-21010 (S.D. Fla.), paras. 8–9.

76. Superseding Indictment, U.S. v. Washington Vasconez Cruz et al., Case No. 09-cr-21010 (S.D. Fla.).

77. Superseding Indictment, U.S. v. Washington Vasconez Cruz et al., Case No. 09-cr-21010 (S.D. Fla.); U.S. DOJ, "Former Haitian Government Official Convicted in Miami for Role in Scheme to Launder Bribes Paid by Telecommunications Companies," press release, March 13, 2012; and U.S. v. Patrick Joseph, Case No. 1:10-cr-21010 (S.D. Fla.), Plea Agreement filed on February 8, 2012.

78. U.S. DOJ, "Two Telecommunications Executives Convicted."

79. U.S. DOJ, "Two Florida Businessmen Plead Guilty."

80. World Bank, *World Development Report 2011* (Washington, DC: World Bank, 2011), 264, box 8.4, "Bilateral Cooperation against Corruption and Money Laundering in Haiti and Nigeria."

81. U.S. DOJ, "Two Florida Businessmen Plead Guilty."

As of mid-2012, when this case summary was compiled, this case was still ongoing. Duperval pleaded guilty in March 2012 and was sentenced to nine years in jail and ordered to forfeit $497,311 on May 21, 2012. Joseph pleaded guilty in March 2012 and was awaiting sentencing as of May 2012. Grandison, Cruz, Richards, and Cinergy had been indicted but not yet tried.[82] Of the legal actions that have concluded, Diaz and Perez were first two targets, and each pleaded guilty on 22 April 2009 to a single count of conspiracy to violate the FCPA and money laundering laws.[83] Esquenazi, Rodriguez, Antoine, Duperval, and Grandison were jointly indicted on December 4 2009,[84] as was Fourcand, albeit in a different proceeding.[85] Though all five persons in the Esquenazi case initially fought the charges, circumstances changed somewhat when on February 1, 2010 Fourcand signed a plea agreement admitting his guilt and accepting one count of Engaging in Monetary Transactions in Property Derived from Specified Unlawful Activity, a money laundering violation under 18 U.S.C. §1957.[86] Having been arrested in Haiti and remanded to U.S. custody to stand trial, and with damning admissions from Fourcand, Antoine signed a plea agreement on 19 February[87] and appeared in court on12 March 2010 to change his plea from not guilty to guilty on count 9 of the indictment (18 U.S.C. §1956(h), Conspiracy to Commit Money Laundering).[88]

With Diaz, Perez, Fourcand, and even one of the foreign officials himself having pleaded guilty, the accused had added incentive to settle. Esquenazi and Rodriguez, however, did not accept a settlement, and their case went to a jury trial. Both were convicted on all 21 counts of the indictment (including conspiracy, FCPA violations, and money laundering).[89] Whereas Diaz, Perez, Fourcand, and Antoine had all been sentenced to terms of imprisonment between 2 and 4.75 years,[90] Rodriguez received the harsher sentence of 7 years, and Esquenazi the sentence of 15 years—the lengthiest ever handed down in a foreign bribery case.[91]

One of the unique features of this case is the restitution order handed down during the sentencing of the coconspirators. Though all the defendants who have been found

82. Superseding Indictment, U.S. v. Washington Vasconez Cruz et al., Case No. 09-cr-21010 (S.D. Fla.).
83. U.S. DOJ, "Two Florida Businessmen Plead Guilty."
84. U.S. DOJ, "Florida Businessman Pleads Guilty."
85. Criminal Information, U.S. v. Jean Fourcand, Case No. 10-cr-20062 (S.D. Fla., February 1, 2010).
86. Plea Agreement, U.S. v. Jean Fourcand, Case No. 10-cr-20062 (S.D. Fla., February 1, 2010).
87. Plea Agreement [Antoine], U.S. v. Joel Esquenazi, Carlos Rodriguez, Robert Antoine, Jean Rene Duperval, and Marguerite Grandison, Case No. 09-cr-21010 (S.D. Fla., February 19, 2010).
88. Change of Plea [Antoine], U.S. v. Joel Esquenazi, Carlos Rodriguez, Robert Antoine, Jean Rene Duperval, and Marguerite Grandison, Case No. 09-cr-21010 (S.D. Fla., March 12, 2010).
89. U.S. DOJ, "Two Telecommunications Executives Convicted."
90. U.S. DOJ, "Florida Businessman Sentenced to 57 Months in Prison for Role in Foreign Bribery Scheme," press release, July 30, 2010; on Perez, "Former Controller of a Miami-Dade County Telecommunications Company Sentenced to 24 Months in Prison for His Role in Foreign Bribery Scheme," January 21, 2011; on Antoine, "Former Haitian Government Official Sentenced to Prison for His Role in Money Laundering Conspiracy Related to Foreign Bribery Scheme," June 2, 2010; and on Fourcand, "Florida Businessman Pleads Guilty."
91. U.S. DOJ, "Executive Sentenced to 15 Years in Prison for Scheme to Bribe Officials at State-Owned Telecommunications Company in Haiti," press release, October 25, 2011.

guilty have been subject to significant financial forfeiture orders, these are of secondary priority to the repayment of restitution, meaning that any money recovered shall go toward the victim before court fines and costs are paid.

The government of Haiti is referenced in the sentencing transcripts of Diaz as the victim of the scheme, and he was ordered to pay restitution of $73,824.20 to the nation, payable to the clerk of courts who shall, upon receipt, forward the money to the victims.[92] Esquenazi, Rodriquez, Perez, Fourcand, and Antoine were held liable to make joint and several restitutions in the amount of $2,200,000.[93] Whether or not any payments to Haiti have been made is unknown at this time.

6. Innospec (United Kingdom and United States)

Innospec Inc. (Innospec USA) is a U.S.-registered company listed on the New York Stock Exchange. Its primary business includes the manufacture and sale of fuel and power-related chemicals. Two of Innospec USA's subsidiary structures are the U.K.-registered Innospec Ltd. (Innospec UK) and the Switzerland-registered Alcor Chemic Vertriebs GmbH.[94]

The U.S. DOJ, SEC, and Office of Foreign Asset Control began investigating Innospec USA in 2005, after the company was outed in the United Nations Independent Inquiry Committee into the OFFP report issued that year.[95] U.S. authorities alerted the United Kingdom's SFO in October 2007, and it subsequently opened an investigation into Innospec UK.[96] The Innospec companies admitted to having violated international economic sanctions by providing kickbacks to the government of Iraq while participating in the UN OFFP[97] as well as by providing cash, gifts, and travel reimbursements to Iraqi officials.[98] The companies also admitted to having paid an estimated $8 million in bribes to government officials in Indonesia.[99]

Talks of a "global settlement" between these agencies and the Innospec companies began in 2008, as there was concern that Innospec might be facing over $650 million dollars

---

92. Transcript of Sentencing Hearing, U.S. v. Juan Diaz, Case No. 09-cr-20346 (S.D. Fla. July 30, 2010), 22–24.

93. See the Judgments of U.S. v. Joel Esquenazi and U.S. v. Carlos Rodriguez, Case No. 09-cr-21010 (S.D. Fla., October 26, 2011).

94. Plea Agreement, Attachment A: Statement of Facts. United States v. Innospec Inc., Case No. 1:10-cr-61 (D.D.C., March 17, 2010), paras. 1–5. It is to be noted that the Statement of Facts also names two further Innospec subsidiaries: the Sweden-registered Innospec Sweden AB and the Mexico-registered Bycosin S.A. However, the misconduct attributed to these two companies involves circumventing U.S. regulations against trading with Cuba rather than bribery (or related offenses).

95. U.K. SFO, "Innospec Limited Prosecuted for Corruption by the SFO," March 18, 2010.

96. Judgment, Regina v. Innospec Ltd., 2010, EW Misc 7 (EWCC, March 18, 2010), para. 6.

97. Plea Agreement, Attachment A: Statement of Facts. United States v. Innospec Inc., paras. 33–102, sets forth the actions of the Innospec companies in regard to particular Iraq contracts.

98. Plea Agreement, Attachment A: Statement of Facts. United States v. Innospec Inc., paras. 103–112.

99. Judgment, Regina v. Innospec Ltd., 2010, paras. 3–5.

in fines and other penalties across the two jurisdictions, an amount that would have rendered the company insolvent, which was an outcome neither jurisdiction sought, given the complete admission of wrongdoing and cooperation on Innospec's part.[100]

Eventually, in late 2009, a settlement was reached. The United States agreed to prosecute Innospec for the conduct in Iraq, and Innospec USA pleaded guilty to charges (made by the DOJ[101] and SEC[102]) of conspiracy, foreign bribery, and book and record violations. The SFO prosecuted Innospec UK simultaneously, and Innospec UK pleaded guilty to one count of conspiracy to corrupt (under Section 1 of the Criminal Law Act 1977).[103] Charging documents and settlement agreements were filed on March 18, 2010.

The joint settlements in 2010 between Innospec and the jurisdictions of the United States and United Kingdom are notable for several reasons. In the U.K. prosecution of Innospec Ltd., the wholly owned British subsidiary of the U.S. company Innospec Inc., the ruling of Lord Justice Thomas is unique in that it elaborates at length on some of the major issues arising in a collaborative multijurisdictional settlement. Chief among the issues are the division of enforcement responsibilities between cooperating jurisdictions, the calculation of offsets for financial penalties to account for settlements reached in other jurisdictions, and practical and equitable issues engendered when seeking to provide reparations to a jurisdiction whose officials have been bribed.

Lord Justice Thomas pointed out that the coordination between the U.S. and U.K. authorities were not without certain setbacks. An initial offer by the SFO to split the enforcement and financial penalties on a 50/50 basis with the United States ("based upon the fact that the criminality had been orchestrated and arranged from the United Kingdom in respect of the corruption in both Iraq and Indonesia") was rebuffed by the DOJ, which countered with an eventually accepted proposal that the total financial penalties should be divided roughly into thirds, being shared out as follows: DOJ ($14.1 million), U.S. SEC and Office of Foreign Assets Control ($11.2 million and $2.2 million, respectively), and the SFO ($12.7 million).[104]

The Lord Justice further noted that he had reluctantly agreed, upon acceptance of the plea by Innospec USA in the U.S. Federal Court, to restrict any U.K. penalties to the agreed-upon $12.7 million. He also stated that, had he not had to take into consideration an offset for the U.S. enforcement action and the prosecutorial agreement

100. Judgment, Regina v. Innospec Ltd., 2010, para. 7.
101. U.S. DOJ, "Innospec Inc. Pleads Guilty to FCPA Charges and Defrauding the United Nations; Admits to Violating the U.S. Embargo against Cuba," press release, March 18, 2010.
102. U.S. SEC, "SEC Files Settled Foreign Corrupt Practices Act Charges against Innospec, Inc. for Engaging in Bribery in Iraq and Indonesia with Total Disgorgement and Criminal Fines of $40.2m," litigation release no. 21454, March 18, 2010.
103. U.K. SFO, "Innospec Limited Prosecuted for Corruption by the SFO," press release, March 18, 2010. Also see the draft indictment available at the SFO website, http://www.sfo.gov.uk/media/105631 /innospec%20annex%204%20draft%20indictment.pdf.
104. Judgment, Regina v. Innospec Ltd., 2010, paras. 11–13.

(which he considered to be neither within the powers of the director of the SFO nor constitutionally legitimate[105]), he would have ordered a penalty of more than $100 million.[106]

In addition, of the $12.7 million to be made available by the Innospec companies to the SFO, the original settlement proposal decreed that "a confiscation penalty of $6.7m would be made in respect of the Indonesian corruption and ... a civil recovery order of $6m of which $5m would be paid to the UN Development Fund for Iraq."[107] The return of money to Iraq was to be orchestrated as a civil recovery order to avoid infringement on the principle of *ne bis in idem*/double jeopardy, given the criminal case settled in the United States.[108] This was rejected by the Lord Justice, who questioned the rationale of ordering reparations in the case of Iraq but not in the case of Indonesia, despite the misconduct being apparently equal in seriousness in both places.[109] He also highlighted the logical disconnect between filing charges concerning Iraqi misconduct in the United States but ordering reparations be paid only to Iraq from the United Kingdom, which had charges of conspiracy only in relation to the acts in Indonesia.[110] Lord Justice Thomas expressed objections to the confiscation as part of the settlement agreement, and he eventually ordered that the entire financial penalty be forfeit as a criminal fine payable to the British Crown.[111]

Several individuals were also charged in the United States over the matter. Criminal charges (one count of conspiracy and one count of violating the FCPA) were filed and settled against Ousama M. Naaman, a dual Canadian/Lebanese citizen who had been extradited for the role he played as Innospec's agent in Iraq.[112] Naaman and David Turner, a business director at Innospec USA who had played a role in the Indonesian bribery, also accepted civil settlements with the SEC later that year.[113] Finally, in 2011, Paul Jennings, the erstwhile head of Innospec USA, accepted a settlement with the SEC over his role in approving the bribery payments made by the Innospec companies.[114]

7. Johnson & Johnson (Greece, United Kingdom, and United States)

Johnson & Johnson (J&J) is a U.S. conglomerate that wholly owns a group of medical device businesses operating under the DePuy brand, including one in the United States

---

105. Judgment, Regina v. Innospec Ltd., 2010, para. 43.
106. Judgment, Regina v. Innospec Ltd., 2010, para. 41.
107. Judgment, Regina v. Innospec Ltd., 2010, para. 17.
108. Judgment, Regina v. Innospec Ltd., 2010, para. 37.
109. Judgment, Regina v. Innospec Ltd., 2010, paras. 31–37.
110. Judgment, Regina v. Innospec Ltd., 2010, para. 31.
111. Judgment, Regina v. Innospec Ltd., 2010, para. 47.
112. U.S. DOJ, "Innospec Agent Pleads Guilty to Bribing Iraqi Officials and Paying Kickbacks Under the Oil for Food Program," press release, June 25, 2010.
113. U.S. SEC, "SEC Files Settled Charges against David P. Turner and Ousama M. Naaman."
114. U.S. SEC, "SEC Charges Former CEO of Innospec for Role in Bribery Scheme," press release, January 24, 2011.

and the U.K.-headquartered DePuy International (collectively referenced as DePuy).[115] J&J admitted that, acting through subsidiaries (notably DePuy), employees, and agents, it "paid bribes to public doctors and administrators in Greece, Poland, and Romania ... including cash and inappropriate travel [using] slush funds" and that it engaged in "sham civil contracts with doctors, and offshore companies."[116] In its U.S. SEC settlement, J&J also acknowledged that it had won humanitarian contracts in the UN's OFFP by paying kickbacks to Iraqi officials.[117]

The case originated in February 2006, when J&J received a subpoena from the U.S. SEC concerning the OFFP matter.[118] Beginning in March 2006, J&J conducted an internal investigation.[119] In November 2006, J&J also learned of an investigation by Polish authorities concerning special advantages granted to public officials at public hospitals.[120] By February, 2007, J&J had started to cooperate with the U.S. DOJ and SEC.[121]

In October 2007, the DOJ transmitted information to the United Kingdom concerning U.K.-based subsidiary DePuy International,[122] leading the SFO to commence an investigation.[123] On December 1, 2009, the SFO announced the arrest of Robert Dougall, former vice president of market development of DePuy International on charges of conspiracy to corrupt (under the Criminal Law Act of 1977) with respect to illicit payments in Greece.[124] On April 14 2010, Dougall entered a guilty plea and received from Justice Bean in the Southwark Crown Court a reduced sentence of one year's incarceration. Significantly, the SFO gave Dougall credit for cooperating fully and substantively in the broader J&J and DePuy corruption investigations, as the SFO's first ever "cooperating defendant" in a corruption investigation.[125]

While the U.S. and U.K. investigations were pending, Greek authorities initiated an investigation into J&J's corrupt activities in the Greek public health system and froze

---

115. Information, United States v. DePuy, Inc., Case No. 11-cr-099 (D.D.C., April 8, 2011), paras. 2–4.

116. Deferred Prosecution Agreement, U.S. v. DePuy, Case No. 11-CR-099 (D.D.C., April 8, 2011); U.S. SEC, "Johnson and Johnson to Pay More Than $70m in Settled FCPA Enforcement Action," litigation release no. 21922, April 8, 2011.

117. Complaint, SEC v. Johnson & Johnson, Case No. 11-cv-00686-EFH (D.D.C., April 8, 2011), para. 2.

118. Johnson & Johnson (J&J), FORM 10-K, *Annual Report* for the period ending February 1, 2011, "Notes to Consolidated Financial Statements," 69–70.

119. U.K. SFO, "DePuy International Limited Ordered to Pay 4.829m Pounds in Civil Recovery Order," press release, April 8, 2011.

120. J&J, *Report of the Special Committee of the Board of Directors of Johnson & Johnson* (New Brunswick, NJ: J&J, June 27, 2011), 113.

121. In February 2007, J&J voluntarily disclosed information about the scheme to the DOJ and SEC. See J&J, FORM 10-K, 69–70.

122. U.K. SFO, "DePuy International Limited Ordered to Pay."

123. U.K. SFO, "Former Vice President of DePuy International Ltd. Charged with Corruption," press release, December 1, 2009.

124. U.K. SFO, "Former Vice President of DePuy International Ltd. Charged."

125. U.K. SFO, "British Executive Jailed for Part in Greek Healthcare Corruption," press release, April 14, 2010.

€5.785 million in assets of the Greek subsidiary DePuy Hellas.[126] That matter is still pending. Sources indicate that the asset freeze shall remain in place until the case is tried. The Polish authorities had also opened an investigation into J&J's corrupt activities there. Reportedly, all four jurisdictions, the United States, United Kingdom, Greece, and Poland, shared evidence through MLA in a timely fashion.

On April 8, 2011, the U.S. DOJ and SEC jointly announced settlements. In a DPA with the DOJ, DePuy admitted to the substance of the allegations, that is to say, having paid bribes to officials in Greece, Poland, and Romania.[127] Simultaneously, without admitting to or denying the allegations, J&J consented to the entry of a civil court order by the SEC over the same material facts.[128] The U.S. DOJ acknowledged that its investigation was significantly assisted by authorities in Greece (8th Ordinary Interrogation Department of the Athens Court of First Instance, Athens Economic Crime Squad), Poland (5th Investigation Department of the Regional Prosecutor's Office in Radom, Poland), and the United Kingdom (Serious Fraud Office, Fraud Squad of the West Yorkshire Police).[129] J&J was fined $21.4 million in criminal penalties and disgorged $48.6 million of allegedly illicit profits and prejudgment interest.[130] The fine had been reduced in light of the anticipated resolution of the U.K. charges and because of J&J's cooperation.[131]

On the same day, April 8, 2011, the SFO settled its investigation of J&J by means of a civil recovery order, acknowledging the actions taken in the United States. The SFO settlement concerned the conduct of the U.K. subsidiary of J&J in Greece between 1998 and 2006. The director of the SFO noted that the SFO had "worked with the DOJ to find a solution that served the interests of justice and the company's desire to put illegal activity behind it and move on."[132] The SFO announced that, taking into account the international actions concerning the same material allegations (the U.S. criminal and civil settlements as well as a further restraint of €5.785 million by Greek authorities), their "most appropriate" available course of action was to enter a civil recovery order, under the Proceeds of Crime Act of 2002, in the amount of £4.829 million, to which DePuy International had consented.[133] Thus, the end result of the J&J case (as of early 2013) has been a DPA agreement in the United States with a $21.4 million fine; a U.S. civil disgorgement and prejudgment interest of $48.6 million; a Greek freeze of almost €6 million; and a civil recovery order by the SFO of almost £5 million. While all of the legal actions by the United States, United Kingdom, and Greece concerned the same

126. U.K. SFO, "Former Vice President of DePuy International Ltd. Charged."
127. U.S. DOJ, "Johnson & Johnson Agrees to Pay $21.4m Criminal Penalty to Resolve Foreign Corrupt Practices Act and Oil for Food Investigations," press release, April 8, 2011.
128. U.S. SEC, "Johnson & Johnson to Pay More Than $70m in Settled FCPA Enforcement Action," litigation release no. 21922, April 8, 2011.
129. U.S. DOJ, "Johnson & Johnson Agrees to Pay $21.4m."
130. U.S. DOJ, "Johnson & Johnson Agrees to Pay $21.4m."
131. U.S. DOJ, "Johnson & Johnson Agrees to Pay $21.4m."
132. U.K. SFO, "DePuy International Limited ordered to pay 4.829m pounds."
133. U.K. SFO, "DePuy International Limited ordered to pay 4.829m pounds."

unlawful conduct carried out in Greece, different legal tools were used to address it to take account of the applicable legal principles.

The SFO explained that, on the facts of this case, because criminal sanction of the Greek conduct was achieved by the conclusion of a DPA in the United States with UK DePuy International Limited's U.S. parent company, a U.K. prosecution was prevented by the principles of double jeopardy, a universal principle in common law jurisdictions.[134] The underlying purpose of the double jeopardy rule is to stop a defendant from being prosecuted twice for the same offense in different jurisdictions. The SFO opined that under U.K. law, the U.S. DPA had the legal character of a formally concluded prosecution and punished the same conduct in Greece that had formed the basis of the SFO investigation: in short, a prosecution would not have been appropriate. Nonetheless, a civil proceeding in the United Kingdom, resulting in the civil recovery order, was an entirely appropriate method by which to sanction the conduct.[135]

On February 12, 2013, Greek prosecutors brought criminal corruption charges related to state hospital purchases from DePuy. Five company officials have been charged with bribery and money laundering over deals between 1998 and 2006. The names of the five officials were not released, and it was unclear whether they were still employed by DePuy. The charges accuse the five of paying more than €16 million ($21.5 million) in bribes to Greek doctors to promote company products.[136]

The J&J case showcases four important trends in settlements. First, it illustrates synergistic benefits from timely cooperation among authorities in at least four countries—Greece, Poland, the United Kingdom, and the United States—which in this case led to substantial settlements in the United States and the United Kingdom, an asset freeze in Greece, and ongoing proceedings in Poland. Second, the cases demonstrate that the creative nature of settlements may mitigate the effects of *ne bis in idem* and double jeopardy rules through the interplay of various remedies: in this case the United States obtained criminal and civil penalties, the United Kingdom opted for a civil order only, and Greece obtained a provisional remedy preserving opportunities to pursue further asset recovery. While the legal principles of *ne bis in idem*/double jeopardy shaped the outcomes, they did not prevent any jurisdiction from finding a way to punish the corrupt conduct. Third, the result was facilitated by the desire of the company to put an end to its legal troubles through a "global settlement," showing that, in the context of foreign bribery cases, the speedy resolution offered by settlement is often attractive enough to defendants to incentivize their cooperation and negotiation with enforcement authorities. Finally, the United Kingdom matter introduced the concept of the *cooperating defendant* in U.K. corruption enforcement, with a natural person pleading

---

134. Civil law systems have analogous principles.
135. U.K. SFO, "DePuy International Limited ordered to pay 4.829m pounds."
136. Associated Press, "Greek Prosecutors Bring Corruption Charges over State Hospital Deals with DePuy," Fox News, http://www.foxnews.com/world/2013/02/12/greek-prosecutors-bring-corruption-charges-over -state-hospital-deals-with-depuy/.

guilty and receiving a reduced sentence for his assistance in providing evidence for the case against a related company.

8. Mabey & Johnson (Ghana, Iraq, Jamaica, and United Kingdom)

Mabey & Johnson (Mabey) was the first major U.K. company to be convicted of foreign bribery, in 2009. The case is significant for three reasons. First, it represents a settlement in which the company admitted corruption and was ordered to pay reparations: a total of £1,415,000. Second, an international organization played a role; the corrupt conduct was first exposed by the UN, which informed the U.K. authorities. Third, the company's management faced strong incentives to settle; the final phase of the investigation was motivated by the company's self-disclosure to the SFO and the settlement by the company's desire to resolve the matter.

Mabey is a U.K. company that focuses on steelwork, engineering, and bridge building.[137] In May of 2001, Mabey signed a contract with the government of Iraq to supply 13 modular bridges.[138] While UN and U.K. economic sanctions severely restricted foreign businesses from working with Iraq, a humanitarian program, the UN's OFFP, made allowance for Iraq to export oil at a fair price provided that all proceeds were deposited into a UN escrow account set up for the benefit of the Iraqi people.[139] The OFFP escrow account financed Mabey's €4,222,643 contract for the bridges. Mabey had inflated the contract by adding a 10 percent surcharge on top of the initial estimate and used the excess money (paid out in two disbursements of £231,228 and €191,036) to fund kickbacks to Iraqi officials in violation of the sanctions.[140]

Mabey had a well-established practice of employing agents to help it win contracts in various nations, financing their support by factoring in a commission (typically 5 to 15 percent) as part of their offered contract prices.[141] With regard to Jamaica and Ghana, Mabey knew of corrupt relationships between its agents and influential officials. The company agreed to pay bribes to those officials, deductible from the agent's commissions.[142] Mabey has admitted to similar corrupt misconduct, as well as the direct payment of bribes to officials, in Madagascar, Angola, Mozambique, and Bangladesh, though no charges have been filed.[143]

Mabey's misconduct in Iraq was first uncovered by the UN Independent Inquiry Committee into the OFFP, which published its final report on the manipulation of the

---

137. Prosecution Opening Note [Iraq], Regina v. Mabey & Johnson Ltd. Reference No. T2009 7513, Crown Court at Southwark, September 25, 2009, para. 1.
138. Prosecution Opening Note [Iraq], Regina v. Mabey & Johnson Ltd., paras. 28–29.
139. Prosecution Opening Note [Iraq], Regina v. Mabey & Johnson Ltd., para. 12.
140. Prosecution Opening Note [Iraq], Regina v. Mabey & Johnson Ltd., paras. 53, 72, 79.
141. Prosecution Opening Note [Jamaica, Ghana], Regina v. Mabey & Johnson Ltd. Reference No. T2009 7513, Crown Court at Southwark, 25 September 2009, paras. 5–6.
142. Prosecution Opening Note [Jamaica, Ghana], Regina v. Mabey & Johnson Ltd., para. 7.
143. Prosecution Opening Note [Jamaica, Ghana], Regina v. Mabey & Johnson Ltd., paras. 16, 188.

program in October 2005 and made a referral to the U.K. authorities in December 2005. Following the provision of additional funding from the U.K. Treasury (with the support of the attorney general), the SFO commenced an investigation in May 2007.[144] Meanwhile, the company's other more widespread bribery practices had come to light inadvertently when Mabey began a legal action December 28, 2006, against former employees and agents seeking damages for fraud and conspiracy having to do with consultancy payment involved in the Jamaican bridge contracts.[145] Mabey's management came forward, making a voluntary disclosure of the bribery offenses to the SFO in February 2008. The SFO then commenced a second investigation of the company.[146]

The company entered into an arrangement with the SFO in which it agreed to plead guilty to two counts of conspiracy to corrupt and to accept financial penalties, to be assessed by the court.[147] In terms of asset recovery, in the U.K. plea agreement, Mabey had agreed with the SFO that it would pay reparations to the Development Fund for Iraq, to Jamaica, and to Ghana.[148]

At its sentencing on September 25, 2009, Mabey was subject to a confiscation order of £1,100,000, a fine totaling £3,500,000, and costs of £350,000 to the SFO and was ordered to implement a first-year monitoring program at maximum cost of £250,000.[149] The court ordered Mabey to pay reparations of £658,000 to Ghana, £139,000 to Jamaica, and £618,000 to Iraq, totaling £1,415,000.[150] The SFO noted in written evidence presented before the International Development Committee of the U.K. House of Commons that, as of late 2011, the Iraqi reparations had been paid to the Development Fund for Iraq, that the "client" in Jamaica had accepted the reparations payment, and that Ghana has refused to accept the payment due to "the reluctance of the Ghanaian authorities to accept that any corruption was involved."[151]

Of interest, the court documents in Mabey's U.K. case provide the names of and evidence given against foreign officials. The prosecution's opening note in the case named all officials alleged to have received bribes, not just in Jamaica and Ghana, but also in the four other disclosed, but uncharged, instances of corruption: Angola, Bangladesh, Madagascar, and Mozambique.[152] (This disclosure set off subsequent investigations in at least one other nation. The Office of Contractor General of Jamaica sought MLA from the SFO. The information gathered from the assistance culminated in a report by

---

144. Prosecution Opening Note [Iraq], Regina v. Mabey & Johnson Ltd., para. 15.

145. Judgment, Mabey and Johnson Ltd. v. Danos & Ors (2007) EWHC 1094 (Ch) (May 11, 2007), paras. 1–7.

146. U.K. SFO, "Mabey & Johnson Ltd. Sentencing," press release, September 25, 2009.

147. U.K. SFO, "Mabey & Johnson Ltd. Sentencing."

148. Prosecution Opening Note [Iraq], Regina v. Mabey & Johnson Ltd., para. 102.

149. U.K. SFO, "Mabey & Johnson Ltd. Sentencing."

150. U.K. SFO, "Mabey & Johnson Ltd. Sentencing."

151. U.K. House of Commons IDC, *Financial Crime and Development Eleventh Report of Session 2010–12, Vol. I,* Ev [evidence] 38), Annex B, "Notes on Other Cases by the Serious Fraud Office."

152. Prosecution Opening Note, Regina v. Mabey & Johnson Ltd., paras. 45–97 [Jamaica], paras. 107–125 [Ghana], and paras. 132–185 [concerning the officials of the four other nations].

Jamaica that concluded,[153] among other things, that there was enough *prima facie* evidence of corruption on the part of a public official to compel the contractor general to refer the matter to the Jamaican commissioner of policy and director of public prosecutions.[154] No further information appears to be available concerning the outcome of that referral and subsequent investigation.)

On February 23, 2011, the SFO announced the sentencing of three high-ranking individual employees of Mabey who had been prosecuted for sanctions violations in the Iraqi kickback scheme.[155] Former sales manager Richard Gledhill had accepted a settlement in which he pleaded guilty to the charge and gave evidence against the two others; he was sentenced to eight months' imprisonment and suspended from being a company director for two years.[156] Former managing director Richard Forsyth and former sales director David Mabey, who were both found guilty at trial on February 10, 2011, were sentenced to 21 months' and 8 months' imprisonment, respectively. Each was disqualified from acting as a company director for two years and ordered to pay combined prosecution costs of £200,000.[157]

An SFO lawyer mentioned that the situation in *R v. Mabey & Johnson* and similar cases "stand testament to the fact that in certain cases the level of criminality is such that even where there has been a self-referral and full cooperation, a criminal prosecution is the only proper outcome."[158]

In what then-SFO director Richard Alderman described as the "the final act" in the Mabey case, on January 13, 2012, Mabey Engineering (Holdings) Ltd., parent company to Mabey, consented to the entry of an £131,201 forfeiture order under Part 5 of the Proceeds of Crime Act 2002, which was recognized as representing the dividends earned though Mabey's corrupt activities.[159]

9. Macmillan Publishers (United Kingdom and World Bank)

In 2010–11, the U.K.-based Macmillan Publishers Ltd. settled corruption allegations by the World Bank and the U.K. authorities in a case that illustrated two points: first, the

153. Office of Contractor General of Jamaica, *Special Report of Investigation Conducted into the Allegations of Corruption and Irregularity that are Related to Certain Government of Jamaica Bridge Building Contracts that were Awarded to the British Firm of Mabey and Johnson Limited* (Kingston: Ministry of Transport and Works, October 2009).

154. Office of Contractor General of Jamaica *Special Report,* 159–162, referencing recommendations 1 and 6.

155. U.K. SFO, "Mabey & Johnson Ltd.: Former Executives Jailed for Helping Finance Saddam Hussein's Government," press release, February 23, 2011.

156. U.K. SFO, "Mabey & Johnson Ltd.: Former Executives Jailed."

157. U.K. SFO, "Mabey & Johnson Ltd.: Former Executives Jailed."

158. Robert Amaee, U.K. SFO, speech delivered to the World Bribery and Corruption Compliance Forum, London, September 14, 2010.

159. U.K. SFO, "Shareholder Agrees Civil Recovery by SFO in Mabey & Johnson," press release, January 13, 2012.

important role that settlements by international organizations can play in assisting national corruption investigations, and second, the benefits of an international organization and a national government collaborating expeditiously to resolve corruption cases against legal persons.

In April 2010, Macmillan admitted committing bribery during the course of a World Bank–administered education initiative in South Sudan funded by the South Sudan Multi-Donor Trust Fund.[160] The tender involved the provision of educational materials in South Sudan and was not successful.[161] Macmillan admitted the corrupt conduct in the settlement of a World Bank administrative proceeding, accepting debarment for six years from World Bank tenders, and subsequently reached a civil settlement with the U.K. SFO to forfeit £11,263,852.28 (and costs of £27,000) for unspecified unlawful conduct in connection with business activities in Africa (specifically, in Rwanda, Uganda, and Zambia).[162]

Macmillan was first investigated by the Integrity Vice Presidency of the World Bank, the Bank's unit tasked with investigating fraud and corruption in Bank projects.[163] The World Bank uncovered a bribery scheme and referred its findings to the U.K. authorities at the Overseas Anti-Corruption Unit (OACU) of the City of London Police.[164] In December 2009, OACU police searched Macmillan's headquarters in Oxford, U.K.[165]

After being made aware of these investigations but prior to any formal prosecution, Macmillan voluntarily cooperated and sought a resolution with the World Bank. Around March 2010, Macmillan decided to self-disclose potential violations to the SFO, at which point the SFO directed Macmillan to follow the SFO's published guidance on the matter.[166]

Macmillan's 2010 settlement with the World Bank was the first settlement ever in the Bank's administrative sanctions system of debarment. Previous cases had all undergone a fuller litigation process, with no opportunity for future cooperation by the defendants. The Bank found that Macmillan's conduct called for an eight-year debarment, but in light of the company's early cooperation in the investigation, the Bank decided it was appropriate to reduce the debarment to six years.[167] Macmillan promised to implement a series of remedial measures, including a risk assessment, new ethical

160. World Bank, "The World Bank Group Debars Macmillan Limited for Corruption in World Bank –supported Education Project in Southern Sudan," press release no: 2010/370/INT, April 30, 2010.
161. U.K. SFO, "Action on Macmillan Publishers Limited," press release, July 22, 2011, http://www.sfo.gov .uk/press-room/press-release-archive/press-releases-2011/action-on-macmillan-publishers-limited.aspx.
162. U.K. SFO, "Action on Macmillan Publishers Limited."
163. World Bank, "The World Bank Group Debars Macmillan Limited."
164. City of London Police, "OACU Case Ends with £11m Pay Out," press release. July 29, 2011, http://www .cityoflondon.police.uk/CityPolice/Media/News/290711OACUcaseendswith%C2%A311mpayout.htm
165. City of London Police, "OACU Case Ends with £11m Pay Out."
166. U.K. SFO, "Action on Macmillan Publishers Limited"; U.K. SFO, "Corporate Self-Reporting," October 9, 2012, http://www.sfo.gov.uk/bribery--corruption/corporate-self-reporting.aspx.
167. World Bank, "The World Bank Group Debars Macmillan Limited."

framework, and a staff training program.[168] Under the settlement agreement, successful completion of such measures coupled with continued cooperation may allow Macmillan to reduce the debarment further by up to three years.[169]

On July 22, 2011, the SFO entered into a civil settlement with Macmillan in the High Court, under Part 5 of the 2002 Prevention of Crime Act. Macmillan was required to forfeit £11,263,852.28 (and costs of £27,000) and to appoint an independent company monitor.[170] Under the U.K. incentive system, the monetary sanctions are allocated as follows: the Home Office retains 50 percent, 18.75 percent goes to the prosecuting authority, 18.75 percent goes to the investigating authority, and 12.5 percent goes to Her Majesty's Court Service.

The SFO's case centered on potential bribery and corruption risk in Rwanda, Uganda, and Zambia, which were identified through SFO's cooperation with the OACU and the World Bank. In reaching a resolution with Macmillan the SFO considered the company's self-disclosure, full cooperation with authorities, internal compliance regime reassessment, the previously arranged World Bank debarment, and the company's decision "to cease all live and prospective public tenders in its Education Division business, in East and West Africa regardless of the source of funds" at a significant cost in terms of lost revenue and forfeit bid securities. The SFO also found that Macmillan products and materials were of a satisfactory enough quality and price to have been viable for the original tender, regardless of any potentially illicit circumstances concerning the winning of contracts.[171]

10. Mercator/Giffen et al. (Kazakhstan, Switzerland, and United States)

According to an August 6, 2010, indictment handed down in the District Court of the Southern District of New York, in 1992 James H. Giffen received the "semi-official" title of Counselor to the President of Kazakhstan Nursultan Nazarbayev, a position from which he advised the Republic of Kazakhstan on transactional matters concerning the sale of oil and natural gas resources.[172]

According to the indictment, Giffen allegedly arranged an agreement with the Kazakh Ministry of Oil and Gas Industries in which his company, Mercator Corporation, would receive significant success fees if it able to develop a lucrative foreign investment strategy for the nation's energy sector.[173] Between 1995 and 2000, Giffen was alleged to have

---

168. Macmillan Publishers Limited, "Macmillan Publishers Moves to Address Concerns over Its Education Business in Southern Sudan," press release, May 6, 2010.
169. World Bank, "The World Bank Group Debars Macmillan Limited."
170. U.K. SFO, "Action on Macmillan Publishers Limited."
171. U.K. SFO, "Action on Macmillan Publishers Limited."
172. Second Superseding Indictment, U.S. v. James H. Giffen, Case No. 1:03-cr-00404 (S.D.N.Y., August 4, 2004), para. 3.
173. Mercator was "his company" in that he was the principal shareholder, board chairman, and chief executive officer. Second Superseding Indictment, U.S. v. James H. Giffen, paras. 2, 4.

received $135 million in both success fees and funds diverted from oil transactions, some of which (at least $20 million) was transmitted directly and through intermediaries into secret Swiss bank accounts held by three senior Kazakh officials. Funds were also used to buy luxury gifts for officials in order to establish and retain Giffen's lucrative business relationships within the nation.[174] Additionally, some money from these deals allegedly went to Giffen, his acquaintances, and certain co-conspirators as kickbacks.[175]

In a sworn statement filed in 2003 seeking the arrest of Giffen, the FBI declared that the investigation had uncovered one such instance of corrupt payments concerning a mid-1990s deal. Mobil Oil Corp. entered into an agreement to purchase a 25 percent interest in the Tengiz oil field at a cost of $1.05 billion.[176] J. Bryan Williams, a close personal friend and business associate of Giffen[177] and senior executive at Mobil, was selected to represent his employer in finalizing the deal with Kazakhstan. Mobil made a side agreement with Mercator; the latter company would receive an additional 5 percent of the sale price ($52.5 million) for "its services to the Republic." Mobil wired the money in three payments between August 3, 2005 and May 17, 2006.[178]

Giffen and his companies and associates were investigated by the United States. Media reports have claimed that the General Prosecutor's Office of Kazakhstan asserted that Giffen had not broken any Kazakh laws and would not face investigation domestically, though such information has not been found in any official statement.[179]

The U.S. investigations had begun in the late 1990s, and the first prosecutions occurred in 2003. They did not conclude until 2010. In 2003 Williams pled guilty to conspiracy to defraud the U.S. Internal Revenue Service and tax evasion on income held in an undisclosed, secret Swiss bank account in the name of Alqi Holdings, Ltd. About $2 million of this income had been obtained as a kickback in connection with the Tengiz deal through Mercator.[180] Williams received a sentence of 46 months imprisonment and was required to make restitution of $3.512 million to the U.S. government.[181]

Giffen was originally charged in 2003 with 62 felonious counts ranging from conspiracy to FCPA violations to money laundering to mail and wire fraud.[182] By the end of his case, Giffen pleaded guilty to one count of failing to disclose control of a Swiss bank

---

174. Second Superseding Indictment, U.S. v. James H. Giffen, paras. 5–6.

175. Second Superseding Indictment, U.S. v. James H. Giffen, para. 6; and Superseding Information, U.S. v. J. Bryan Williams, Case No. 03-cr-406, (S.D. N.Y. June 12, 2003), para. 10.

176. Complaint, U.S. v. James H. Giffen, Case No. 1:03-cr-00404 (S.D.N.Y., March 23, 2003), paras. 7–18.

177. Superseding Information, U.S. v. J. Bryan Williams, para. 3.

178. Complaint, U.S. v. James H. Giffen, paras. 7–18.

179. Sabrina Tavernise, "World Business Briefing: Europe; No Kazakhstan Inquiry on Consultant," *New York Times*, July 11, 2000, http://www.nytimes.com/2000/07/11/business/world-business-briefing -europe-no-kazakhstan-inquiry-on-consultant.html.

180. U.S. DOJ, "Former Mobil Executive Sentenced on Tax Evasion Charges In Connection with Kazakhstan Oil Transactions," press release, September 18, 2003.

181. Amended Judgment, U.S. v. J. Bryan Williams, Case No. 03-cr-406 (S.D. N.Y. October 29, 2003).

182. Original Indictment, U.S. v. James H. Giffen, Case No. 1:03-cr-00404 (S.D.N.Y., April 2, 2003).

account on his income tax return, a misdemeanor, and his judgment required only the payment of a $25 assessment fee.[183] Mercator pleaded guilty to one count of making an unlawful payment to a senior government official of the Republic of Kazakhstan, in violation of the FCPA, and received a fine of $32,000 and an assessment fee of $400.[184]

Given that FCPA enforcement actions over the past decade have entailed increasingly high penalties and natural persons involved are more and more likely to receive significant penalties, including prison terms, this case has invited much scrutiny.[185] This case did, in fact, involve a significant monetary sanction.

Prior to the execution of the plea agreements with Giffen and Mercator, a significant amount of money relevant to this scheme had been frozen and seized by the U.S. government. In May 2007, the United States brought an *in rem* action seeking civil forfeiture of funds in a bank account that had been frozen by the Swiss government.[186] The United States alleged that the funds were traceable to unlawful payments to senior Kazakh officials in connection with the oil and gas transactions arranged by Mercator for Kazakhstan. The court entered a Final Order on June 1, 2009.[187] The terms of the Mercator plea agreement called for, among other things, the renunciation of any claim to these funds:

"The defendant withdraws and relinquishes any and all right, title and interest it may have, directly and indirectly, on any legal, factual or other basis, in any manner-or forum, to the following: Any and all funds formerly on deposit in Account No. 1 0 17789E in the name of Orel Capital Ltd. at Credit Agricole Indosuez bank in Geneva, Switzerland, which funds include approximately $84 million frozen by the Swiss government in or about August 1999, and which funds (a) are the subject of a civil forfeiture action brought by the United States in this District (No. 07 Civ. 3559 (LAP)); and (b) are being used to benefit the citizens of Kazakhstan, pursuant to agreements entered into by the United States and the Republic of Kazakhstan and endorsed as Orders of the Court in the civil forfeiture action."[188]

In 2007, a trilateral MOU was executed among the governments of Kazakhstan, Switzerland, and the United States, by which the aforementioned $84 million was specified for return to Kazakhstan to establish the BOTA Foundation, an independent not-for-profit foundation. The foundation was formally launched in May 2008, with

---

183. Judgment, U.S. v. James H. Giffen, Case No. 1:03-cr-00404 (S.D.N.Y., November 19, 2010).

184. Judgment, U.S. v. Mercator Corporation, Case No. 1:03-cr-00404 (S.D.N.Y., November 22, 2010).

185. See, for instance, Andy Spalding, "Is the Giffen Case America's BAE?," *The FCPA Blog*, August 12, 2010, http://www.fcpablog.com/blog/2010/8/12/is-the-giffen-case-americas-bae.html.

186. U.S. DOJ, "New York Merchant Bank Pleads Guilty to FCPA Violation; Bank Chairman Pleads Guilty to Failing to Disclose Control of Foreign Bank Account," press release, August 6, 2010.

187. Final Order, U.S. v. Approximately $84m on Deposit in Account no. T-94025 in the Name of the Treasury of the Ministry of Finance of the Republic of Kazakhstan, Case No. 2:07-cv-03559 (S.D.N.Y., June 1, 2009).

188. Plea agreement, U.S. v. Mercator Corporation, Case No. 1:03-cr-00404 (S.D.N.Y., August 6, 2010).

the goal of improving the lives of Kazakh children and youth suffering from poverty.[189] The BOTA board of trustees and program manager, with the supervision of the World Bank, oversee financial management of these funds.[190] The Foundation will also benefit from interest earned on the $84 million.[191]

11. Schneider Electric (Lesotho)

This case concerns the settlement of corruption allegations against Schneider Electric SA as part of a larger scandal. A significant number of companies had participated in corrupt activities to secure tenders on the Lesotho Highlands Water Project (LHWP). The intertwining cases make a complex web, but only the Schneider case, which was resolved by settlement, will be addressed here.[192]

Schneider is the descendant of a company founded in 1871 as Spie Batignolles (Spie 1), that became Schneider SA in a 1995 merger and finally known by its present name in 1999.[193] In 1997, Schneider offloaded the Spie Batignolles brand and properties onto a company named Gesilec, which continued to conduct business under that name (Spie 2).[194]

The LHWP, financed in part by the World Bank, was conceived in the 1950s and took shape in the 1980s as one of the largest public sector development projects in Africa at the time. Its purpose was the creation of hydroelectric power–producing dams in Lesotho and high-capacity tunnels to facilitate the export of fresh water to neighboring South Africa.[195] The Lesotho Highlands Development Authority (LHDA) was the main

---

189. "Amended Memorandum of Understanding Among the Governments of the United States of America, the Swiss Confederation, and the Republic of Kazakhstan," May 2008, http://star.worldbank.org /corruption-cases/sites/corruption-cases/files/documents/arw/Kazakhstan_Oil_Switzerland_MOU-CH -US-KZ_BOTA_FDN_2008.pdf.

190. World Bank, "Kazakhstan BOTA Foundation Established," news release no: 2008/07/KZ, June 4, 2008.

191. BOTA Foundation, "Who We Are > Frequently Asked Question 2: What is the origin of the initial capital of the foundation? What amount is it?" http://www.bota.kz/en/index.php. See also from the website the BOTA Foundation's *Independent Auditor's Report and Special Purpose Financial Statements for the Year Ended December 31, 2010.*

192. Though we cannot make any representation as to its accuracy, for informative source materials and a substantial explication of the broader Lesotho Highlands Water Project scandal, see the case study prepared by the Information Portal on Corruption and Governance in Africa (IPOC), http://www.ipocafrica.org/index.php?option=com_content&view=article&id=71&Itemid=66.

193. Judgment, Schneider Electric SA v. Director of Public Prosecutions (CRI/APN/751/2003) [2003] LSHC 150 (11 December 2003), Lesotho High Court, 4–10.

194. Judgment, Schneider Electric SA v. Director of Public Prosecutions, 4–10.

195. World Bank, *Implementation Completion Report: The Kingdom of Lesotho Highlands Water Project Phase 1A (Loan 3393 - LSO),* report no. 1916 (Washington, DC: World Bank, December 13, 1999), ii, para. 2.

implementation agency responsible for all project activities in Lesotho.[196] During the time relevant to this case, Masupha Ephraim Sole served as the CEO of the LHDA.[197]

Irregularities uncovered during an audit undertaken by Ernst & Young in the mid-1990s led to the dismissal of Sole from his position at the LDHA; subsequent civil litigation initiated by Sole would reveal undeclared bank accounts belonging to him in Switzerland.[198] A conviction obtained by Lesotho authorities against Sole (and subsequently upheld on appeal), and a guilty plea agreement entered by Schneider, also in Lesotho, confirm that Schneider provided bribes to Sole in the late 1980s to early 1990s in order to win tenders on construction contracts.

The World Bank assisted Lesotho in its investigation by providing extensive evidentiary support, making Bank staff available for interviews, and connecting the prosecution with various project funding agencies and European Union antifraud officials. Assistance to the legislative process was also offered by the U.S Embassy, which provided the Lesotho judiciary with funding to access Internet resources such as the Lexis-Nexis legal research tool during the course of the proceedings.[199]

The investigation and prosecution of Sole and the other involved parties was led by Guido Penzhorn.[200] Starting in 1998, Penzhorn successfully pursued MLA with France and Switzerland, obtaining access to relevant bank records from these jurisdictions and lauding the "prompt and efficient" Swiss handling of "what eventually became a complex and multi-layered application" that would have to be fought all the way up to the level of the Swiss Federal Appeal Court.[201] Penzhorn noted that the success of the LHWP prosecutions was "largely based on bank records" from this Swiss MLA. Further support from the European Anti-Fraud Office "impacted directly" on the conviction of Schneider.[202]

With possession of these critical records, Penzhorn was then able to get gain the cooperation of one involved conspirator, Jacobus Michiel Du Plooy, who had previously rejected such settlement overtures:

---

196. World Bank, *Implementation Completion Report: The Kingdom of Lesotho*, ii, para. 2.

197. Judgment, Rex v. Ephraim Masupha Sole et al. (CRI/T/111/99) [1999] High Court of Lesotho (May 20, 2002), 18.

198. *Combating Multilateral Development Bank Corruption: U.S. Treasury Role and Internal Efforts, Hearing Before the Senate Committee on Foreign Relations*, 108th Cong. (204) (testimony of Guido Penzhorn SC, "Comments on the current Lesotho Bribery Prosecutions," July 21, 2004, para. 3).

199. "Case Study Lesotho: Demonstrating the Need to Support Investigations and Prosecutions," in *The International Financial Institutions: A Call for Change, Report to the Senate Committee on Foreign Relations*, 2011th Cong. (March 10, 2010), 34.

200. *Combating Multilateral Development Bank Corruption: U.S. Treasury Role and Internal Efforts, Hearing Before the Senate Committee on Foreign Relations*, para. 3.

201. *Combating Multilateral Development Bank Corruption: U.S. Treasury Role and Internal Efforts, Hearing Before the Senate Committee on Foreign Relations*, para. 11.

202. *Combating Multilateral Development Bank Corruption: U.S. Treasury Role and Internal Efforts, Hearing Before the Senate Committee on Foreign Relations*, paras. 11, 12.

In the Du Plooy case, several offers were made to Du Plooy to turn Crown witness. Each offer was declined. (Such offers were also made to other accused. This was done as part of our overall mandate to not only secure convictions but to get to the bottom of this whole mess.) It was only when all the preliminary issues had been decided in favor of the prosecution and Mr. Du Plooy now literally had his back against the wall and facing a long term of imprisonment that he came forward, tendering a plea of guilty and offering to cooperate.[203]

Schneider originally fought the charges with a motion claiming that, due to various mergers and divestitures, it was not the appropriate Spie Batignolles descendant to be charged in the bribery matter. Interestingly, this defense, asserting that all assets and liabilities had been divested to Spie 2, now owned by Gesilac, left Schneider at risk due to representations made at the time of the transfer of the Spie Batignolles identity.[204] Justice Nomngcongo rejected the company's efforts, asserting that Schneider was materially the same company that had performed the corrupt acts as Spie 1.[205] Facing both the criminal case in Lesotho and a potential legal challenge by Spie 2, Schneider quickly agreed to settle the matter, pleading guilty to 16 counts of bribery on February 25, 2004.[206]

This case is unusual among international settlements investigated in this study in that (i) it was pursued by the nation whose official had been bribed, (ii) the bribe recipient was a primary and initial focus of prosecution, and (iii) the conviction of the official, affirmed in the court of appeal, was concluded in advance of settlement with the bribe-giving company. Penzhorn underscores the import of the Sole trial as providing a ruling necessary for the successful resolution of Schneider (and all such efforts to prosecute common law bribery in multinational bribery cases). To wit, Justice Cullinan held that "the country where the recipient of the bribe is a public official has jurisdiction, irrespective of where the bribe agreement was entered into or where the bribe money was paid. It is the integrity of that country's institutions that are undermined and which accordingly suffers the harmful effects."[207]

Lesotho imposed a penalty of M 10,000,000 (about $1,400,000) on Schneider. At the time of this writing, the disposition of these funds after receipt is unknown.[208]

---

203. Guido Penzhorn, "Three Strikes against Graft: Assessing the Impact of High-Profile Corruption" (presentation made at the Institute for Security Studies Seminar, March 15, 2004), para. 17, http://journal.probeinternational.org/2004/03/15/three-strikes-against-graft/.
204. Judgment, Schneider Electric SA v. Director of Public Prosecutions, 8–9.
205. Judgment, Schneider Electric SA v. Director of Public Prosecutions, 8–9.
206. *Combating Multilateral Development Bank Corruption: U.S. Treasury Role and Internal Efforts, Hearing Before the Senate Committee on Foreign Relations*, para. 6.
207. Guido Penzhorn, "Three Strikes against Graft," para. 6, http://journal.probeinternational.org/2004/03/15/three-strikes-against-graft/.
208. *Combating Multilateral Development Bank Corruption: U.S. Treasury Role and Internal Efforts, Hearing Before the Senate Committee on Foreign Relations*, para. 6.

12. Siemens AG (Germany, Greece, Italy, Nigeria, United States, and others)

Siemens is a German multinational company that engages in private and public sector business around the world in telecommunications, power generation, transportation, and medicine, among other areas.[209] Upon settlement of charges against Siemens AG by the United States (in which Siemens accepted guilt)[210] on December 15, 2008, U.S. authorities stated that "for [Siemens'] business operations overseas, bribery was nothing less than standard operating procedure," indicating that "from the 1990s through 2007, Siemens engaged in a systematic and widespread effort to make and to hide hundreds of millions of dollars in bribe payments across the globe."[211] Between 2001 and 2007 (Siemens became listed on the New York Stock Exchange in 2001), Siemens and its affiliates paid out and concealed over $800 million in bribes using secret slush funds, shell companies, phony consulting fees, and falsified records.[212] From at least 1999, if not earlier, Siemens AG has been investigated for foreign bribery by a variety of jurisdictions.[213]

Proceedings in various countries have resulted in at least five settlements relevant to this study. First, in November 2006, Siemens entered into a *pattegiamento* in Milan, Italy. Second, German authorities entered into two separate settlements with Siemens. On October 4, 2007, the Munich prosecutor's office entered into a settlement with Siemens for $201 million, and on December 15, 2008, Siemens simultaneously resolved allegations with the United States (both DOJ and SEC) and Germany (Munich prosecutor's office) for an additional $395 million. Third, In July, 2009, the World Bank settled with a Russian affiliate of Siemens that agreed to pledge $100 million to settle administrative allegations of fraud in World Bank projects. Fourth, on or about November 22, 2010, Nigeria agreed to withdraw charges in an out-of-court settlement with Siemens for an unspecified large sum. Finally, in April 2012, Greece announced that a settlement had been reached with Siemens, requiring (and receiving) ratification from the Parliament of the Hellenic Republic. It should be noted that the wide scope of Siemens business activities generated a multiplicity of investigations and legal actions elsewhere, including in Australia; Austria; Azerbaijan; China; Israel; Liechtenstein; Norway; Switzerland; and Taiwan, China. None of these inquiries are as of yet known to have resulted in enforcement actions or settlements.

---

209. Statement of Offense, U.S. v. Siemens Aktiengesellschaft, Case No. 08-cr-367 (D.D.C. December 15, 2008), para. 1.

210. Statement of Offense, U.S. v. Siemens Aktiengesellschaft, Defendant's Acceptance.

211. U.S. DOJ, "Transcript of Press Conference Announcing Siemens AG and Three Subsidiaries Plead Guilty to Foreign Corrupt Practices Act Violations," transcript no. 08-1112, December 15, 2008.

212. U.S. DOJ, "Transcript of Press Conference Announcing Siemens AG and Three Subsidiaries Plead Guilty." It is also important to note that prior to Germany's implementation of the OECD Convention in 1999 companies were not prohibited by German law from participating in overseas bribery or taking tax deductions for bribe payments to foreign officials; Statement of Offense, U.S. v. Siemens Aktiengesellschaft, Case No. 08-cr-367-RJL (D.D.C., December 15, 2008), paras. 36–37.

213. Statement of Offense, U.S. v. Siemens Aktiengesellschaft, para. 37.

First, beginning with Italy, prosecutors in Milan had been investigating Siemens since about 2003 concerning bribes paid by Siemens AG to win contracts from the Italian company Enel.[214] In November, 2006, Siemens reported an end to the Italian legal proceedings in the Enel matter, when Siemens AG and two charged, former employees entered into a *patteggiamento* with the Milan public prosecutor.[215] Siemens agreed to pay a €0.5 million fine and to give up €6.121 million of profit relating to the Enel contracts. Siemens also accepted a one-year debarment, a ban prohibiting it from entering into contracts with the Italian public administration. This part of the *patteggiamento* was discharged through the one-year ban imposed on Siemens by preliminary injunction that expired on May 14, 2005. The *patteggiamento* was endorsed by the Court of Milan on July 25, 2006, and entered into force on November 11, 2006.

Second, with respect to the United States and Germany, a payment of €201 million was imposed based on a settlement related to the telecommunications group. On December 15, 2008, the U.S. DOJ, SEC, and the Munich public prosecutor's office announced a major coordinated, international, three-agency settlement of Siemens matters not previously settled in a 2007 German arrangement with the Siemens telecommunications group.[216] In its plea agreement with the U.S. DOJ, Siemens AG accepted responsibility for, among other things, acts occurring between 2000 and 2002 wherein four Siemens entities—Siemens SAS of France, Siemens Sanayi ve Ticaret A.S. of Turkey, Osram Middle East FZE, and Gas Turbine Technologies S.p.A.—had inflated contract tenders in order to provide 10 percent kickbacks to Iraqi officials in the context of the UN OFFP.[217] The United States fined Siemens AG $448.5 million for violating the internal controls and the books and records provisions of the FCPA.[218] The SEC required Siemens AG to disgorge $350 million in illicit profits to settle an SEC civil suit.[219] The same day, using administrative procedure under German law, the Munich prosecutor's office entered into a settlement in which Siemens paid fines and disgorged sums totaling €395 million.[220] The German cases covered profits made in the medical area and in transportation systems in Maracaibo and Valencia (República Bolivariana de Venezuela) and in China, namely, for specific instances of bribery different from the ones prosecuted in the United States. In both

---

214. Statement of Offense, U.S. v. Siemens Aktiengesellschaft, paras. 51–52.
215. Legal Proceedings, *Annual Report, 2007*, Siemens AG, 162–63; *Penale contemporaneo* (Italian legal review, specialized in criminal law), http://www.penalecontemporaneo.it/upload/Trib.%20Milano,%20 25.7.2006%20_sent._%20GUP%20Varanelli%20_Confisca_.pdf.
216. U.S. DOJ, "Siemens AG and Three Subsidiaries Plead Guilty to Foreign Corrupt Practices Act Violations and Agree to Pay $450m in Combined Criminal Fines," press release, December 15, 2008.
217. Statement of Offense, U.S. v. Siemens Aktiengesellschaft, Case No. 08-cr-367 (D.D.C., December 15, 2008), paras. 95-98.
218. U.S. DOJ, "Siemens AG and Three Subsidiaries Plead Guilty to Foreign Corrupt Practices Act Violations and Agree to Pay $450m in Combined Criminal Fines," press release, December 15, 2008.
219. Simultaneously in the United States, Siemens settled bribery allegations against three other Siemens subsidiaries: Siemens S.A. of Argentina, Siemens S.A. of Venezuela, and Siemens Bangladesh Limited. Each subsidiary admitted to conspiracy to commit bribery within their respective nations and paid an additional $500,000 fine. See U.S. DOJ, "Siemens AG and Three Subsidiaries Plead Guilty."
220. U.S. DOJ, "Siemens AG and Three Subsidiaries Plead Guilty."

settlements, German prosecutors used administrative law, since the German Criminal Code does not provide for liability of legal persons.

Third, in July 2009, the World Bank settled by agreement administrative allegations of fraud in the World Bank–financed Moscow Urban Transport Project. Siemens (i) agreed voluntarily to refrain from bidding on Bank projects for two years, (ii) agreed that its Russian affiliate would be debarred from World Bank contracting for four years, and finally (iii) pledged $100 million to combat corruption, an amount over which the World Bank Group holds audit and veto rights.[221]

Fourth, in late 2010 Nigeria, a country whose officials had been bribed, agreed to a settlement. Nigeria had filed criminal charges against Siemens and its employees. In exchange for the company entering into an out-of-court settlement in which Siemens made a payment to Nigeria in the "mid-double-digit Euro million range," Nigeria agreed to an end to all current and future actions, including "the initiation of any criminal, civil, or other actions—such as a debarment" against Siemens and its employees.[222]

Finally, a unique development in enforcement of antibribery by the use of settlements is the historic "Settlement Agreement between the Hellenic Republic and Siemens" (called here, the Settlement). After a lengthy negotiations process, the Hellenic Republic (Greece) and Siemens announced an accord in April 2012. Since the settlement was negotiated and conducted by the legislative branch rather than under the authority of courts or prosecutors, it was extralegal by its very nature. Beyond the vastness and complexity of the issues addressed, it occurred in a country with no framework for settlements within the judicial system. The mechanism for the settlement was ratification by the Greek Parliament and entry into effect through publication in the Official Government Gazette which occurred in April 2012.

In this settlement, Siemens agreed to (i) a waiver of €80 million in obligations owed by the Greek government to Siemens, with the explicit acknowledgement that this write-off would not constitute a donation for the purposes of Greek tax law; (ii) the provision of €90 million to finance various entities and endeavors advancing the Greek public interest (including the support of Greece's anticorruption platform); (iii) a further investment of €100 million to Siemens' activities within Greece; and (iv) a structured plan to consider and develop further investment opportunities within Greece. Siemens further agreed to pay all legal expenses.

---

221. World Bank, "Siemens to Pay $100m to Fight Corruption as Part of World Bank Group Settlement," press release no. 2009/001/EXT, July 2, 2009.

222. Mohammed Bello Adoke, "2010 Ministerial Media Briefing on the Activities of the Federal Ministry of Justice," December 22, 2010, 11, paras. 36–40, provided to the study by the Nigerian Economic and Financial Crimes Commission; and Siemens AG, *Third Quarter Results FY 2011: Legal Proceedings*, July 28, 2011, http://www.siemens.com/press/pool/de/events/2011/corporate/2011-q3/2011-q3-legal-proceedings-e.pdf.

Significantly, the matter being settled in Greece was defined quite broadly as "any and all matters, claims, and allegations to date, whether known or unknown relating to corruption; payments to (or promises to pay) third parties; other illegal activities on the part of Siemens, including without limitation all matters investigated by any Greek, German, or U.S. authority or [Siemens' law firm], including matters covered by Siemens' 2008 settlement with the German authorities and the SEC and DOJ in the United States." Absent clarification to the contrary, this settlement appears to give Siemens blanket immunity from any Greek enforcement action for any and all prior bad acts the company has ever potentially committed prior to this agreement coming into effect.

This broad immunity provision mirrors the one allowed for in the settlement reached between the U.K.'s Serious Fraud Office and BAE Systems Plc in 2010, which invited the censure of the presiding justice in that case.[223] Such a term runs contrary to the more specifically targeted immunity (covering only fully disclosed misconduct known to a government) that one most often sees in U.S. DOJ settlement agreements. However, one particular difference between these two arrangements is that Siemens must inform the Greek authorities (independently or upon request) of any other facts deemed relevant to ongoing criminal prosecutions relating to *individuals* who may have had a criminal role in the conduct being settled and who have not been immunized from prosecution. Contrast that with the BAE matter, wherein the SFO agreed that it "shall not prosecute any person in relation to conduct other than conduct connected with the Czech Republic or Hungary."[224]

13. Statoil (Norway and United States)

Statoil ASA is state-owned Norwegian petroleum enterprise that has been partially privatized.[225] In the early 2000s, Statoil sought to obtain a contract to develop the South Pars oil and gas field in Iran.[226] In late 2001, an Iranian official approached Statoil and proposed a consultancy arrangement whereby the company would "(i) pay a 'success fee' payable upon Statoil's being awarded a participation interest in the development of the South Pars Project; (ii) provide money for 'charities' of the Iranian Official's choice;

---

223. See Sentencing Remarks of Justice Bean, Regina v. BAE Systems Plc, para. 5: "The Settlement Agreement is, with respect, loosely and perhaps hastily drafted. In paragraph 6 'any person' is not defined, and paragraph 10 is not, at least expressly, confined to conduct preceding the agreement. But the heart of the matter is paragraph 8, whereby the SFO agreed that there would be 'no further investigation or prosecutions of any member of the BAE Systems Group for any conduct preceding 5 February 2010.' It is relatively common for a prosecuting authority to agree not to prosecute a defendant in respect of specified crimes which are admitted and listed in the agreement: this is done, for example, where the defendant is an informer who will give important evidence against co-defendants. *But I am surprised to find a prosecutor granting a blanket indemnity for all offenses committed in the past, whether disclosed or otherwise.* The U.S. Department of Justice did not do so in this case: it agreed not to prosecute further for past offenses which had been disclosed to it." [Emphasis added.]
224. See Sentencing Remarks of Justice Bean, Regina v. BAE Systems Plc, para. 2(6).
225. Statoil ASA, *Annual Report and Accounts 2004* (Stavanger, Norway: Statoil, March 9, 2005), 106.
226. Deferred Prosecution Agreement, U.S. v. Statoil ASA, Case No. 06-cr-960 (S.D.N.Y.), October 9, 2006, 1.

and (iii) make payments through an offshore company."[227] The identity of this Iranian official was later confirmed as Mehdi Hashemi Rafsanjani, and Statoil later admitted that he "must probably be considered a public official in Iran," being both son to a former president of the country and the then-head of an Iranian state oil company subsidiary, the Iranian Fuel Optimizing Organization.[228]

In early 2002, Statoil signed a $15,200,000 contract[229] to develop the gas fields with Horton Investment Ltd.,[230] a Turks and Caicos Islands company registered to an in-name-only owner in London.[231] These machinations allowed Statoil to avoid identifying Rafsanjani, as disclosing such a relationship might have imperiled Statoil's ability to obtain Iranian business.[232] Statoil later admitted that as a result of this contract, Rafsanjani used his influence to provide Statoil with nonpublic information and bid tenders concerning Iranian energy projects.[233] In October 2002, Statoil received the contract to develop the South Pars oil and gas field.[234] In 2002 and 2003, Statoil paid invoices to Horton amounting to $5,200,000, before the contract was terminated when the illegal conduct came to light.[235]

On September 6, 2003, the Norwegian newspaper *Dagens Næringsliv* disclosed the Horton contract.[236] Within the month, Statoil's board chairman, CEO, and head of international exploration and production each resigned, and the contract was terminated.[237]

On September 11, 2003, the Norwegian National Authority for Investigation and Prosecution of Economic and Environmental Crime (Økokrim) filed preliminary charges against Statoil for violating Norway's anticorruption statutes.[238] During the period of alleged misconduct the Norwegian penal code had been amended, so acts prior to July 4, 2003, fell under Section 128 of the penal code (amended and entered into force in 1999 in an implementation of the OECD Anti-Bribery Convention).[239] Acts after this date came under Section 276 a and b of the revised law.[240] On September 11, Økokrim also raided Statoil's offices for evidence.[241]

---

227. Deferred Prosecution Agreement, U.S. v. Statoil ASA, 3.
228. Statoil ASA, "Keiserud Report: No Basis for Criminal Liability," press release, Stavanger, Norway, June 18, 2004.
229. Deferred Prosecution Agreement, U.S. v. Statoil ASA, 3.
230. Økokrim, "Statoil-saken," press release (in Norwegian), Oslo, April 22, 2009.
231. U.S. SEC, Cease-and-Desist Order, in the Matter of Statoil ASA, Administrative Proceeding File No. 3-12453, October 13, 2006, 2.
232. Deferred Prosecution Agreement, U.S. v. Statoil ASA, 3.
233. Deferred Prosecution Agreement, U.S. v. Statoil ASA, 3.
234. Information, U.S. v. Statoil, ASA, Case No. 06-cr-960 (S.D.N.Y.), October 13, 2006, para. 12.
235. Deferred Prosecution Agreement, U.S. v. Statoil ASA, 6–7.
236. Økokrim, "Statoil-saken."
237. Statoil ASA, "Statoil Accepts Økokrim Penalty in the Horton Case," press release, October 14, 2004.
238. Statoil ASA, "Horton Agreement: Statoil Will Assess Penalty Notice," stock market announcement, June 29, 2004.
239. OECD *Phase 3 Report on Implementing the OECD Anti-Bribery Convention in Norway* (Paris: OECD, 2000), 1.
240. Statoil ASA, "Horton Agreement."
241. U.S. SEC, Cease-and-Desist Order, in the Matter of Statoil ASA, 7.

In June of 2004, Økokrim concluded its investigation and prosecution by issuing penalty notices to Statoil for NKr 20,000,000 (an estimated $3,000,000) and to former Statoil employee Richard Hubbard for NKr 200,000 (an estimated $30,000) for Section 276c violations (trading-in-influence) of the anti-bribery law.[242] Statoil did not contest the orders and paid the fines.[243]

On June 29, 2004, Statoil issued a release stating that Økokrim, having determined that it was unable to demonstrate that the "company has paid bribes to Iranian decision makers with the intention of securing commercial advantages in Iran," had altered the charge from foreign bribery to a trading–in-influence (Section 276 c) offense. Statoil argued that Økokrim found that the real purpose of the suspect agreement was to influence decision makers in the oil and gas industry for the benefit of Statoil but that there was no basis for claiming any such influence was exercised.[244] While in its evaluation of Norway the OECD's Working Group on Bribery expressed concern about this decision by Økokrim to downgrade the offense (a foreign bribery offense conveys much steeper penalties), the working group also noted questions about whether the person bribed could have been considered a foreign public official and acknowledged some questions about "whether extensive cooperation is needed from the foreign public official's country to establish that the person bribed was a foreign public official."[245]

Concurrent with the efforts of Norway, the U.S. DOJ and SEC opened investigations into Statoil violations of the FCPA.[246] Statoil settled with both agencies, entering into a DPA with the DOJ that included a $10.5 million fine and accepting a cease-and-desist order from the SEC.

In setting its fine, the U.S. authorities took into account the penalties already paid by Statoil in Norway. In light of the fine paid to Økokrim, the U.S. DOJ reduced by $3 million the ordered penalty of $10.5 million payable to the U.S. Treasury.[247] As usual under DPAs, Statoil was required to retain an independent compliance consultant for the three-year term of the agreement.[248] After the three-year term of the DPA ended, the charges against Statoil were dismissed by the U.S. DOJ.[249]

14. TSKJ Consortium (Nigeria, United Kingdom, and United States)

In order to secure contracts related to the construction of liquefied natural gas (LNG) facilities on Bonney Island, Nigeria, a group of energy concerns formed a joint venture

---

242. Økokrim, "Statoil-saken"; Statoil ASA, "Statoil Accepts Økokrim Penalty in the Horton Case," press release, October 14, 2004.
243. Økokrim, "Statoil-saken."
244. Statoil ASA, "Horton Agreement."
245. Government of Norway, *Follow-Up Report on the Implementation of the Phase 2 Recommendations* (Paris: OECD, 2007), para. 8.
246. U.S. SEC, Cease-and-Desist Order, In the Matter of Statoil ASA, paras. 7–16.
247. Deferred Prosecution Agreement, U.S. v. Statoil ASA, 14–15.
248. Deferred Prosecution Agreement, U.S. v. Statoil ASA, 7.
249. Nolle Prosequi, U.S. v. Statoil ASA, Case No. 06-cr-960 (S.D.N.Y.), November 18, 2009.

called the TSKJ Consortium. The name was based on the first initial of the member companies (each of which held a 25 percent interest):

- Technip SA, a French company[250]
- Snamprogetti Netherlands B.V., a subsidiary of the Italian company ENI SpA and later sold with an indemnity agreement to Saipem SpA[251]
- Kellogg, Brown, and Root LLC (Kellogg, Brown & Root), a U.S. company formerly known and incorporated as KBR Inc., a subsidiary of the U.S. company Halliburton Co. and comprising, as a limited liability partner, the U.K.-based M.W. Kellogg Ltd. (Kellogg),[252] another Halliburton subsidiary
- JGC Corporation, a Japanese company formerly called Japan Gas Co.[253]

To win the LNG contracts, which had been valued at roughly $6 billion, the members of TSKJ conspired to funnel over $180 million worth of bribes to Nigerian public officials.[254] Acting through a subsidiary shell company in Madeira called LNG services, TSKJ entered into contractual consulting agreements with agents who used two companies, Tri-star Investment Ltd. and Marubeni Inc., to serve as conduits for the bribe money.[255] Tri-star was alleged to have been used to route $132 million to high-level Nigerian officials and Marubeni $50 million for lower level officials.[256] (How these activities originally came to the attention of authorities is not known.)

According to the U.S. DOJ, cooperative inquiries were jointly conducted in France, Italy, Switzerland, the United Kingdom, and the United States.[257] These investigations resulted in a significant number of legal actions brought forth against those persons and companies alleged to have been involved, and most of those actions that had been completed at the time of writing were concluded through settlement agreements.

The first charges in this case were leveled by the U.S. government against Kellogg, Brown, & Root executive Albert Jack Stanley in 2008 and were settled by guilty plea on September 3 of the same year.[258] Stanley pled guilty to two counts—conspiracy to violate the FCPA and conspiracy to commit mail and wire fraud—and agreed to cooperate in

---

250. Deferred Prosecution Agreement, U.S. v. Technip S.A., Case No. 10-cr-439 (S.D. Tex), June 28, 2010.
251. Deferred Prosecution Agreement, U.S. v. Snamprogretti, Case No. 10-cr-460 (S.D. Tex), July 7, 2010.
252. See Plea Agreement, U.S. v. KBR, Case No. 09-cr-071 (S.D. Tex), Feb 11, 2009; and U.K. SFO, "MW Kellogg Ltd. to Pay 7m Pounds in SFO High Court action," press release, 16 February 2011.
253. Deferred Prosecution Agreement, U.S. v. JGC Corp., Case No. 11-cr-260 (S.D. Tex), April 6, 2011.
254. U.S. DOJ, "Former Officer and Director of Global Engineering and Construction Company Pleads Guilty to Foreign Bribery and Kickback Charges," press release, September 3, 2008.
255. U.S. DOJ, "UK Solicitor Pleads Guilty for Role in Bribing Nigerian Government Officials as Part of KBR Joint Venture Scheme," press release, March 11, 2011.
256. U.S. DOJ, "UK Solicitor Pleads Guilty."
257. U.S. DOJ, "Former Officer and Director of Global Engineering and Construction Company Pleads Guilty."
258. U.S. DOJ, "Former Officer and Director of Global Engineering and Construction Company Pleads Guilty."

the continuing investigation.[259] Stanley's plea agreement initially called for a seven-year prison sentence and the payment of $10.8 million restitution to his former employer, being the victim of the second count. It was anticipated that the restitution would be satisfied by the liquidation of several Credit Suisse bank accounts in Switzerland that Stanley holds in the name of various companies.[260] Stanley additionally consented to an order restraining him from further conduct in violation of relevant SEC provisions.[261] He eventually received a lesser sentence.[262]

After Stanley agreed to testify as a cooperating witness, all the TSKJ partners reached settlement terms with the U.S. government regarding FCPA violations. Kellogg, Brown, & Root reached a plea agreement with the U.S. DOJ. SEC settlements were reached with KBR Inc. and Halliburton on February 11, 2009, resulting in $579 million total monetary penalties and disgorgement.[263] JGC accepted a DPA with the DOJ on April 6, 2011, resulting in $218.8 million total penalties.[264] Technip accepted a DPA with the DOJ and an SEC settlement on June 28, 2010, resulting in $338 million total penalties and disgorgement.[265] Finally, Snamprogetti accepted a DPA with the DOJ, and SEC settlements were reached with both Snamprogetti and parent company ENI on July 7, 2010, resulting in $365 million total penalties and disgorgement.[266]

Individuals charged with FCPA violations due to their roles in the bribery scheme include Wojciech J. Chodan, a sales vice president at Kellogg and consultant who reported to Stanley, and Jeffrey Tesler, an agent of the TSKJ consortium.[267] Though co-indicted on February 17, 2009, they did not settle the charges against them until after the TSKJ partners had concluded agreements.[268] On December 6, 2010, Chodan accepted a plea agreement that required, among other terms, the forfeiture of illicit funds originating from the scheme held in Swiss bank accounts amounting

---

259. Plea Agreement, U.S. v. Stanley, Case No. 08-cr-597 (S.D. Tex, 2008), September 3, 2008.

260. Plea Agreement, U.S. v. Stanley.

261. Consent of Defendant, SEC v. Stanley, Case No. 08-cr-2680 (S.D. Tex, 2008), September 3, 2008.

262. On February 23, 2012, Stanley was sentenced to 30 months in prison for conspiring to violate the FCPA and also ordered to pay the $10.8 million in restitution to KBR (as the victim of the kickback scheme). U.S. DOJ, "Former Chairman and CEO of Kellogg, Brown & Root Inc. Sentenced to 30 Months in Prison for Foreign Bribery and Kickback Schemes," February 23, 2013.

263. See Plea Agreement, U.S. v. KBR; Consent of Defendant KBR, SEC v. Halliburton & KBR, Case No. 4:09-cr-399 (S.D. Tex.), February 11, 2009; and Consent of Defendant Halliburton and Final Order, SEC v. Halliburton & KBR, Case No. 4:09-cr-399 (S.D. Tex.), February 11, 2009.

264. Deferred Prosecution Agreement, U.S. v. JGC.

265. See Deferred Prosecution Agreement, United States v. Technip S.A.; and U.S. SEC, "SEC Charges Technip with Foreign Bribery and Related Accounting Violations—Technip to Pay $98m in Disgorgement and Prejudgment Interest; Company Also to Pay a Criminal Penalty of $240m," litigation release no. 21578, June 28, 2010.

266. See Deferred Prosecution Agreement, U.S. v. Snamprogretti; and U.S. SEC, "SEC v. ENI, S.p.A. and Snamprogetti Netherlands, B.V.," litigation release no. 21588, July 7, 2010.

267. Indictment, U.S. v. Tesler and Chodan, Case No. 09-cr-098 (S.D. Tex.), February 17, 2009.

268. Indictment, U.S. v. Tesler and Chodan.

to $726,885.[269] On March 11, 2011, Tesler, the controller of Gibraltar-based Tri-Star, also pled guilty to conspiracy to violate and violation of the FCPA after losing a lengthy extradition proceeding in the United Kingdom.[270] His plea agreement called for the forfeiture of $148,964,568, which is at the time of writing the largest amount ever ordered of a natural person for FCPA-related offenses.[271]

On February 16, 2011, the U.K. SFO announced that a settlement action taken in High Court resulted in an order, under Part 5 of the Proceeds of Crime Act 2002, for Kellogg to forfeit £7,028,077. While Kellogg was not accused of participation in the Bonney Island scheme, this amount represented share dividend income attributable to illicit venture.[272]

The outcomes of investigations in France, Italy, and Switzerland are unknown at this time.

Nigeria, while not credited by the U.S. DOJ in any available press releases as having cooperated with the FCPA investigations of TSKJ, is known to have conducted its own investigation of the Bonney Island bribery scheme. In the course of this inquiry, charges were filed against TSKJ members and other individuals thought to be complicit in the bribery enterprise.

Halliburton, Snamprogetti, JGC, and Technip have all released statements or disclosures announcing settlement of the charges with Nigeria, including a combined total return of $127.5 million comprising penalties, attorneys' fees, and other expenses,[273] as has been publicly acknowledged by the Federal Government of Nigeria (FGN).[274]

The following statement by Halliburton is typical of these releases except for the noteworthy final provision, in which the company has additionally agreed to help the Nigerian government attempt recovery of funds held in Switzerland.

> Pursuant to this agreement, all lawsuits and charges against KBR and Halliburton corporate entities and associated persons have been withdrawn, the FGN agreed not to bring any further criminal charges or civil claims against those entities or persons, and Halliburton agreed to pay $32.5 million to the FGN and to pay an additional $2.5 million for FGN's

---

269. Plea Agreement [as to Defendant Chodan], U.S. v. Chodan, Case No. 09-cr-098 (S.D. Tex.), December 6, 2010. Chodan was sentenced to one year of probation and ordered to pay a $200,000 fine.

270. U.S. DOJ, "UK Solicitor Pleads Guilty."

271. U.S. DOJ, "UK Solicitor Pleads Guilty." Tesler was sentenced to 21 months in prison followed by two months of supervised release and was sentenced to pay the agreed amount.

272. U.K. SFO, "MW Kellogg Ltd. to pay 7m pounds in SFO High Court action."

273. Halliburton, "Halliburton Confirms Agreement to Settle with Federal Government of Nigeria," press release, Houston, TX, December 21, 2010; Saipem, "Snamprogetti Netherlands BV enters agreement with Federal Government of Nigeria," press release, Milan, December 20, 2010; JGC Co., *Consolidated Financial Statements Summary for the Period Ending March 31, 2011,* (Tokyo: JGC Co., May 13, 2011), 2; and Technip SA, *Reference Document 2010 Including the Annual Financial Report,* Autorité des marchés financiers filing (Paris: Technip SA, March 24, 2011), 175.

274. Mohammed Bello Adoke, "2010 Ministerial Media Briefing on the Activities of the Federal Ministry of Justice," December 22, 2010, 11, paras. 36–40.

attorneys' fees and other expenses. Among other provisions, Halliburton agreed to provide reasonable assistance in the FGN's effort to recover amounts frozen in a Swiss bank account of a former TSKJ agent and affirmed a continuing commitment with regard to corporate governance. Any charges related to this settlement will be reflected in discontinued operations.[275]

At the time of writing, the status of this asset recovery effort is unknown. From the wording of the statement, and lacking official documentation from Nigeria, we are unable to discern if these funds are the same that the U.S. government has asserted a claim over in the cases of Tesler, Chodan, and/or Stanley or if instead they represent other funds that might have been held by other parties.

---

275. Halliburton, "Halliburton Confirms Agreement to Settle."

Appendix I. Forms of Legal Remedies Relevant to Foreign Bribery Cases

Appendix 1 describes the basic forms of monetary sanctions that may be the components of a settlement: confiscation (also known as forfeiture), compensation, disgorgement, restitution, fines, and reparations and their variations. While labeling these forms carries some limitations as the terms vary from jurisdiction to jurisdiction, defining these terms provides a context for the case examples discussed in this study. In most instances, whether a case is settled or completes the full criminal or other enforcement process, these same basic financial components will be used. Some components, such as restitution and reparations, will generally be paid to the injured parties (or "victims"), and others, such as fines, will generally be paid to the state. For each term we provide a basic definition, an explanation of where that money generally goes, and an example from the case studies in chapter 6.

1. Confiscation: Criminal, Civil, and Administrative

Confiscation is the permanent deprivation of assets by order of a court or other competent authority. In some jurisdictions, it is called *forfeiture*. Confiscation of the proceeds of bribery (or any offense) may be ordered whether or not any loss or other disadvantage has been incurred by the wronged party, which may include governments of a bribed official, competitors, and consumers, among others. There are three basic kinds of confiscation: (i) criminal confiscation, (ii) non-conviction-based confiscation (NCB), and (iii) administrative confiscation. Criminal confiscation requires a criminal conviction by trial or guilty plea establishing guilt beyond a reasonable doubt or sufficient to "intimately convince" the judge or the jury. Once a defendant is convicted, a final order of confiscation can be entered by the court, often as part of the sentence. NCB confiscation usually involves obtaining an order for forfeiture of a specific piece of property. Administrative confiscation occurs through an administrative process as established by relevant authorities, without the need for a conviction or even a judicial determination.[1]

Generally, confiscation is paid to the prosecuting state treasury, unless the confiscation order specifies that a portion of it shall paid to victims, such as a confiscation order that

---

[1]. See Jean-Pierre Brun, Clive Scott, Kevin M. Stephenson, and Larissa Gray, *Asset Recovery Handbook: A Guide for Practitioners* (hereinafter ARH) (Washington, DC: World Bank, 2011), 6.1.3., http://star.worldbank.org/star/publication/asset-recovery-handbook.

includes a subpart for compensation. As noted in chapter 4, parties must meet certain criteria in order to be considered victims.

The Mabey & Johnson case provides an example of confiscation. The company was subject to a confiscation order of £1,100,000 as well as a fine, costs, and reparations.

2. Compensation: Criminal and Civil

In both common law and civil law jurisdictions, the court may issue a compensation order in a criminal case where a victim has been identified in the proceedings and has proved that it has suffered damage.[2] The compensation order (like a restitution order) will often form part of the confiscation and will be paid out before other penalties are paid.

The prosecuting authority can choose, on behalf of victims, to pursue compensation through a civil process. The civil remedy can also be pursued through private law suits, in which a victim country or a nongovernmental organization (NGO) can engage a private counsel to bring the civil claim.[3] The civil claim through tort and contract damages are paid to compensate a plaintiff for loss, injury, or harm directly caused by a breach of duty (including criminal law), immoral conduct, and precontractual fault.[4] Beyond the government of the bribed official (or an NGO), plaintiffs may include, for example, harmed consumers, shareholders, or unsuccessful bidders.[5] Where a bribery of the public official has occurred, the plaintiff generally has to prove the defendant's breach of duty, actual damage, and the causal link between the offense and the damage or assets. Proof of breach of duty in a tort claim in the United Kingdom, for example, would be made through a statement provided by the attorney general of the victim state.[6]

3. Disgorgement: Civil Remedy Variation on Confiscation

Disgorgement is a species of civil remedy in common law jurisdictions. Unlike confiscation, this remedy is not derived from statute but from the courts' equitable power to correct unjust inequality. Disgorgement is the forced giving up of profits obtained

---

2. There can be variance in the ways in which different jurisdictions interpret legal remedies. For example, the Swiss use of a compensation order is akin to confiscation in some jurisdictions and disgorgement in the United States.

3. The recent case of Transparency International in France is an example. See chapter 4, box 4.2.

4. ARH, 169–171.

5. See, e.g., Korea Supply Co. v. Lockheed Martin Corp., 29 Cal. 4th 1134, 63 P.3d 937 (Cal. 2003). In this case, a competitor who did not win a contract because the winner paid bribes to Korean officials established a tort claim. See generally Olaf Meyer, ed., *The Civil Law Consequences of Corruption* (Sinzheim, Germany: Nomos, 2009).

6. An example is the case against former president of Zambia Frederick Chiluba in the United Kingdom, in which the court granted a global order to freeze over £500 million worth of assets.

illegally. A court may order wrongdoers to pay back illegal profits, with interest, to prevent unjust enrichment. It is not meant to be punitive. In an enforcement action, disgorgement is paid to the enforcing state.

In practice, disgorgement and confiscation achieve the same goal of separating proceeds from wrongdoers. In the United States, disgorgement is the most frequently used tool by the U.S. Securities and Exchange Commission (SEC) to recover proceeds in cases involving violations of the Foreign Corrupt Practices Act by issuers of securities registered in the United States. Disgorgement in the United States is almost always accompanied by prejudgment interest and a civil fine. Disgorgement may be combined with additional tools such as civil and criminal forfeiture and restitution. For example, in the case brought against Alcatel by the SEC, the company was ordered to pay $45.372 million in disgorgement and $92 million in criminal fines.

4. Restitution: Criminal and Civil

Restitution is closely related to compensation, disgorgement and tort/contract remedies. It is based on the principle that a person who has suffered loss as a result of a wrong committed against him or her must be restored as nearly as possible to the circumstance in which he or she existed before the damage took place. Restitution can be either civil or criminal. In some jurisdictions, as part of a criminal conviction, the court has the power to order the guilty party to pay restitution to the victim in an amount of the costs incurred by the victim as a result of the guilty party's actions. In a simple example, if a corrupt official steals government property and sells it, the court may order the defendant to pay back the value of the stolen property, to restore the victim to the financial position it was in before the crime. This power is typically defined by statutes. On the civil side, restitution is closely linked with and sometimes indistinguishable from compensation.

In some cases, restitution may be agreed upon as part of the plea agreement and later approved by the court. Moreover, to receive restitution, the victim must be included in or addressed by a plea agreement or other settlement agreement and/or must meet requirements such as direct harm and damages. It may be that the absence of an identified victim during the process (see chapter 2, section 4) is one of the reasons that there is very little restitution to victims of corruption. According to the database compiled for this study, restitution is rarely used in foreign bribery cases.

As an example of restitution, in the Haiti Teleco case a U.S. court ordered an individual defendant to pay restitution of $73,824 to Haiti.

5. Fines: Criminal and Civil

Criminal and civil fines are provided for by statute in many jurisdictions. Fines are often punitive in nature and may not be related to the value of the ill-gotten gains.

Fines are almost always paid to the state treasury of the prosecuting jurisdiction. For example, in the Alstom Network case, the company was required to pay Sw F 2.5 million as a criminal fine to Switzerland. In the United States, there is usually a base fine and escalation depending on the value received.

6. Reparations: Gratuitous and/or Voluntary Payments

Reparations in foreign bribery cases are generally gratuitous or voluntary payments undertaken by a wrongdoer as an effort to repair damage done or to express remorse.

For example, in the BAE case in the United Kingdom, the company agreed to make a voluntary payment to Tanzania, where bribes were allegedly paid. In another example, Alstom SA paid Sw F 1 million to the International Committee of the Red Cross for its projects in the three countries where Alstom had engaged in illegal payments.

Appendix II. U.K. Remedies

1. Criminal Remedies

- **Confiscation:** paid to Her Majesty's Courts Service, determined before other penalties
  - *Compensation* is a subset of confiscation and is available to registered victims.
- **Fines:** paid to the Treasury, determined after confiscation
  - *Costs* can be assessed as part of fines and are paid to the Crown Prosecution Service or the prosecuting agency.

The net confiscation (confiscation less fines and costs) is distributed under the Asset Recovery Incentivization Scheme (ARIS) as follows:

- 50.00 percent to the Home Office (general treasury)
- 18.75 percent to the prosecuting agency
- 18.75 percent investigating authority
- 12.5 percent to Her Majesty's Courts Service.

The funds returned to a law enforcement agency must be used for further Proceeds of Crime Act activities directed toward asset recovery and cannot be placed in the agency's general operating funds.

The Serious Fraud Office (SFO) may count as an investigating or prosecuting service or as both on the same case. The Overseas Anti-Corruption Unit of the City of London Police (OACU) may be an investigating service, with the Crown Prosecution Service or the SFO prosecuting.

2. Civil Remedies

Civil Recovery Order funds go to a court-appointed trustee and then to the Home Office, which proceeds under ARIS with distributions made in the same way as under criminal asset recoveries.

Appendix III. Settlements Cases Database: Methodology

As the settlements study team embarked on its research, it became evident that a great deal of invaluable work had already been done to collect and analyze past prosecutions and settlements of foreign bribery and related cases by other organizations, most notably by the Organisation for Economic Co-operation and Development (OECD) and the Asian Development Bank. The OECD also had compiled its annual Enforcement Data Table, providing statistics on its members' enforcement of the Convention on Combating Bribery of Foreign Public Officials in International Business Transactions (Anti-Bribery Convention). For each member country, this data include the number of convictions and settlements, which were further broken down by legal persons and individual defendants (natural persons) and whether criminal and civil forms of prosecution had been employed.

StAR Database of Settlements of Foreign Bribery and Related Cases

The StAR Database of Settlements of Foreign Bribery and Related Cases (Settlements Database) consulted the OECD Enforcement Data Table as its starting point, but with the key difference that the Settlements Database identifies cases by their names. As shown in the following sections, the Settlements Database also includes additional fields that enable the study team to extract and analyze data pertaining to issues at the heart of its study. By constructing the database, we sought to help firmly ground in actual cases the debate surrounding settlements.

Another distinguishing feature of the Settlements Database is the inclusion of cases that countries themselves have not reported as foreign bribery cases, because they were settled under nonforeign bribery laws (e.g., the Netherlands and UN Oil-for-Food Programme cases) or because the countries did not report them as settlements owing to the narrow scope of their definition of a case as a settlement. Many of these are included in this study's broad definition of settlements (e.g., Siemens cases in Germany). Due to limitations in time and because new settlements continue to take place, the Settlements Database does not purport to be exhaustive. However, we are confident that it includes all known cases from jurisdictions that have been most active in prosecuting foreign bribery and related cases.

The entire Settlements Database is published on the website of the Stolen Asset Recovery (StAR) Initiative as of fall 2013. As with StAR's ongoing Asset Recovery Watch project[1]—the first systematic and the most comprehensive database of completed and active international asset recovery cases—the Settlements Database is free and publicly accessible online, with search filters and source documents provided for ease of access by all interested persons. The Settlements and Asset Recovery Watch databases aim to help fulfill StAR's mandate of creating a common base of knowledge with which to conduct informed discussions on these issues of critical importance to the international community.

1. Details of the Settlements Cases Database

The new database features the potential for extensive research and analysis within a number of parameters.

1.1 Time Period Covered

The cases in the database occurred from 1999 through July 3, 2012. While, most notably, the United States had entered into settlements agreements in foreign bribery and related cases prior to 1999, this year was chosen as the starting point so as to be consistent with the OECD Enforcement Data Table's starting point. While new settlements cases continue to take place, the database was closed to new entries as of the end of July 3, 2012, so as to permit the team to tally and extract data for the body of the study.

1.2 "Case" Defined

In looking at the OECD Enforcement Data Table and in discussion with officials of the U.S. Department of Justice, it became clear that the United States counts and reports its cases differently from other member countries.[2] While all other countries report one case as involving one legal person or one individual defendant, the United States considers as one "matter" a set of related cases involving legal persons and individuals and that "matter" number is the one recorded in the Enforcement Data Table. So as to provide a common basis for comparison, the Settlements Database broke down the U.S. "matters" to their subcomponents. For example, in U.S. Matter #5 involving the Bonny Island Liquefied Natural Gas Bribe Scheme,[3] the criminal cases against the JGC Corporation, the Snamprogetti Netherlands B.V., and so on were each entered into the Settlements Database as a separate case. This method also enabled the study team to see which companies had been prosecuted in other jurisdictions for the same or related underlying misconduct.

---

1. Accessible at StAR Corruption Cases Search Center, http://star.worldbank.org/corruption-cases/?db=All.
2. OECD Working Group on Bribery, 2101 Data on Enforcement of the Anti-Bribery Convention (Paris: OECD, 2010), http://www.oecd.org/dataoecd/47/39/47637707.pdf.
3. See U.S. DOJ, *Steps Taken to Implement and Enforce the OECD Convention on Combating Bribery of Foreign Public Officials in International Business Transactions* (Washington, DC: U.S. DOJ, 2011), http://www.oecd.org/dataoecd/18/8/42103833.pdf.

The practice of collecting individual cases under the umbrella heading of a "matter" was, we believed, also useful. So as to avoid confusion with U.S. reporting methodology, however, the Settlements Study calls this umbrella heading "case clusters."

1.3 Sources Used

The Settlements Database builds on research that had been conducted for the StAR Asset Recovery Watch cases database (http://star.worldbank.org/corruption-cases /?db=All), the StAR *Asset Recovery Handbook: A Guide for Practitioners,* and other StAR publications. These publications can be located in entirety at StAR's website: http://star.worldbank.org/star/.

A wealth of primary sources was available for use in the database in open source. They were supplemented in a limited number of cases with secondary sources to fill in gaps in information. No official sources were available for a small number of settlement cases reported in the media; these were not included in the Settlements Database.

Among the main sources of information were the following:

- OECD: The country-specific Phase 3 and Phase 2 reports pertaining to the implementation of the Anti-Bribery Convention, as compiled by the OECD Directorate for Financial and Enterprise Affairs: http://www.oecd.org/about/0,3347,en _2649_34859_1_1_1_1_1,00.html.

See in particular, tabs for Statistics and Information by Country.

- Asian Development Bank/OECD Anti-Corruption Initiative for Asia and the Pacific, *The Criminalization of Bribery in the Asia and the Pacific: Frameworks and Practices in 28 Asian and Pacific Jurisdictions; Thematic Review and Final Report* (Paris and Manila: OECD and ADB, 2010), http://www.oecd.org/dataoecd /2/27/46485272.pdf.
- United Nations Office on Drugs and Crime (UNODC): The background and text of UN Convention against Corruption (UNCAC), available at http://www.unodc .org/unodc/en/treaties/CAC/;

Travaux Préparatoires of the negotiations for the elaboration of UNCAC, available at http://www.unodc.org/unodc/en/treaties/CAC/travaux-preparatoires.html.

- Enforcement agencies' websites, including:
  o U.S. Department of Justice (DOJ): http://www.justice.gov/criminal/fraud /fcpa/cases/d.html
  o U.S. Securities and Exchange Commission (SEC): www.sec.gov
  o U.K. Serious Fraud Office: http://www.sfo.gov.uk
  o Switzerland's Office of the Attorney General: http://www.bundesanwaltschaft .ch/bundesanwaltschaft/index.html?lang=en

- Company websites: Company-issued annual reports, statements, or other required legal filings with regulatory agencies such as the U.S. SEC: http://www.sec.gov/edgar.shtml.
- Civil society organizations: Most notably, Transparency International, *Progress Report 2011: Enforcement of the OECD Anti-Bribery Convention* (London: Transparency International, 2011), http://www.transparency.org/whatwedo/pub/progress_report_2011_enforcement_of_the_oecd_anti_bribery_convention; and Transparency International UK, *Deterring and Punishing Corporate Bribery: An Evaluation of UK Corporate Plea Agreements and Civil Recoveries in Overseas Bribery Cases* (London: Transparency International, 2012).
- Private law firms, companies, and media organizations: Various law firms in the United States and elsewhere provide information and analysis of foreign bribery cases. The most long-standing and systematically organized collection of U.S. cases is by the Shearman and Sterling law firm, http://fcpa.shearman.com/.

Trace International provides information on both U.S. and non-U.S. cases, https://secure.traceinternational.org/Knowledge/Compendium.html. Trace and Shearman databases both provide links to source documents.

Two blogs—the *FCPABlog* and *Wall Street Journal Risk & Compliance Journal* also provide timely information on case developments.

- Other Sources:
  - For legal documents, the World Legal Information Institute at Worldlii.org and related free country or regional legal resources, countries' courts for free or at small cost (U.S. PACER for federal cases), and the World Bank Law Library proved invaluable.
  - The study team's February 2012 mission to Germany, Switzerland, and United Kingdom; the study's March 2012 Experts Roundtable meeting in Washington, D.C.; and additional interviews and discussions with and research assistance by experts all contributed in helping to fill in gaps in information of the cases in the Settlements Database.

2. Explanation of Fields and a Sample Entry

The Settlements Database comprises five categories of fields:
1. *Main background:* fields pertaining to the name of the case, when and where the settlement took place, location of the foreign public officials, and a summary of the case
2. *Form of settlement:* fields allowing users to sort by civil or criminal settlement; settlements pertaining to a legal person (i.e., company) or an individual defendant (natural person); the legal form of settlement (guilty plea, Non-Prosecution Agreements, etc.); and the monetary sanctions imposed

3. *Monetary sanctions:* organized by total amount and then broken down into the type(s) imposed, plus a field for known amounts returned or ordered to be returned to the victim country or other, third-party entity
4. *Offenses:* fields recording both alleged and settled offenses, and UNCAC and OECD Anti-Bribery Convention articles implicated in the case
5. *Sources used:* self-explanatory

See table A3.1 for a breakdown of fields and table A3.2 for a sample entry.

TABLE A3.1	Fields and Their Breakdowns in the Settlements Database	
Field name	Field category	Explanation/Notes
Case cluster	Main background	Umbrella name for group of related cases
Name of case	Main background	Case names: almost always as reported or referred to by the jurisdiction of settlement; parent company name followed by involved subsidiary or name of individual defendant
Jurisdiction of settlement	Main background	Self-explanatory
Jurisdiction of settlement: enforcement agency	Main background	Self-explanatory
Country/jurisdiction of foreign public official(s)	Main background	As identified in the official documents pertaining to the case, the location of the recipients or alleged recipients of foreign bribery payments
Date of settlement(s)	Main background	Self-explanatory
Other jurisdictions of settlement	Main background	Due to limitations in the study's time and resources, no comprehensive research has been undertaken to complete this field; information has been noted where readily available or referenced from open sources.
Settlement with individual or legal person?	Form of settlement	Self-explanatory
Form of settlement (administrative, civil, or criminal)	Form of settlement	U.S. SEC cases noted as civil although some involved administrative proceedings, so as to avoid double counting

(continued next page)

Field name	Field category	Explanation/Notes
Legal form of settlement	Form of settlement	Legal basis for settlement, as labeled by the jurisdiction of enforcement (examples: Non-Prosecution Agreement, *patteggiamento*, penalty notice)
Monetary sanctions (types)	Form of settlement	Monetary settlement types as labeled by the jurisdiction of enforcement (examples: confiscation, criminal fine, disgorgement of profits, legal costs)
Total monetary sanctions (US$)	Monetary settlement	Self-explanatory; date of settlement used for purposes of currency conversion
Amount of sanction: Criminal fine/penalty	Monetary settlement	Breakdown of the "total monetary sanctions" field
Amount of sanction: other criminal—amount (type)	Monetary settlement	Breakdown of the "total monetary sanctions" field
Amount of sanction: Civil disgorgement of profits	Monetary settlement	Breakdown of the "total monetary sanctions" field
Amount of sanction: Civil prejudgment interest	Monetary settlement	Breakdown of the "total monetary sanctions" field
Amount of sanction: Civil fine/penalty	Monetary settlement	Breakdown of the "total monetary sanctions" field
Amount of settlement: Other civil—amount (type)	Monetary settlement	Breakdown of the "total monetary sanctions" field
Amount of settlement (US$) returned/ordered to be returned to "victim" jurisdiction or other designated third-party/entity	Monetary settlement	Self-explanatory

(continued next page)

TABLE A3.1 Fields and Their Breakdowns in the Settlements Database *(continued)*

TABLE A3.1	Fields and Their Breakdowns in the Settlements Database (*continued*)	
Field name	Field category	Explanation/Notes
UNCAC articles implicated (on offenses and international cooperation): • Articles 15–27 (including Art. 16 bribery of foreign public officials, Art. 23 laundering of proceeds of crime, Art. 26 liability of legal persons, Art. 27 participation and attempt) • Art. 38 cooperation between national and international authorities • Art. 43 international cooperation (general) • Art. 44 extradition • Art. 46 mutual legal assistance	Offenses	Self-explanatory
OECD Anti-Bribery Convention articles implicated (on offenses and international cooperation): Art. 1 bribery of foreign public official (including conspiracy and attempt) Art. 2 responsibility of legal persons Art. 7 money laundering Art. 8 accounting (books and records/internal controls) Art. 9 mutual legal assistance Art. 10 extradition	Offenses	Self-explanatory

(continued next page)

TABLE A3.1	Fields and Their Breakdowns in the Settlements Database (*continued*)	
Field name	**Field category**	**Explanation/Notes**
Offenses: Alleged	Offenses	Offenses alleged by jurisdiction of settlement
Offenses: Settled	Offenses	Offenses settled on between the jurisdiction of settlement and defendants
Public procurement contract or state-owned enterprise (SOE) involved? (yes/no/ unknown)	Offenses	Self-explanatory: case may involve more than one (alleged) misconduct—the field is marked YES if at least one of the (alleged) misconducts involved public procurement contract or state-owned enterprise.
Summary	Main background	Self-explanatory
Sources	Main background	Sources used have been saved as PDFs, and they will be available on the website. The database will also provide web links for easy access by users, but note that links may become defunct over time.

TABLE A3.2 Sample Entry in Settlements Database

Case cluster	Siemens AG
Name of case	Siemens AG
Jurisdiction of settlement	United States
Jurisdiction of settlement: Enforcement agency	Department of Justice (DOJ)
Country/jurisdiction of foreign public official(s)	Argentina, Bangladesh, Iraq (UN Oil-for-Food), República Bolivariana de Venezuela
Date of settlement(s)	2008-12-15
Other jurisdictions of settlement	Germany, World Bank
Settlement with individual or legal person?	Legal person
Type of settlement (administrative, civil, or criminal)	Criminal
Legal form of settlement	Guilty plea
Monetary sanction (types)	Criminal fine
Total monetary sanction (US$)	$448,500,000
Amount of sanction: Criminal fine/penalty	$448,500,000
Amount of sanction other criminal: Amount (type)	$0
Amount of sanction: Civil disgorgement of profits	NA
Amount of sanction: Civil prejudgment interest	NA
Amount of sanction: Civil fine/penalty	NA
Amount of sanction civil: Amount (type)	NA
Amount of settlement (US$) returned/ordered to be returned to victim jurisdiction or other designated third-party/entity	$0
a. UNCAC articles implicated (on offenses and international cooperation): • Articles 15–27 (including Art. 16 bribery of foreign public officials, Art. 23 laundering of proceeds of crime, Art. 26 liability of legal persons, Art. 27 participation and attempt) • Art. 38 cooperation between national and international authorities • Art. 43 international cooperation (general) • Art. 44 extradition • Art. 46 mutual legal assistance	Art. 16. Art. 23, Art. 26, Art. 43

(continued next page)

b. OECD Anti-Bribery Convention articles implicated (on offenses and international cooperation): • Art. 1 bribery of foreign public official (including conspiracy and attempt) • Art. 2 responsibility of legal persons • Art. 7 money laundering • Art. 8 accounting (books and records/internal controls) • Art. 9 mutual legal assistance • Art. 10 extradition	Art. 1, Art. 2, Art. 7, Art. 8
Offenses : Alleged	Falsification of books and records
Offenses: Settled	Falsification of books and records
Public procurement contract or SOE (YES, if in at least one location of misconduct)	YES
Summary	According to the June 2011 United States Report to the OECD, "On December 11, 2008, Siemens Aktiengesellschaft (Siemens AG), a German corporation, and three of its subsidiaries were charged in separate criminal informations filed in the U.S. District Court for the District of Columbia for their roles in a scheme to bribe foreign officials in several countries. Siemens AG was charged with two counts of violating the internal controls and books and records provisions of the FCPA, while Siemens SA - Argentina was

(continued next page)

charged with conspiracy to violate the books and records provisions. In addition, Siemens Bangladesh Limited (Siemens Bangladesh) and Siemens SA–Venezuela (Siemens Venezuela) were each charged with one count of conspiracy to violate the antibribery and books and records provisions of the FCPA. According to court documents filed in these criminal cases, beginning in the mid-1990s, Siemens AG engaged in systematic efforts to falsify its corporate books and records and knowingly failed to implement existing internal controls. As a result of Siemens AG's knowing failures in and circumvention of internal controls, from the time of its listing on the New York Stock Exchange on March 12, 2001, through approximately 2007, Siemens AG made payments totaling approximately $1.36 billion through various mechanisms. Of this amount, approximately $554.5 million was paid for unknown purposes, including approximately $341 million in direct payments to business consultants for unknown purposes. The remaining $805.5 million of this amount was intended in whole or in part as corrupt payments to foreign officials in Asia, Africa, Europe, the Middle East and the Americas, which were to be paid through various mechanisms, including cash desks and slush funds.

The criminal charges against Siemens AG and its three subsidiaries stem from bribery schemes and related accounting misconduct involving its operations in Iraq, Argentina, Venezuela, and Bangladesh."

Source: U.S. DOJ, *Steps Taken to Implement and Enforce the OECD Convention on Combating Bribery of Foreign Public Officials in International Business Transactions,* Information as of May 31, 2011, Siemens Aktiengesellschaft (Siemens AG) case summary, 70–73.

(continued next page)

TABLE A3.2	Sample Entry in Settlements Database (*continued*)
Sources	U.S. DOJ, *Steps Taken to Implement and Enforce the OECD Convention on Combating Bribery of Foreign Public Officials in International Business Transactions,* Information as of May 31, 2011, Siemens Aktiengesellschaft (Siemens AG) Case Summary at 70-73, accessed at http://www.oecd.org/dataoecd/18/8/42103833.pdf;
	U.S. v. Siemens AG, Case No. 1:08-cr-367-RJL (D.D.C.), Information filed December 12, 2008, accessed at http://www.justice.gov/criminal/fraud/fcpa/cases/siemens/12-12-08siemensakt-info.pdf; Plea Agreement filed December 15, 2008, accessed at http://www.justice.gov/criminal/fraud/fcpa/cases/siemens/12-15-08siemensakt-plea.pdf;
	Statement of Offense filed December 15, 2008, accessed at http://www.justice.gov/criminal/fraud/fcpa/cases/siemens/12-15-08siemens-statement.pdf;
	Government Sentencing Memorandum filed December 12, 2008, accessed at http://www.justice.gov/criminal/fraud/fcpa/cases/siemens/12-12-08siemensvenez-sent.pdf; Judgment filed January 6, 2009, accessed at http://www.justice.gov/criminal/fraud/fcpa/cases/siemens/01-06-09siemensakt-judgment.pdf.
	U.S. Department of Justice, "Siemens AG and Three Subsidiaries Plead Guilty to Foreign Corrupt Practices Act Violations and Agree to Pay $450 Million in Combined Criminal Fines," press release, December 15, 2008, accessed at http://www.justice.gov/opa/pr/2008/December/08-crm-1105.html.

administrative confiscation. A nonjudicial mechanism for confiscating proceeds of crime or assets used or involved in the commission of an offense.

assets. Assets of every kind, whether corporeal or incorporeal, movable or immovable, tangible or intangible, and legal documents or instruments evidencing title to or interest in such assets.[1] The term is used interchangeably with *property*.

asset confiscation. The permanent deprivation of property by order of a court or other competent authority. The term is used interchangeably with *forfeiture*. Confiscation takes place through a judicial or administrative procedure that transfers the ownership of specified funds or assets to the state. The persons or entities that held an interest in the specified funds or other assets at the time of the confiscation or forfeiture lose all rights, in principle, to the confiscated or forfeited funds or other assets.

central authorities. The entity designated by a jurisdiction to receive requests for mutual legal assistance from other jurisdictions. The central authority may deal with these requests itself or forward them to the appropriate authority.

compensation. A pecuniary remedy that is awarded to a victim identified in proceedings and who is proved to have suffered damages. See appendix 1.

confiscation. The permanent deprivation of assets by order of a court or other competent authority.[2] The term is used interchangeably with *forfeiture*. The persons or entities that hold an interest in the specified funds or other assets at the time of the confiscation lose all rights, in principle, to the confiscated funds or other assets. See appendix 1.

conviction-based confiscation. Describes all forms of confiscation that require the defendant to be convicted of an offense before confiscation proceedings can be initiated and confiscation can take place.

criminal confiscation. See *conviction-based confiscation.*

defendant. Any party who is required to answer the complaint of a plaintiff in a civil lawsuit before a court, or any party who has been formally charged or accused of violating a criminal statute.

---

1. United Nations Convention against Corruption (UNCAC), Article 2(e).
2. UNCAC, Article 2(g).

Deferred Prosecution Agreement. A form of settlement used in the United States whereby the prosecution can propose to a defendant a written agreement in which the defendant admits responsibility and undertakes certain obligations in exchange for the prosecutor filing charges but not immediately taking further action on them (in legal parlance, *deferring* action) and dismissing them at a later time once the defendant has satisfactorily fulfilled his side of the agreement.[3]

disgorgement. The act of giving up profits obtained by illegal or unethical acts on demand or by legal compulsion, to prevent unjust enrichment. This is a type of civil remedy available in common law jurisdictions. See appendix 1.

double jeopardy. The principle that a person, natural or legal, should not be subject to a second prosecution for the same offense after legitimate acquittal or conviction, nor should a person be subject to multiple punishments for the same offense. See also the *ne bis in idem* principle.

fines. Criminal or civil monetary sanctions, which are often punitive in nature. See appendix 1.

focal point. A single, readily accessible office or official with designated authority to communicate with other jurisdictions with respect to mutual legal assistance requests and other related matters and whose contact details are provided through the Internet and/or other media.

forfeiture. See *confiscation.*

freeze of assets. A temporary prohibition on the transfer, conversion, disposition, or movement of property or temporary assumption of custody or control of property on the basis of an order issued by a court or other competent authority.[4] The term is used interchangeably with *seizure* and *restraining.*

informal assistance. Any activity or assistance that is provided without the need for a formal mutual legal assistance (MLA) request. There may be legislation that permits this type of practitioner-to-practitioner assistance, including MLA legislation.

legal persons. Refers to bodies corporate, foundations, partnerships, or associations or any similar bodies that can establish a permanent customer relationship with a financial institution or otherwise own property.

---

3. The Deferred Prosecution Agreement was introduced in the United Kingdom subsequent to the drafting of this study. For more information, please see background available at the U.K. Serious Fraud Office, http://www.sfo.gov.uk/about-us/our-policies-and-publications/deferred-prosecution-agreements --consultation-on-draft-code-of-practice.aspx.
4. UNCAC, Article 2(d).

letters rogatory. A formal request from a court to a foreign court for some type of judicial assistance. It permits formal communication between the judiciary, a prosecutor, or law enforcement official of one jurisdiction and his or her counterpart in another jurisdiction. A particular form of *mutual legal assistance.*

mutual legal assistance. The process by which jurisdictions seek and provide assistance in gathering information, intelligence, and evidence for investigations, in implementing provisional measures, and in enforcing foreign orders and judgments.

mutual legal assistance request. Distinguished from informal assistance, a mutual legal assistance request is typically a request in writing that must adhere to specified procedures, protocols, and conditions set out in multilateral or bilateral agreements or domestic legislation. These requests are generally used to gather evidence (including through coercive investigative techniques), obtain provisional measures, and seek enforcement of domestic orders in a foreign jurisdiction.

mutual legal assistance treaty (MLAT). A bilateral treaty that creates clear and binding obligations between two jurisdictions for cooperation on mutual legal assistance and sets out efficient and comprehensive procedures to be applied. These treaties are typically not limited in scope to a range of offenses but apply to any criminal activity that falls within their scope of application. MLATs typically create a closer relationship between the signatory states than multilateral conventions and are customized to fit that relationship.

ne bis in idem. Latin for "not twice for the same." A principle applied in civil law systems mainly meaning that a person (natural or legal) may not be tried for a criminal offense for which that person has previously been finally convicted or acquitted. See *double jeopardy.*

non-conviction-based confiscation (NCB confiscation). Confiscation for which a criminal conviction is not required. As its name suggests, an NCB confiscation does not require trial or a criminal conviction, but only a noncriminal confiscation proceeding. The NCB proceeding may, or may not, parallel a criminal proceeding.[5]

Non-Prosecution Agreement (NPA). A form of settlement used in the United States whereby the prosecution can propose to a defendant a written agreement to admit responsibility and undertake certain obligations in exchange for the prosecutor not filing charges. See chapter 1, 4.4 United States.

---

5. For more information on NCB proceedings and remedies, see Jean-Pierre Brun, Clive Scott, Kevin M. Stephenson, and Larissa Gray, *Asset Recovery Handbook: A Guide for Practitioners* (Washington, DC: World Bank, 2011), 11–12; 106–107; 156–157, http://star.worldbank.org/star/publication/asset-recovery -handbook; and Theodore S. Greenberg, Linda M. Samuel, Wingate Grant, and Larissa Gray, *Stolen Asset Recovery: A Good Practices Guide for Non-Conviction-Based Asset Forfeiture* (Washington, DC: World Bank, 2009).

OECD Anti-Bribery Convention. OECD Convention on Combating Bribery of Foreign Public Officials in International Business Transactions. Entered into force 15 February 1999.

originating jurisdiction. A jurisdiction that asks for the assistance of another jurisdiction for the purpose of assisting an investigation or prosecution or enforcing a judgment. See also *requesting jurisdiction.*

partie civile. French for *civil party.* In some civil law systems, a party injured as a direct result of a criminal offense can apply to join the criminal proceedings as a civil party, with a view to obtaining access to the case file and related evidence as well as to pursuing damages in the context of the criminal case.

politically exposed person (PEP). Individuals who are, or have been, entrusted with prominent public functions, for example, heads of state or of government; senior politicians; senior government, judicial, or military officials; senior executives of state-owned corporations; and important party officials. Business relationships with family members or close associates of PEPs involve reputational risks similar to those with PEPs themselves. The definition is not intended to cover middle ranking or more junior individuals in the foregoing categories.

proceeds of crime. Any asset derived from or obtained, directly or indirectly, through the commission of an offense.

reparations. Gratuitous or voluntary payments undertaken by a wrongdoer in an effort to repair the damage done or an expression of remorse. See appendix 1.

requested jurisdiction. A jurisdiction that is asked to provide assistance to another jurisdiction for the purpose of assisting a foreign investigation or prosecution or enforcing a judgment.

requesting jurisdiction. A jurisdiction that asks for the assistance of another jurisdiction for the purpose of assisting with a domestic investigation or prosecution or enforcing a judgment.

restitution. The principle that a person who has suffered loss as a result of a wrong committed against him or her must be restored as nearly as possible to the circumstance in which he or she was before the damage took place. See appendix 1.

State Party. A country that has ratified or acceded to a particular treaty and is therefore legally bound by the provisions in the instrument.

UNCAC. United Nations Convention against Corruption. Entered into force on 14 December 2005.